THE FIRST TEENAGERS

THE WOBURN EDUCATION SERIES

General Series Editor: Professor Peter Gordon

The Victorian School Manager *by Peter Gordon*

Selection for Secondary Education by *Peter Gordon*

The Study of Education
A Collection of Inaugural Lectures *edited by Peter Gordon*

Volume I: Early and Modern
Volume II: The Last Decade
Volume III: The Changing Scene
Volume IV: End of an Era?

The Education of Gifted Children by *David Hopkinson*

Games and Simulation in Action
by Alec Davison and Peter Gordon

Slow Learners - A Break in the Circle
A Practical Guide for Teachers in Secondary Schools
by Diane Griffin

The Middle School - High Road or Dead End?
by John Burrows

Music in Education
by Malcolm Carlton

Teaching and Learning Mathematics
by Peter Dean

Unequal Educational Provisions in England and Wales:
The Nineteenth-Century Roots
by William E. Marsden

Dictionary of British Educationists
by Richard Aldrich and Peter Gordon

History of Education: The Making of a Discipline
edited by Peter Gordon and Richard Szreter

Educating the Respectable:
The Story of Fleet Road School, Hampstead, 1879–1903
by W. E. Marsden

Teaching the Humanities
edited by Peter Gordon

Education and Policy in England in the Twentieth Century
by Peter Gordon, Richard Aldrich and Dennis Dean

The Private Schooling of Girls: Past and Present
edited by Geoffrey Walford

The State and Higher Education
by Brian Salter and Ted Tapper

James Kay-Shuttleworth: Journey of an Outsider
by R. J. W. Selleck

Teaching Science
edited by Jenny Frost

Educational Reconstruction:
The 1944 Education Act and the Twenty-First Century
by Gary McCulloch

The First Teenagers: The Lifestyle of Young Wage-Earners in Interwar Britain
by David Fowler

International Yearbook of History Education
edited by Alaric Dickinson, Peter Gordon, Peter Lee and John Slater

THE FIRST TEENAGERS:

THE LIFESTYLE OF YOUNG WAGE-EARNERS IN INTERWAR BRITAIN

DAVID FOWLER

The Queen's University of Belfast

THE WOBURN PRESS

LONDON

First published in 1995 in Great Britain by
THE WOBURN PRESS
Newbury House, 900 Eastern Avenue,
London IG2 7HH, England

and in the United States of America by
THE WOBURN PRESS
c/o ISBS, Inc.
5804 N.E. Hassalo Street, Portland, Oregon 97213-3644

British Library Cataloguing in Publication data
Fowler, David
First Teenagers: Lifestyle of Young
Wage-Earners in Interwar Britain. -
(Woburn Education Series)
I. Title II. Series
305.2350941

ISBN 0-7130-0195-X (cloth)
ISBN 0-7130-4018-1 (paper)

Library of Congress Cataloging in Publication data
Fowler, David.
  The first teenagers: the lifestlye of young wage-earners in
interwar Britain/David Fowler.
    p. cm. — (The Woburn education series)
  Includes bibliographical references and index.
  ISBN 0-7130-0195-X — ISBN 0-7130-4018-1 (pbk.)
    1. Teenagers—Employment—Great Britain—History—20th century.
2. Unemployment—Great Britain—History—20th century. 3. Labor
market—Great Britain—History—20th century. 4. Youth as
consumers—Great Britain—History-20th century. 5. Life style-
conditions—20th century. 6. Great Britain—Social
conditions—1918–1945. I. Title. II. Series.
HD6276.G7F68 1995
331.3'47'0941—dc20   94-3714
                                                        CIP

Printed in Great Britain by
Bookcraft (Bath) Ltd, Midsomer Norton, Avon

Contents

List of Tables

Abbreviations

BL	British Library
CAB	Cabinet Papers
DCS	Day Continuation School
GMRO	Greater Manchester Record Office
HO	Home Office Papers
JEB	Juvenile Employment Bureau
JIC	Junior Instruction Centre
JLB	Jewish Lads' Brigade
JOC	Juvenile Organisations Committee
JUC	Juvenile Unemployment Centre
LAB	Ministry of Labour Papers
LCC	London County Council
LEA	Local Education Authority
LFBC	London Federation of Boys' Clubs
MCL	Manchester Central Library
MDBSA	Manchester and District Boy Scouts' Association
MEC	Manchester Education Committee
MEPO	Metropolitan Police Papers
MOA	Mass Observation Archive
NCPM	National Council of Public Morals
PRO	Public Record Office, Kew
SAA	Scout Association Archives
YCL	Young Communist League
YHA	Youth Hostel Association

Acknowledgements

I began researching this book in 1983. Many people since then have heard me expound on my revisionist account of the origins of the British teenager; but before they are identified and thanked I must register my earliest debts.

First of all, I would like to thank the Economic and Social Research Council (ESRC) of London for funding my doctoral research on young wage- earners, undertaken at the University of Manchester between 1983 and 1988. The Faculty of Arts at Manchester also awarded me some funding in the later stages of my doctoral work which, along with some teaching at the University of Salford, saved me from penury in those early days.

New benefactors emerged when I undertook further research for the book after gaining my PhD in 1988. The School of Economic and Social Studies at the University of East Anglia, where I held a temporary lectureship in economic and social history from 1991 to 1992, made a significant contribution financially towards the publication of this book. Not only did the School generously support research trips to London; they also provided a grant to cover typing expenses, and supplied the services of a secretary, Mrs Sue Rowell of the Department of Economics at UEA. I am very grateful to Sue for delivering an impeccable manuscript (at least typographically!).

My current employer, The Queen's University of Belfast, has greatly assisted my research and I am especially grateful to the Academic Council of Queen's and to Professor John Spencer, Director of the School of Social Sciences, for providing financial support that made possible a long period of research in the British Library during the summer vacation of 1993 and, earlier in the year, a visit to the Vimto Archive in Manchester. The results of my recent research, however, will be incorporated in my next book *Youth Culture In The Twentieth Century*, due to be published by Macmillan in 1996.

The following study took shape under the very competent supervision of Professor Michael E. Rose of the Department of

Economic History in the University of Manchester. His vast experience and constant encouragement helped me to complete my thesis in good time. From an early date, he also showed great faith in my potential to become a professional historian. I thank him for all of this. Dr John Springhall of the University of Ulster at Coleraine has always taken a serious interest in my research, for which I am grateful, and he and Dr David Morgan made some useful suggestions on how my thesis might be turned into a book.

For stimulating discussions during the research and writing of this book I thank: Greg Anderson, John Armstrong, Stephen Constantine, Andrew Davies, Steve Fielding, Simon Gunn, Bernard Harris, Lorraine Harrison, Patrick Joyce, Alan Little, Andrew Martin, Michael Miller, Alastair Reid, Andrew Sturdy and Simon Thurlbeck. For inviting me to present aspects of my research at research seminars and conferences I am grateful to: the Business History Unit of the London School of Economics; the Centre for Social History, University of Warwick; the Economic History Society of the United Kingdom; the Institute of Historical Research (University of London); Manchester History Workshop; the Social History Society of the United Kingdom; the University of East Anglia (School of English and American Studies); the University of Lancaster (Department of History); the University of Liverpool (Department of Economic History and Department of History); the University of Manchester (Department of History); and the University of York (Department of Economics and Related Studies and Department of History).

I am, of course, grateful to those librarians and archivists who have allowed me to consult material included in this study (see the bibliography for the archives and libraries I have utilised). I thank my publisher, The Woburn Press, for their very positive response to my manuscript and I am grateful to the Hulton Deutsch Picture Library for permission to reproduce the cover illustration. Finally, I thank two of my students at Queen's, Caroline Martin and Ciaran Hartigan, for helping me to decide which cover illustration to use.

Introduction

> ....today's teenagers...are living in a world more than usually different from that of their parents....These young people have tastes, in dress, in amusements and in many other things, widely different from and more costly than any their parents were able to entertain....A particularly strong imaginative effort is needed by anyone over 35 – by middle-class parents as much as by working-class parents – to understand the true quality of the lives of this generation...[1]

Thus did a government committee appointed in November 1958 to review the youth service of England and Wales depict the lives of 1950s teenagers. The apparent novelty of the youth culture of that period was a view widely held at the time and expounded on in the popular and highbrow press; in novels such as Colin MacInnes's *Absolute Beginners* (1959), which chronicled the emergence of teenage culture in London; in market research; working-class autobiographies, and academic works.[2] Historians, sociologists, anthropologists and media writers remain convinced of the pertinence of this interpretation.[3]

The present study seeks to establish that the affluent teenager and the emergence of a distinctive teenage culture, at least in Britain,[4] were not post-war developments but products of the interwar years. This task is not as narrowly conceived as it might appear. It involves not simply an analysis of developments in the leisure sphere – for example, changes in the levels of disposable income those in their teens possessed; or changes in the leisure supply, involving the emergence of a youth market for leisure goods and services[5] – but also careful consideration of the economic circumstances that made these changes possible: the buoyant state of the labour market for young wage-earners; the occupational and geographical mobility of the teenage labour force; their workplace campaigns to secure wage increases, holidays with pay and so on and the structure of youth unemployment at this period. There are also favourable demographic circumstances to consider. Such

1

issues are central to the present study, which seeks to survey the lifestyles of boy and girl wage-earners from the moment they entered full-time employment at 14 as 70 per cent of 14-year-olds did as late as 1938.[6]

Strictly speaking, the terminal age of those featured in this study goes slightly beyond the teens since those employed as apprentices, a significant proportion of the young labour force and an important voice at the workplace, remained such until they reached 21. Those who analysed teenagers' lifestyles during the 1950s, however, did not restrict themselves to a consideration of 13-19-year-olds. Mark Abrams, who pioneered market research on the British teenager, defined teenagers as young people 'from the time they leave school to the age at which they marry'.[7]

The need for a systematic survey of young wage-earners' lives at a significant period in their history has been emphasised by social historians working in this field;[8] but, as yet, no such history has emerged. More than a decade ago the social historian Harry Hendrick, in a review of J. R. Gillis's *Youth and History, Tradition and Change in European Age Relations 1770-Present* (1974) and John Springhall's *Youth, Empire and Society: British Youth Movements, 1883-1940* (1977), appealed for 'a more comprehensive and perceptive history of youth' than he regarded these two studies.[9] 'We should not', he remarked, 'confine that history to boy scouts, club members, public schoolboys or delinquents. Such historical categorisation ignores the everyday experiences of the mass of young people who left barely any record of their grievances, their problems, or their aspirations.'[10] Historians since have produced important studies of the male youth problem of late Victorian and Edwardian Britain;[11] delinquency during the nineteenth and early twentieth centuries;[12] adolescence in Britain;[13] premarital sex;[14] and books and articles on the ideological origins of British youth movements.[15] But no monograph has appeared, until now, on the lives of 'the mass of young people' in recent British history.[16]

It is worth pausing to consider the terms used in the book and to explain why some have been eschewed. Since wage-earners in their teens are the principal focus, this is how they are sometimes referred to. This might appear anachronistic. Was the concept of people 'in their teens' unknown during the 1920s and 1930s? A dictionary search has revealed two things. First, young people 'in their teens' have been recognised as a distinct group in Britain since the seventeenth century. The *Oxford English Dictionary* (*OED*) records, for example, that in 1693 the following statement appeared in a dancing magazine: 'Your poor young things, when they are once in the teens, they think they shall never be married.'[17] Second, the dictionary evidence highlights the inappropriateness of terms such as 'adolescent' and 'youth' for the subjects of this study. The former, as defined by the *OED*, denotes 'a youth between childhood and manhood'.[18] The term is problematic for two reasons. First, it is too vague and does not refer specifically to the teenage years. Second, it has male connotations. The latter term has been eschewed for the same reasons.[19]

The following study draws heavily on archival records and, in its coverage of certain issues, utilises archival sources either not hitherto consulted by historians working in the field of youth history, or underutilised. The analysis of youth unemployment in Chapter 3, for example, draws upon the records of the Juvenile Employment Bureaux (JEBs), which administered the unemployment insurance scheme for 14–18-year-olds. These provide answers to a series of questions germane to the debate over youth unemployment at this period: its scale; structure (the age, sex, occupational, and geographical distribution of the young unemployed); the duration of bouts of unemployment; the day-to-day administration of the unemployment insurance scheme for young wage-earners; the work of the Juvenile Unemployment Centres (JUCs), and the impact of unemployment on those in their teens. Historians of youth unemployment have not, so far, used these immensely valuable records.[20] Underexploited sources, used extensively here, include the records of the lads' club movement and those of more obscure youth organisations such as the Pioneer Club for Girl Clerks and Typists.[21] Other institutional records (census reports, Home Office papers, Ministry of Labour reports and correspondence, police records, and parliamentary papers, for example), along with newspaper and magazine evidence, and reports produced by independent social investigators, help to build up a vivid picture of the lifestyles and preoccupations of the young wage-earners of interwar Britain. The oral historian Stephen Humphries rejected manuscript and printed records in his study *Hooligans or Rebels? An Oral History of Working-Class Childhood and Youth, 1889-1939* (1981) on the grounds that these were produced by middle-class adults who had a 'biased and distorted view of...working-class youth'.[22] Such sources do shed light, however, on the behaviour and concerns of young wage-earners. The fact that they were written by middle-class adults should not deter the historian with a critical and probing mind.

Oral evidence has not been neglected. Use is made, for example, of the extensive oral history archive at Manchester Metropolitan University, comprising over 300 tapes and transcribed interviews with people from the north-west of England.[23] These reminiscences provide interesting detail on, for example, youth movements from the point of view of their recipients (as do the official records, to a large extent) and other aspects of youth culture, such as dance halls and cinemas.[24] Social investigators, of course, interviewed young wage-earners and quoted them extensively in their reports and surveys.[25] These contemporary accounts (used here) proved as valuable as retrospective accounts from individuals who were not always able to recall the minutiae of their lives during their teens sixty or seventy years on.

The geographical focus of the book is broader than that entrusted to the government committee on the youth service cited earlier. Material relating to Scotland is included, though the bulk of the study relates principally to England and Wales. Included also are chapters and sections of chapters with a regional orientation. These serve a number of purposes. They, in some cases, illustrate general themes in detail; for example, the weekly pattern of teenage consumerism.[26] They focus attention also on events of significance for the teenage group at this period; for example, the apprentices' strikes during 1937.[27] Local studies, in addition, throw up new or underused sources which enable general historical judgements on particular issues to be tested.[28] They, furthermore, cast new light on issues which attracted the attention, and frequently concern, of contemporaries; the labour market behaviour of young wage-earners, the focus of Chapter 1, is a good example of such an issue. As to the occupational groups featured in the study, both manual and white-collar workers are discussed; but more attention is devoted to the former, who constituted a much higher percentage of the young labour force than the latter.[29]

INTRODUCTION

NOTES

1. See Ministry of Education, *The Youth Service in England and Wales*, Report of the Committee Appointed by the Minister of Education in November 1958, Cmnd 929 (London, 1960), p.31.
2. On the newspaper evidence see J. Davis, *Youth and the Condition of Britain: Images of Adolescent Conflict* (London, 1990), Ch. 7. See also C. MacInnes, *Absolute Beginners* (London, 1959); idem, *England, Half English* (London, 1961), pp.45–60; M. Abrams, *The Teenage Consumer* (London, 1959); R. Hoggart, *The Uses of Literacy: Aspects of Working-class Life with Special Reference to Publications and Entertainments* (Middlesex, 1957), Ch. 8(A); T.R. Fyvel, *The Insecure Offenders: Rebellious Youth in the Welfare State* (Middlesex, 1961): '...young people of today have far more money to spend than their parents ever had...who in their own young days grew up under the constant threat of unemployment...This new spending power of the young has also produced another phenomenon...whole new industries...have sprung up to supply the new market, and so we have the new commercial "youth culture"', pp. 131–3.
3. See, for example, J. Stevenson, *British Society, 1914–45* (Middlesex, 1984): '...a distinct "teenage" culture was to await the affluence of the years after the Second World War....', (though Stevenson is one of the few historians to acknowledge the existence of 'relatively affluent young people' before the Second World War), pp.246–7; J. Springhall, *Coming of Age: Adolescence in Britain, 1860-1960* (Dublin, 1986): '...a...teenage market...was not discovered until the late 1950s in Britain....', p.218; J. Davis, *Youth and the Condition of Britain:* 'The rise of youth...as a distinct consumer group was a phenomenon of the post-war economic boom...', p.118. For similar assessments by earlier historians see E.J. Hobsbawm, *Industry and Empire: An Economic History of Britain since 1750* (London, 1968): '"Youth" as a recognisable group...emerged in the 1950s; both commercially as the "teenage market", and in habits and behaviour...', p.250; H. Hopkins, *The New Look: A Social History of the Forties and Fifties in Britain* (London, 1963), Ch. 31. For sociologists' observations see S. Hall and T. Jefferson (eds), *Resistance Through Rituals: Youth Sub-Cultures in Post-War Britain* (London, 1976): 'Our subject...is Youth Cultures: our object, to explain them as a phenomenon, and their appearance in the post-war period', p.9; D. Hebdige, 'Towards a Cartography of Taste 1935–1962' in B. Waites, T. Bennett and G. Martin (eds), *Popular Culture: Past and Present* (1982, repr. Kent, 1986), Ch. 9; S. Frith, *Sound Effects: Youth, Leisure and the Politics of Rock* (London, 1983), Ch. 8, 'Children in the 1950s had different experiences from their 1930s parents, derived from new leisure opportunities. Teenagers had money to spend and new goods to spend it on...', p.184; idem, *The Sociology of Youth* (Ormskirk, 1984), Ch. 2. For an anthropological study which points to the uniqueness of 1950s youth culture see B. Martin, *A Sociology of Contemporary Cultural Change* (Oxford, 1981): '...For the first time in British history, there were working-class adolescents with considerable sums of money which they could legitimately spend on their own pleasures. The result was what we now accept as a distinctive culture and a specialised commodity and service market devoted to the leisure activities of youth – music, fashion, cosmetics, drink, bowling alleys, amusement parks...' p.138. For media accounts see, for example, M. Pye, 'R.I.P. The Teenager, 1942–1978', *The Sunday Times*, 30 July 1978; S. Frith, 'Time To Grow Up', *New Society*, 4 April 1986, pp.12–14 ('In the 1950s.. [m]aterial conditions, had made new youth cultures possible...', p.14).
4. On the origins of teenage culture in the United States see J. Gilbert, *A Cycle of Outrage: America's Reaction to the Juvenile Delinquent in the 1950s* (Oxford, 1986), Ch. 12; T. Doherty, *Teenagers and Teenpics : The Juvenilization of American Movies in the 1950s* (London, 1988), *passim*.
5. See below, Ch. 4.
6. J. Jewkes and S. Jewkes, *The Juvenile Labour Market* (London, 1938), p.11. See also Appendix, Tables 1.1 and 1.2, which reveal that in the census years 1921 and 1931 over 70 per cent of those in their teens were either in full-time employment, or seeking it.
7. Abrams, *Teenage Consumer*, p.3.
8. See, for example, Harry Hendrick's recent comments on the need for a study of young wage-earners' experience in recent British history, in *Images of Youth: Age, Class, and the Male Youth Problem, 1880–1920* (Oxford, 1990), 'No attempt is made here to write the history of

5

youth "from below"....I recognise that such an approach will be necessary if there is to be a total history of age relations...', p.8.

9. *Social History*, Vol.3, No.2 (May 1978), pp.249-52.
10. Ibid., p.252.
11. Hendrick, *Images of Youth*.
12. S. Humphries, *Hooligans or Rebels? An Oral History of Working-Class Childhood and Youth, 1889–1939* (Oxford, 1981); V. Bailey, *Delinquency and Citizenship: Reclaiming the Young Offender, 1914–1948* (Oxford, 1987). See also on this subject G. Pearson, *Hooligan: A History of Respectable Fears* (London, 1983); E. Dunning, P. Murphy and J. Williams, *The Roots of Football Hooliganism: An Historical and Sociological Study* (London, 1988).
13. J. Springhall, *Coming of Age*.
14. S. Humphries, *A Secret World of Sex. Forbidden Fruit: The British Experience, 1900–1950* (London, 1988). On courtship and marriage see also J. Gillis, *For Better, For Worse: British Marriages 1600 to the Present* (Oxford, 1985).
15. See below, Ch. 6.
16. Popular histories of post-war teenagers have, however, been produced. See, for example, P. Everett, *You'll Never Be 16 Again: An Illustrated History of the British Teenager* (London, 1986); The Conran Foundation, *14–24: British Youth Culture* (London, 1986).
17. *Oxford English Dictionary*, Vol.XI (Oxford, 1970), p.141.
18. *Oxford English Dictionary*, Vol.I (Oxford, 1970), p.123.
19. *Oxford English Dictionary*, Vol. XII (Oxford, 1970), p.77.
20. See below, Ch. 3.
21. See below, Ch. 6.
22. Humphries, *Hooligans or Rebels?*, p.3.
23. On the archives' holdings see A. Linkman and B. Williams, 'Recovering the People's Past: the archive rescue programme of Manchester Studies', *History Workshop*, 8 (Autumn 1979), pp.111–26.
24. See below, Chs. 4 and 6.
25. Numerous contemporary social surveys are cited below and the Mass Observation Archive at the University of Sussex contains much useful material relating to the 1930s.
26. See below, Ch. 4, *passim*.
27. See below, Ch. 2.
28. See below, Ch. 3.
29. See Appendix, Tables 1.3 and 1.4.

1

'Industrial Nomads'?: The Labour Market Behaviour of Young Wage-Earners in Interwar Britain

'No father with an assured income would throw his child into the labour market to sink or swim at 14', a London youth leader remarked in August 1928.[1] During the interwar years, however, the vast majority of the teenage age group left school at the earliest opportunity. In practice, this meant that even at the end of the period, in 1938, seven out of every ten children entered the adult labour market at the age of 14.[2] And yet, despite this, remarkably little is known about young people's experiences in the labour market at this period. Historians have certainly devoted scant attention to the subject. Little is known, for instance, about basic questions such as how young people found employment; why they chose to enter specific occupations, and how often they changed jobs. More is known about youth unemployment in interwar Britain, but historians are still divided over whether the 14–18 age group were afflicted by unemployment or not.[3]

These serious gaps in historical knowledge regarding those in their teens are surprising, especially given that issues such as those raised above perplexed academics, educationists and youth workers at the time. They were exclusively concerned about young wage-earners from the working class. Ernest S. Griffith and R. A. Joseph, who worked for a University Settlement in Liverpool, argued that the typical working-class boy in that city was 'an industrial nomad' who held down a job for no more than nine months on average.[4] Such behaviour, they felt, prevented boys from learning any useful industrial skills, exposed them to periodic bouts of unemployment in their teens, and restricted them to casual labouring jobs as adults.[5]

Other middle-class professionals were worried about the labour market behaviour of working-class girls. Joan L. Harley, a research student at Manchester University during the 1930s, believed they were open to all kinds of dangers once they left the protective environment of school and entered the adult world of work. On becoming a wage-earner the 14-year-old girl, she argued, immediately became 'unstable (in) character'; a malady brought on by 'the business of wage-earning and in the excitement of the independence which wage-earning brings'.[6] But how accurately did middle-class investigators depict the labour market for young wage-earners at this period? How realistic were their impressions of an abrupt transition from school to wage-earning status; of the apparently nomadic labour market behaviour of those in unskilled or blind-alley occupations; and of the apparently highly stratified juvenile labour market? Were their concerns shared by young wage-earners? Such questions are addressed in this chapter.

The Teenage Workforce

The occupations those in their teens entered are difficult to identify. To judge by the questions asked in social surveys, hardly anything was known about the occupations 14- and 15-year-olds entered on leaving school. They were not admitted to the unemployment insurance scheme until 1934 and were largely hidden from statistical records of any kind before that date. 'Comparatively few remain in school beyond the age of fourteen', the authors of the *Merseyside Survey* (1934) pointed out:

> From then for the space of two years they disappear from public view until at sixteen they become insurable... What happens to them when they leave school? Do they soon secure work and begin to earn a living? How do they get work and how long do they manage to retain it? What sort of wages do they earn and how many hours a day do they work? What are their leisure interests? How many of them join a club or similar organisation which may be of assistance in keeping them 'straight'? What proportion attend continuation classes in order to improve their education after leaving school? These are only a few of the questions to which answers would be of interest.[7]

Similar questions were asked by Jewkes and Winterbottom in their survey of juvenile unemployment in Lancashire and Cumberland, published in 1933. 'How rapidly', they asked, 'were school leavers obtaining employment? Were they obtaining "progressive" or blind-alley jobs? Were secondary school leavers more successful in gaining jobs than elementary school leavers?'[8]

Owing to the inability of census data on juveniles to provide answers to any of these questions, academics – the economist John Jewkes of the University of Manchester, for example, and D. Caradog Jones at the University of Liverpool – were forced to undertake detailed and painstaking sample surveys of adolescents and their early industrial experiences.[9] Jewkes's research team in the Department of Economics and Commerce at Manchester began research on juvenile employment and unemployment in September 1931. In their first enquiry, they attempted to trace the early employment 'histories' of all school-leavers in Lancashire over the period between August 1930 and July 1931.[10] They discovered that the official employment agencies for juveniles had little idea of the employment circumstances of 14- and 15-year-olds in their areas. The majority of the Juvenile Employment Bureaux throughout the county were only able to provide the enquiry with information on the most recent school-leavers; namely, those who left school in July 1931, two months before the Jewkes team's research was begun. This led the author of the team's first publication to conclude: 'A continuous and detailed study of the constitution of the labour force in the first two years of working life and of the trends affecting it is a condition precedent to any effective control of the flow of juveniles into industry.'[11]

But the gaps in the statistical records kept by local authorities on 'new entrants into industry' had still not been rectified by 1939. In a study of the working conditions of shop and office workers, J. Hallsworth found that: 'Statistics as to the extent of child and juvenile labour and the effects of legislation on such labour are not compiled and published annually by the responsible Government Departments in England and Wales or in Scotland.'[12]

A number of contemporary studies also drew attention to the difficulties involved in using existing statistical data to calculate the incidence of unemployment among young people. Jewkes and Winterbottom, after two major attempts to measure the extent of juvenile unemployment in Lancashire, declared in a 1933 study: 'At the present time it is impossible for any individual or any authority to state how many children between the ages of fourteen and eighteen years are unemployed.' This, they argued, was principally

9

due to the two-year 'gap' noted earlier which, until the Unemployment Act of 1934, meant that 14- and 15-year-olds were not obliged to register themselves for employment if unemployed, and had no incentive to do so since they received no unemployment benefit until 1934.[13]

It would appear, therefore, that the two-year period during which the majority of young people in the interwar years left school and entered full-time employment was as much a subject for speculation and concern, even by the 1930s, as one about which anything concrete was known. The Jewkes team attempted to rectify this by employing voluntary workers to visit the homes of 2,000 elementary school-leavers in St. Helens, Burnley, Warrington, Ashton-under-Lyne and Atherton at three to four month intervals between 1934 and 1936.[14] Joan L. Harley did a similar thing in Manchester in 1935; but her efforts to maintain contact with 169 ex-elementary and ex-central school girls were much less successful.[15] There is, therefore, a basic lack of meaningful statistical data on the employment and unemployment record of young workers at this period.

We can, of course, draw on the evidence produced in printed census reports. The 'juvenile' workforce was enumerated both in 1921 and in 1931.[16] But what needs to be emphasised is that the way in which the census authorities went about this, drawing up 'condensed lists' of the juvenile occupational structure of individual towns and cities, conceals at least as much as it reveals about the young labour force. Census reports only record the number of 'juveniles' in a particular occupation on a single day of the year, for instance. In fact, the Census of 1921 does not even do this since the number of 'juveniles' who were out of work at the time this Census was taken was not enumerated. Second, the fact that the above exercise was undertaken on only two occasions throughout the entire interwar period thus produces an essentially static picture of the young labour force in these years. No impression is given in census tables, for instance, about the duration of employment and they throw little light on the movement between occupations. As we shall see, movement between unskilled or 'blind-alley' jobs and skilled occupations was becoming increasingly common by the interwar period, with the decline of the seven-year apprenticeship and the growing number entering apprenticeships at the age of 16. Third, as both interwar censuses only provided 'condensed lists' of juvenile occupations, an enormous number of individual occupations entered by young people remain hidden behind generalised categories such as 'Metal Worker' or 'Textile Worker'.[17] Such categories invoke a deceptively simple picture of the young labour force. The category 'Metal Worker', for example, lumped together both apprentices and non-apprenticed young workers: 'fitters' and 'fitters' mates'.[18] Such workers would have been more aware of their differences, both in terms of the status attached to their respective occupations and the degree of skill involved, than of any shared interests.[19] These and other problems make census occupational statistics an exceptionally poor guide to the ways in which young people actually experienced the labour market and an even poorer guide to the environment of work.

Nevertheless, because the Census provides the only comprehensive snapshot of the young labour force, its main features are summarised in Tables 1.3 and 1.4 in the Appendix. No systematic attempt is made here to compare the numbers in certain occupations in 1921 and 1931, for obvious reasons. First, the Census definition of the 'juvenile' workforce changed. In 1921, the lower age-limit was 12 and the upper age-limit 19; in 1931, the lower age-limit was 14 and the upper age-limit 20. Second, the occupational categories used in 1921 were not the same as those used in 1931. Those enumerated as 'Transport Workers' at the Census of 1921, for instance, were separated into two occupational groups ('Transport and Communication Workers' and 'Road Transport Workers') at the Census of 1931; 'Embroiderers and Milliners', meanwhile, were grouped together in 1921 (under the general heading of 'Textile Goods and Articles of Dress'); but 'Milliners' were grouped with 'Hat Workers' at the Census of 1931 and 'Embroiderers' were not enumerated at all. Moreover, students were enumerated in 1931, but not in 1921 and so on. Finally, inter-decennial comparisons are made even more difficult by changes which are either hidden from census occupation tables (such as boundary changes);[20] or others which are not really quantifiable (such as changes in the prestige of certain occupations).[21] With these qualifications in mind, some general observations can be made.

A key feature appears to be continuity in the case of both boys' and girls' occupations. In the case of boys, 'Metal Workers' and 'Transport and Communication' workers were the largest occupational 'groups' at both interwar censuses.[22] The principal occupations for girls during the period did not change either. Textiles and personal service were by far the most popular occupations at both censuses.[23] But the emphasis on continuity should not be taken too far. Boys, for instance, were not simply concentrated in the two sectors of metal work and transport. Large numbers also entered agriculture, mining and quarrying, textiles, commerce, clerical work, personal service, labouring jobs, electrical work, and the furniture trades.[24] The same was true for girls, many of whom were clerks and typists, warehouse and storekeepers, transport and communication workers, and even metal workers.[25] Also, in the most popular occupations such as textiles, there was no uniformity of work experience. 'Textile Goods Makers', for instance, were not a homogeneous group but included embroiderers, milliners, tailoresses, dress- and blouse-makers, sewing machinists, and boot-workers; all employed in a variety of trading establishments, small and large. In the Jewish tailoring trades of Manchester, for instance: 'The typical establishment consists of six or a dozen girls working under the Jewish master in a small tenement workshop, frequently under very bad conditions.'[26] Similarly, the raincoat trade of that city was carried on 'in the upper floors of tumble-down houses in the Ancoats district'.[27] On the other hand, the 'average' Manchester tailoring establishment at this period was said to employ 'about 300' workers.[28] The Co-operative Wholesale Society's tailoring firm at Broughton, for instance, employed 300.[29] In another branch of the city's clothing trade, light dressmaking, which included the manufacturing of blouses, the workshops tended to be larger still. Much of the light dressmaking trade of the city was in the hands of large firms such as Tootal, Broadhurst, Lee and Company and Messrs Rylands Limited. S. P. Dobbs noted in 1928 that the former firm: 'not only makes up the garments ready for sale, but itself manufactures the materials from which they are made, and does a huge home and export trade both in piece-goods and finished garments of all kinds'.[30]

Juveniles, then, even those in the same occupation, frequently worked in a variety of industrial settings and performed a range of tasks. 'Textile Workers', to take just one example, were not a homogeneous group but included winders and beamers, spinners and doublers, weavers, card frame tenters, and machine knitters.[31]

Gender and the Youth Labour Market

Jerry White has recently argued that there were 'quite distinct labour markets for boys and girls' in London at this period.[32] This seems questionable, however, in the light of evidence available relating to other cities. In Manchester, in 1936, school-leavers were informed that cardboard boxmaking was '[a] light, clean and non-dangerous occupation for boys and girls'; both male and female 'learners' being recruited at 14.[33] In the printing and bookbinding trade of the city: 'Boys and girls usually start as messengers and after a short period on this class of work are taken into the works where they learn one of the various branches of the trade.'[34] Furthermore, those of either sex who wished to enter office work at Manchester Corporation's offices were elected via a 'Junior Entrants' Examination'. The only requirement for sitting this examination was that candidates were between 14 and 17.[35]

Though they were attracted to the same occupations, however, juveniles may still have experienced gender divisions at the workplace. These may have come into play in the specific tasks assigned to them. One important manifestation of gender divisions at work, according to historians of gender, is that girls (and women) were employed on less 'skilled' tasks than boys (and men).[36] This was certainly the case in, for instance, French polishing, one of the furniture trades:

> More girls are now being engaged in this trade on account of the work in some branches being easily learned, but the better class of work requires a high degree of skill. Girls are often employed on the polishing of oak, but rarely polish mahogany which takes a higher polish.[37]

But in the glovemaking trade girls of 14 and 15 were employed on work considered more 'skilled' than the work undertaken by boys employed in the trade: 'Girls enter this trade as learners at the age of 14 and 15 years. The work is chiefly machining and some parts are fairly skilled. Boys enter as errand boys and apprenticeships are unusual.'[38] A similar situation prevailed in laundry work. Girls were employed as 'sorters' and 'folders' as well as in more 'skilled' work such as ironing, whereas boys were employed in van delivery and collection.[39] Girls' work, then, was not necessarily less skilled than boys' work. The reverse was the case in certain occupations.

13

However, gender divisions were in evidence in certain trades. In the baking and confectionery trade boys were employed on 'light labouring duties', whereas girls were employed on 'simple repetition processes'.[40] The same was true in the boot and shoe trade where 'tall, strong juveniles were required to operate the machines', but women were employed on lighter tasks such as sewing and packing.[41] In addition, certain trades were boys' and men's trades – building, for example[42] – and others were girls' and women's such as machining, millinery, dressmaking, and embroidery.[43] That said, we should not impose a too rigid distinction between boys' and men's work and girls' and women's. Often, trades appealed for 'juvenile' workers of either sex and, as the examples cited illustrate, skilled work was not synonymous with boys' and men's work and unskilled work with girls' and women's.

The Juvenile Labour Shortage

The demand for juvenile labour during this period was insatiable, even in the worst years of the Depression. A Juvenile Employment Bureaux official in Manchester remarked in 1934: 'A year or two ago there were more jobs than boys and girls to fill them'.[44] The records of that city's JEBs bear this out. Between July 1932 and June 1933, for instance, when trade throughout the city was said to be 'very poor', the local JEBs were notified of 10,106 vacancies for 'juveniles' (aged 14-18); but they were only able to supply local employers with 9,339 unemployed juveniles.[45] In fact, a juvenile labour shortage was evident in Manchester throughout the 1930s. In 1934–35, 11,406 'placements' were made by the local JEBs; but they were notified of over 13,000 vacancies.[46] In 1935–36, over 12,000 'placements' were made; the JEBs were informed of 16,250 vacancies.[47] In their annual report for 1936 it was stated that local juveniles enjoyed greater employment choice than at any time in the past and more local employers were notifying the JEBs of vacancies than at any time in the past.[48] Between July and October of 1936, the Manchester JEBs were informed of over 5,000 vacancies.[49] In 1937, the demand for juvenile labour in the city was said to be greater than the supply;[50] and, by 1939, work was said to be 'plentiful' for juveniles.[51]

As regards specific trades, there was by 1934 'an unsatisfied demand' for girls in the local sewing trades; electrical engineering, mechanical engineering, wireless assembly, and shorthand and

14

typing.[52] By 1935, the demand for girls in these occupations 'exceeded the number of girls available' and this was also the case in the cotton industry.[53] From 1938, there was a growing demand for boys in the local aircraft factories and also in the local engineering trade.[54] By 1939, juvenile workers of either sex were in heavy demand in the clothing trades, distributive trades and, as a result of rearmament work, in the engineering and rubber trades.[55] There were wage increases of between 2s 6d and 5s a week for 'juveniles' in these trades in 1938 and employers who failed to apply the wage increases failed to attract or hold juvenile labour.[56]

Why, even in years of trade depression, was there such an insatiable demand for juvenile workers in cities such as Manchester? They were, first and foremost, cheaper to employ than adults even during periods of high adult unemployment. Also, their relative scarcity kept demand buoyant. In this respect, school-leavers entering the labour market of Manchester during the 1930s were at an advantage over those in some parts of the country because there were fewer of them competing for the myriad industrial jobs that a large city such as Manchester could offer young people. Manchester was one of the places where, owing to the decline in the birth rate during the First World War, the juvenile labour supply contracted most sharply. Between 1928 and 1932, in fact, the number of school-leavers entering the labour market of Manchester was only three-quarters of the usual figure throughout the 1920s.[57] The contraction of the juvenile labour supply thus gave rise to an actual shortage of juvenile labour in the city in the 1930s and the flood of post-war children into the labour market in 1934 (the products of the brief post-war baby boom) appears not to have altered this situation.[58]

One manifestation of this was the steady increase in the number of juveniles from outside the city who were found jobs in Manchester. 'In all cases where young people have been brought from other areas', the author of the JEB's report for 1935–36 stated, 'it has been impossible to fill the vacancies by the introduction of local candidates'.[59] Few juveniles from other districts were placed in employment locally during the 1920s (a South Wales boy was found a job with a local engineering firm in 1925);[60] but an increasing number were by the 1930s: 262 in 1932–33; 510 in 1933–34; 466 in 1934–35 and 513 in 1935–36.[61] In the latter year, juveniles were placed in employment locally from as far afield as

Jarrow, South Shields, Stockton-on-Tees, and Sunderland.[62] Others arrived in Manchester from Southport, West Hartlepool, Wrexham, Caernarvon, and Newcastle-upon-Tyne.[63] Many from places on the outskirts of Manchester such as Altrincham, Ashton-under-Lyne, and Glossop were found jobs in the city by the local JEBs.[64]

Juvenile Unemployment

The juvenile labour shortage in cities such as Manchester did not mean, of course, that there was no juvenile unemployment. But official unemployment statistics are difficult to interpret and tell us precious little about the extent of the problem.[65] W. R. Garside has argued that during the interwar years juvenile unemployment was 'an economic and social problem of alarming proportions' and he singled out Manchester as one of the cities that recorded high levels of juvenile unemployment.[66] The evidence cited above does not appear to support this interpretation. In that city, as we have shown, there was a shortage of juvenile labour throughout the 1930s, even when juvenile unemployment elsewhere in the country peaked.[67]

The nature and extent of juvenile unemployment at this period will be examined in greater detail in Chapter 3, but when the economist John Jewkes examined the extent of juvenile unemployment in Lancashire in 1932 he found there were considerable regional variations in its incidence. Unemployment among 'insured' juveniles (16- and 17-year-olds) in the Manchester district – which included Levenshulme, Manchester, Denton, Openshaw, Newton Heath, and Reddish – was only five per cent in June 1932; the lowest rate in the entire county after Lancaster where the figure was four per cent.[68] In Trafford Park, Eccles, Salford, and Altrincham the unemployment rate among 'insured' juveniles was also low in June 1932; about seven per cent.[69] This compared very favourably with the juvenile unemployment situation in some areas. In the Atherton district of Lancashire, which included Wigan, 16 per cent of 'insured' juveniles were unemployed; in the Stalybridge district, which included Stockport and Ashton-under-Lyne, 15 per cent were; in the Oldham district 14 per cent of 'insured' juveniles were unemployed in June 1932; in the St. Helens district, which included Warrington and Widnes, 13 per cent were; in Chorley and Preston 12 per cent were; 12 per cent of 'insured' juveniles were unemployed in the Rochdale district, which included Bury; 11 per cent in the Bolton district; 11 per cent in Blackburn and nine per cent in Burnley, Nelson, and Colne.[70]

Manchester was, above all, a magnet for unemployed juvenile labour in these areas. It drew in increasing numbers of young workers from the surrounding districts, and from much further afield, throughout the Depression years. In contrast, the number of Manchester juveniles found jobs outside the city by the local JEBs was infinitesimal; a mere 80 out of 9,339 'placements' in 1932-33; only 175 out of 11,406 'placements' in 1934-35, and only 147 out of 12,366 'placements' in 1935-36.[71]

The 'Transition' from School to Work: A Myth?

For working-class children, the focus of contemporary and historical debate, the 'transition' from school to wage-earning work allegedly occurred at the age of 14. 'I started in the mill in 1930 when I was fourteen', remarked one of Elizabeth Roberts's Preston respondents. 'The way they used to think then, you had to earn your keep, it wasn't a question of going to learn something where you didn't get a wage for four years, you had to start when you turned fourteen to earn money.'[72] The 'transition' period in question would seem to have been a fairly abrupt one in this case, which is how the middle-class writer Joan L. Harley imagined it for all working-class girls. 'The girl who is able to stay at school until she is at least sixteen', Harley argued, 'has a better chance of making a happy transition from childhood to adult life than the girl who leaves school at fourteen, since most of her time is planned for her.'[73] Harley, as we saw at the beginning of this chapter, believed that 14-year-old girls were open to all kinds of dangers once 'the influence and direction of the school are suddenly withdrawn'. Local Education Authorities (LEAs) such as Manchester Education Committee (MEC), shared this view. In 1928, MEC drew attention to the difficult transition from school to wage-earning work for children of either sex:

> The school leaving age is a difficult one for children who have up to that time received much careful and kindly supervision. The school leaver is thrown into the midst of many new and strange experiences which must be faced without a friendly teacher at hand to advise and help.[74]

But how far do these images of an abrupt transition reflect the reality of wage-earning within the working class? Elizabeth Roberts argues that in the case of working-class girls: 'The period between the ages of about fourteen and twenty-five was distinctive for most girls, bridging as it did childhood and independent adulthood. More women worked for wages during this period than at any other time of their lives.'[75] It is nevertheless a fact that wage-earning work was undertaken by large numbers of girls and boys long before the age of 14 and certainly did not always coincide with the end of schooling as Joan L. Harley, Manchester Education Committee, and Elizabeth Roberts seem to imply. In Preston, one of the three Lancashire towns Elizabeth Roberts's research relates to, 29 per cent of all 12- and 13-year-old girls and 15 per cent of all 12- and 13-year-old boys were in full-time paid employment in 1921.[76] In Blackburn, Bolton, Burnley, Oldham and Rochdale, the percentage of 12- and 13- year-olds in full-time paid work was even higher. In Rochdale, where a higher percentage of 12 and 13 year olds were in work than in any other Lancashire town or city with a population of over 50,000 in 1921, 45 per cent of 12- and 13-year-old girls and 47 per cent of 12- and 13-year-old boys were in full-time paid employment.[77]

These statistics reveal that Elizabeth Roberts's emphasis on the domestic unpaid tasks undertaken by children under 14 is perhaps misplaced since a sizeable proportion were already in full-time employment. They also indicate the ineffectiveness of the 1918 Education Act in eliminating child employment.[78] The Census figures seem to demonstrate that a sizeable proportion of 12- and 13-year-olds simply fell through the supposed safety net provided by the 1918 Education Act.

In discussing the number of young people under 14 in paid employment we are not simply concerned with the number in full-time employment. We also need to focus on those who were employed part-time for wages. The true extent of this form of paid employment is, of course, not known. The authors of the Census ignore part-time paid employment altogether. An investigation by Salford Education Committee into the number of children working for wages outside school hours in that city in 1913 arrived at a figure of 2,363; 590 of these, it was discovered, worked between 20 and 40 hours a week and a further 52 worked more than 40 hours a week.[79]

A similar investigation was undertaken in 1915 by Manchester

Education Committee. It was discovered that 6,081 children attending day schools in the city (4,519 boys and 1,562 girls) were employed outside school hours for wages.[80] The majority were employed either on errand work, in shops, or delivering newspapers and milk.[81] The 1918 Education Act allowed LEAs to establish by-laws in order to 'regulate' the number of schoolchildren who were employed for wages outside school hours. Manchester Education Committee, however, did not exercise this right, before 1920; though by-law legislation passed in that year led, after 1920, to a situation in which: 'In no case can a child under twelve years be employed, whilst the maximum number of hours children between twelve and fourteen can be employed in any one week is seventeen.'[82] Thus, as late as 1920, many 12–14-year-olds were working not insignificant working weeks for wages. In fact, despite by-law legislation, there were still more than 6,000 schoolchildren in Manchester working between 20 and 40 hours a week for wages in 1922.[83] And, according to Spurley Hey, the city's Director of Education, the figure was still around 2,000 in 1928.[84]

Obviously, no official investigation could ever hope to ascertain the true extent of child employment. The investigations mentioned do indicate, however, that the number of children engaged in paid work remained significant throughout the 1920s. This was certainly Robert Roberts's impression. In *The Classic Slum* he described the early employment experiences of boys in Salford in the period from *c*.1910 to 1925 thus:

> Well before they left school, most boys from the undermass had been working part-time in shops or as street traders of some sort. At that time railways held a glamour for the young that has long since faded. Round all the city termini 'station boys' gathered in great numbers daily both to watch all the bustle and excitement and earn coppers by doing odd jobs... In our city, like the rest, errand boys, telegraph boys, van boys swarmed like summer flies.[85]

Joseph Farrington grew up in West Gorton on the outskirts of Manchester during the Depression and as a child sold newspapers to supplement the family income:

> I wasn't supposed to sell. I didn't have a permit. I was too

young. There'd been a law passed. But I used to go round with papers to help my dad out [his father, an iron moulder at Metropolitan Vickers' engineering firm in Trafford Park, was made redundant in 1928]. I used to get fourpence a dozen for the penny papers and sixpence halfpenny a dozen for the Sunday Chrons and Empires on a Saturday night. I used to sell programmes at the football matches at Maine Road and Belle Vue...I used to get nearly as much as my dad sometimes (his father lived off public assistance). Of course it was supposed to be unknown to the authorities...[86]

We can see, then, that the whole notion of an abrupt 'transition' from school to wage-earning work, which middle-class investigators believed working-class children experienced at about the age of 14, is somewhat mythical. It certainly ignores the fact that many working-class children were already in full-time employment by the age of 12 as late as 1921 and a number of others might as well have been, to judge by the number of hours they worked.

'Blind-Alley' Employment: Another Myth?

Despite the fact that paid work was often undertaken long before the age of 14, academic commentators were principally concerned about the job choices of school leavers in the 'unknown years' between 14 and 16. The authors of a 1928 study of boy labour in Liverpool observed: 'In the critical years between 14 and 16, accurate information concerning the boy is of the scantiest, in spite of the profound changes (often for the worse) that take place therein.'[87] Contemporaries were primarily interested in the job choices of boys and, particularly, in their peculiar susceptibility to 'blind-alley' work.[88] They were less interested in the job choices of girls. The authors of the *Merseyside Survey*, for instance, were dismissive about the job choices of the working-class girls of Liverpool:

This division into 'progressive' and 'blind-alley' jobs is less satisfactory when applied to girls. Most of the work performed by the female adolescent is purely mechanical and repetitive in character...most women indeed do not wish to remain at work after they get married.[89]

20

One of the Jewkes studies showed how 32.2 per cent of all the boys who left elementary schools in the Manchester district in July 1932 and 17.4 per cent of all the girls entered 'Retail and Wholesale Trading', a quintessential 'blind-alley' occupation according to Jewkes, which exposed 14–18-year-olds to periods of 'sporadic employment', 'interrupted training', and 'weary and deadening idleness'.[90] The most critical period for boys employed in 'blind-alley' occupations (Jewkes, too, was less concerned about girls) occurred at the age of 16 when employers were likely to sack them rather than begin paying unemployment and health insurance contributions, as most were obliged to do for all the members of the workforce who were 16 or older.[91] Jewkes produced no statistics to support this argument, however, and the extent to which the break at 16 was enforced as opposed to 16-year-olds leaving 'blind-alley' occupations to take up apprenticeships is unclear.[92]

There is some evidence to suggest that the latter course was becoming an established practice by this period. In Liverpool, a number of errand boys who wanted to become tradesmen were 'taking steps to achieve their objective' in 1934.[93] In pointing to the movement from 'unskilled' jobs into 'skilled' work among boys in Liverpool (or, as the *Merseyside Survey*'s authors put it, the movement from 'blind-alley employment' into 'progressive employment'), the authors of the *Merseyside Survey* were undermining the alarmist views of Jewkes and his colleagues in Manchester. 'The figures do not indicate', the authors of the *Merseyside Survey* argued:

> that even the boys who get into blind-alley occupations, if – as is often stated – they are dismissed at 16 or thereabouts, remain long without work. In fact, the big jump in the number 'in progressive employment' at 18 or 21 rather suggests that they succeed in finding steady work.[94]

This might have been true in Liverpool but how far was it also the case elsewhere?

In Manchester, the number of 'Messengers and Porters' over the age of 16 was significantly fewer than the number under 16, in both 1921 and 1931.[95] It is unclear from the Census occupation tables where the majority of 'Messengers and Porters' went on reaching 16. No doubt some were promoted. A number, however, undoubtedly took up apprenticeships. To take one indication of this, there were twice as many 16- and 17-year-old apprentice fitters in Manchester, in both 1921 and 1931, than there were 14- and 15-year-old apprentice fitters.[96] A Ministry of Labour Report on apprenticeship training in 1925 pointed out that the traditional seven-year apprenticeship (where boys entered the trade at 14) had been 'superseded to a very considerable extent by an apprenticeship for five years from the age of 16 years'.[97] This was the case in all the 'Principal Industries'. In the engineering industry, for instance, 48 per cent of all boy apprentices served a five-year apprenticeship in 1925 and only 25 per cent served a seven-year apprenticeship; in precious metals, the corresponding figures were 44 per cent as against 24 per cent; in the chemical industry, 78 per cent as against 11 per cent; in electrical contracting, 70 per cent as against eight per cent; in the furniture trades, 50 per cent as against 20 per cent; in leather and leather goods, 55 per cent as against seven per cent, and in the distributive trades, 26 per cent as against five per cent. The evidence produced in this report also showed that boys entered apprenticeships at 17 and even 18.[98]

Given that apprenticeships were being increasingly deferred at this period in favour of 'semi-skilled' or 'unskilled' work, which invariably was more highly paid, it is misleading to refer to the latter as 'dead-end' or 'blind-alley' employment simply because contemporaries did so. They were primarily concerned with the lack of training such jobs offered. They were much less prepared to admit, however, that such work, at least in the short term, held certain attractions over lengthy periods of training on low pay. Griffith and Joseph of the University Settlement in Liverpool provided an unduly bleak account of the life of 'Messengers and van lads', who were said to be 'in such a precarious position industrially as to make them wonder (if they think at all) whether the world has a use for them.'[99]

They were primarily concerned to establish 'the extent to which a boy is an industrial nomad' as seemed to be implied in the high turnover of jobs among the boys in their study. All the boys in their study were aged 16½, but 215 boys had had 425 jobs between them since leaving elementary schools in Liverpool two and a half years earlier.[100] According to Griffith and Joseph, these figures were 'an understatement of the real position' and the total number of jobs held by these 215 boys was 'in the neighbourhood of 482'; which meant that the average length of time they were in a job 'would appear to be not over nine months'.[101] Officials at the JEBs were as concerned about the frequency of job changes, not only among boys but also among girls. An inquiry into the early employment experiences of those registered for unemployment benefit at JEBs in Manchester in April 1929 revealed how one boy had had 13 jobs since leaving school and one girl 12 jobs.[102] There were 240 boys in the sample: two-thirds of these had had two or more jobs and over half had had three or more jobs. Out of the 147 girls in the sample, only 35 had had fewer than two jobs; over 50 per cent had had three or more jobs.[103] One of the officials involved in the placement work of the JEBs remarked: 'One of the greatest difficulties of the Bureaux was to persuade juveniles to stay in their employment long enough to understand their work.' This official always tried 'to obtain a promise from every juvenile' for whom she attempted to find work that he or she would remain in the occupation for three months.[104] It appears that her advice was not always heeded because, in 1938, 210 14- and 15-year-olds each week changed their jobs through the JEBs in Manchester.[105]

Joan L. Harley's study of 169 girl wage-earners in Manchester, 141 of whom had left local elementary schools at the age of 14, allows an even deeper insight into the occupational mobility of girls during the 1930s.[106] All the girls in her study were under 19 and the majority were either 16 or 17. Over half (56 per cent) had had two or more jobs since leaving school; about a quarter (23 per cent) had had three or more jobs; eight per cent four or more jobs, and one per cent between six and eight jobs.[107] Although only half gave their reasons for leaving their previous job, 38 per cent did so because there was 'no prospect of promotion'; 23 per cent because they disliked the work; 21 per cent because they had been put on short time; only five per cent because they had been dismissed, and the remainder because of long hours (five per cent), poor health (five per cent), or because their jobs had been temporary (five per cent).[108] 'The greatest number of girls', Harley concluded, 'left their jobs because they found better ones'. Some of the girls went to learn a trade; others left to earn more money, work shorter hours, and travel shorter distances to work.[109]

The job changes of the girls in this study did not always meet with the approval of the author, who assumed, quite incorrectly, that the aim of all girls was to move into more 'skilled' work and to improve themselves.[110] Clearly this was not the case since 'a tailor's learner would like to give up her trade to be a despatcher, which is a descent from a skilled to an unskilled occupation'.[111] Also, none of the girls in 'Group 2' and 'Group 3' occupations (skilled, semi-skilled, and unskilled manual jobs) expressed any desire to become 'foreladies'.[112] Despite these problem cases, however, a number of the girls in the study were preparing to move from 'unskilled' work into 'skilled' jobs: a packer (a 'Group 3' occupation) was looking for a job as a shop assistant (a 'Group 2' occupation); three domestic servants ('Group 3') were looking for jobs as nurses ('Group 1'), and a shirt and pyjama machinist ('Group 2') was looking for office work ('Group 1').[113]

The most meaningful evidence available on the job choices of boy and girl wage-earners suggests, then, a high degree of occupational mobility among boys (especially up to the age of 16) and, more surprisingly, a high degree of occupational mobility among girls. The evidence relating to boys is supported by a number of contemporary studies, but especially those undertaken into the boy labour markets of interwar Liverpool and Manchester. The juvenile labour markets Jewkes and his colleagues studied at this period differed in many respects from those of Liverpool and Manchester and other large cities such as London.[114] In small Lancashire towns which were either entirely dependent or largely dependent on a single, declining industry there were a limited number of alternatives open to those juveniles sacked at 16, or put on short time. This led, in certain cases (Barrow-in-Furness, Burnley and St. Helens are the most notorious examples), to high levels of juvenile unemployment which, in Burnley, outlasted the Depression in the cotton industry and in St. Helens persisted into 1936.[115]

In cities such as Manchester, London, and even Liverpool, however, the demand for juvenile labour became so insatiable during the 1930s that juveniles had to be imported from other districts and even regions. The evidence available suggests that the above conditions provided a greater degree of job choice for girls and boys in such cities during the 1930s. This led many young workers to 'experiment' with different jobs.[116]

The Determinants of Job Choice

In stressing the frequency of job changes among teenage wage-earners at this period we are, in some ways, offering a different interpretation of their job choices than is suggested by the work of Diana Gittins and Elizabeth Roberts.[117] Both of these historians stress the overriding influence of parents on the job 'choices' of their children. Diana Gittins's interviews with working-class women revealed that 'it was entirely the parents' decision as to whether their daughters should work, and what sort of work they should do.'[118] Elizabeth Roberts also draws attention to 'young people's lack of choice about the sort of work they did.'[119] 'Choice of work', she argues, 'was very much influenced by parental advice, example, or "string-pulling", so that once they were working they frequently found themselves either directly under a relative, or someone well known to the family.'[120] Roberts, however, was only describing the situation that prevailed in small towns such as Lancaster, Preston and Barrow. Similarly, Gittins was basing her conclusions on oral evidence from small textile towns such as Burnley. The job choices of teenage wage-earners appear to have been much less circumscribed in the cities, although there is some evidence to suggest that parents were initially a guiding influence.

Geoffrey Kershaw began work as an apprentice for Hans Renold of Burnage (a firm which made bicycle chains) in 1918, apparently against his father's wishes. (His father, a brass finisher in West Manchester, had wanted him to stay on at school.) Nevertheless, his father did exercise a certain influence over his son's choice of employment since Mr Kershaw was told: 'I must not go to a place that started at 6 o'clock in the morning'.[121] As an apprentice at Hans Renold's, he began work at eight o'clock. Another man, who served an apprenticeship at the British Westinghouse engineering firm in Trafford Park, Manchester during the 1920s, pointed out:

> it was every father's ambition to get the sons to be an apprentice... Everybody wanted to be an apprentice, and there was plenty of work, nobody was unemployed, every boy got a job of some kind, but they all, all the parents wanted them to be an apprentice.[122]

He went on to remark that some of his friends who began as apprentices left before completing their training: 'Oh yes and some used to...start as a tea boy, an apprentice, and they didn't like what they was doing and then they got a job in something or other, a lot

25

of my friends went out...'.[123] Some apprentices were clearly influenced by the wishes of parents. The correspondence of Manchester firms provides examples. In January 1917, Lloyd's Packing Warehouses Ltd informed Manchester, Salford and Bolton Case Makers' Society that 'Robert Clarkson, who commenced work with us as an apprentice on January 8, only worked two days, the excuse being that his parents considered the trade too dirty.'[124] The previous month an apprentice who had worked at the firm 11 months had left due to his father 'taking him away',[125] and another apprentice had left 'on account of his parents refusing to allow him to stay in the trade'.[126]

We should not, then, underestimate the influence parents could have on the job 'choices' of their children. But neither should we overestimate it. A 14- year-old boy's entry into full-time work could just as easily be seen as a process of bargaining, both with parents and, more surprisingly, with employers:

> When I was about 14 I went to town and there was seven of us waiting for this job... I was last, 'Come in. Are you strong?' I said 'Yes', 'Well I want you to walk down Piccadilly with a sandwich board...I said, 'How much will you pay me?' He said 'Ten bob a week'. I said 'No thank you'. [127]

The above example of a boy wage-earner displaying a considerable degree of autonomy in the labour market is certainly not exceptional. An official at a JEB in a London suburb described how boys 'mainly of the factory type' were unwilling to venture out of the town for work and others demanded certain preconditions such as short hours, good pay and good working conditions before they would accept employment that was deemed 'suitable' by the officials at the bureaux.[128] The whole notion of 'suitable' employment, which underpinned the work of the JEBs, was highly ambiguous. The officials had their own views about what was 'suitable' employment. This did not, however, necessarily coincide with what employers considered 'suitable' work for juveniles and, most importantly, what young wage-earners felt was 'suitable' work.[129]

Officials at the JEBs in Manchester constantly drew attention to the fact that local juveniles decided for themselves what was 'suitable' work. In October 1918, an enquiry into unemployment among local boys ascertained that many were unemployed not through lack of work, but because they demanded a particular job with a specific firm. [130] One 15-year-old who had worked for two years in a cotton manufacturer's warehouse had left his job to work for a local engineering firm and 'persisted in waiting for a vacancy'. Another boy of 15 wanted a job in the electrical engineering industry. He was sent to 13 different firms including five engaged in electrical engineering. In three cases he did not attend for an interview; in another he was engaged but failed to start; while in another case he would not accept the work offered.[131] The conditions that allowed boys such choice over the employment they entered were not unique to the war period. As we have seen, boys and girls were in heavy demand during the 1930s, and this allowed many juveniles a greater degree of job choice in these years.

It seems surprising, therefore, that in discussing the job 'choices' of young people at this period historians have been most concerned to stress the restrictions on job choice. From one direction came parental or familial pressures on children to earn 'the biggest shilling'; from another, employer discrimination and the allegedly stricter demands of the labour market at this period.[132] There were also hereditary factors to be taken into account such as the unenviable labour market position of the 'children of the unskilled'[133] and also physical factors: 'It was still the undersized or ugly or slow-thinking youth who found himself unemployed most frequently and for longest', Jerry White argues in his recent study of interwar Islington.[134]

There are elements of truth in this highly circumscribed picture, but it overlooks a great deal and is overdrawn. Take the labour market position of the 'children of the unskilled', for instance. Jerry White argues that this group were fundamentally disadvantaged in terms of the job opportunities available to them. E. L. Lewis, however, in his 1924 study *The Children of the Unskilled: An Economic and Social Study* was unable to prove that apprentices (or 'skilled' workers) only emerged from 'skilled' families and hardly, if at all, from 'semi-skilled' or 'unskilled' families. Lewis claimed that: 'Children belonging to the families in the first class ('skilled families') are usually taught the value of skilled industry, habits of self-control and perseverance, and are encouraged...to enter skilled work.'[135] 'Skilled' parents, he argued, were more 'progressive' in

27

this respect than 'semi-skilled' or 'unskilled' parents: 'Children belonging to the other two classes ("semi-skilled" and "unskilled" families) have little encouragement from their parents... to enter skilled work.'[136] The author's own statistics showed, however, that among 46 families in the 'first class' (skilled) there were 97 apprentices and among 254 families in the 'second class' (semi-skilled) there were 216 apprentices; that is, there was no direct correlation to support his hypothesis.[137] The author's principal conclusion was, therefore, vague and unspectacular: 'The families in the soundest economic position were, as a rule, able to apprentice a greater number of children than those in poorer circumstances.'[138]

There is more to be said for the physical requirements of certain trades. The plumbing trade required boys of 'a good physique' since 'in addition to heavy jobs, there is often outside work to be done in bad weather'.[139] Millinery required girls 'with artistic ability and dexterity... as neatness is most essential'.[140] Good eyesight was another essential requirement in certain trades, notably embroidery and hosiery.[141] But the physical requirements of certain trades did not automatically exclude the physically handicapped. Artificial flower-making appealed to 'young people, chiefly girls who suffer from certain physical disabilities, as they may sit at their work during the greater part of the day'.[142] Similarly, there were no fixed rules on the types of boys and girls required for office work. The educational requirements varied depending on the individual employer: 'Some employers prefer boys and girls from Elementary Schools at 14 years of age, whilst others prefer older boys and girls from Central and Secondary Schools.'[143]

All of this suggests that the job horizons of young wage-earners at this period were less circumscribed than recent historians have claimed. Job choices were influenced by various pressures (familial and peer group pressures, for example)[144] and also by the requirements of employers; although these were by no means fixed and by no means automatically excluded boys and girls with, for instance, a physical defect. But this is not the whole story. While historians have analysed the influences that restricted the job choices of young wage-earners they have ignored the wealth of contemporary evidence drawing attention to their frequent job changes and thus the autonomy shown by the teenage age group in the 'adult' world of work. In March 1937, a juvenile employment officer in London drew attention to this autonomy. He described a typical day in the life of a Juvenile Employment Bureau official in 'a large dormitory suburb of London':

> A small but sharp-looking youngster approaches the counter... 'Please Sir, can I have another card for Snow Hill? That last job you got me was no good. No prospects, Sir. I did nothing but run errands for the others'. 'I see. But you'll always have to do that at first, you know. How long were you there?' 'Only a day, Sir'. 'A day isn't very long to tell what a job is going to be like'. 'No, but there were no prospects. The other boys said so'. Another vacancy is found for him, and he is sent off to try again.[145]

Job Finding: A Case Study

We must turn, finally, to the most difficult question of all: how teenage wage-earners found jobs. The Ministry of Labour claimed in May 1929 that:

> The work of advising boys and girls between the ages of 14 and 18 on the choice of a career, of endeavouring to obtain for them suitable vacancies, and of ensuring their welfare especially during the early months of employment, is in the hands of specially constituted Juvenile Committees.[146]

But a Committee on Education and Industry, set up by the Ministry of Labour itself, had concluded only two years earlier that 'as regards placing work, the public agencies in England and Wales as a whole do not deal with more than 20 per cent of the situations or of the juvenile workers... and that very likely the percentage is less than 20.'[147] An earlier enquiry by the Ministry of Labour into the 'personal circumstances and industrial history' of 3,331 boys and 2,701 girls, conducted in June and July 1925, discovered that only 18 per cent of the jobs undertaken by those in the survey had been found by the official job-finding agencies.[148]

The *Merseyside Survey* (1934) examined this question in rather more detail using a random sample of 266 'adolescents' from Liverpool (164 boys and 102 girls), all of whom left elementary schools in the city in February 1930 at the age of 14. This enquiry revealed that the largest number (40 per cent of the sample) found work through their 'Own Efforts'; which included jobs obtained in answer to an advertisement. Slightly fewer (34 per cent) found work through the Juvenile Employment Bureaux; seven per cent did so through 'Friends' and 6.6 per cent through 'Parents'. There were slight differences between the sexes. For instance, more girls (41 per cent) found their first job through the Juvenile Employment Bureaux than through their 'Own Efforts' (31 per cent), but fewer boys did (32 per cent as against 37 per cent). Thereafter, however, the number who found work through their 'Own Efforts' rose appreciably in the case of both girls and boys. Half the girls in the sample obtained subsequent posts through their 'Own Efforts' and just over half (51.5 per cent) of the boys. About a third of each sex continued to use the Juvenile Employment Bureaux and 14 per cent of the girls (but only four per cent of the boys) found subsequent jobs through the medium of 'Friends'.[149]

No similar enquiry was undertaken in Manchester during this period and in the absence of such a study it seems worthwhile to consider briefly the work of the city's juvenile employment service. This was set up in January 1914 by a sub-committee of Manchester Education Committee.[150] Accordingly, the service was initially administered from temporary accommodation provided by a local school, St. Anne's School, situated in the city centre. The service was administered from here, however, until 1935 when the headquarters were transferred to a building on Deansgate, also in the city centre. Over the period from 1914 to 1935, Manchester Education Committee set up subsidiary branches of the main service in four suburbs: Levenshulme (1918), Newton Heath (1918), Openshaw (1918), and Withington (1935). All of these branch bureaux were administered from schools with the exception of Withington's which was administered from the local town hall.[151] This meant that the atmosphere at the bureaux was extremely formal. The officials certainly made no attempt to extinguish the atmosphere of the school and, it appears, they sought to preserve it. A *Manchester Evening News* reporter visited the city centre bureau in 1934 and described the atmosphere thus:

> In a backwater just off the Deansgate traffic tide in Manchester there is a quiet building which would remind you of any ordinary council school. Today I went in and walked through an upper room which had all the atmosphere of a classroom – dozens of healthy boys and girls sitting in rows

of forms, facing a desk, with men and women who looked like teachers moving about. There was the schoolroom air of order and discipline.[152]

The author of this report even referred to the bureau's supervisor, E. G. Greenwell, as 'the headmaster'. The bureaux' own literature evokes the officious nature of the service provided. In the annual report for 1934, for instance, it was pointed out:

Juveniles are not encouraged to pay unnecessary calls at the Bureau after their first interview and registration. Vacancies are not filled by the selection from those juveniles who happen to be on the premises, but a careful selection from the complete registers is made, and the most suitable boy or girl summoned to attend by post card.[153]

At a national level, the service the JEBs provided attracted criticism on a number of grounds. Among the most frequently cited was the impersonal nature of the service.[154] One juvenile employment officer, writing in May 1936, argued that school-leavers would not automatically resort to the service for advice about jobs until it changed its name. The word 'Bureau', he remarked was, 'an unpleasant word with unfortunate associations' and the term 'juvenile' was 'odious' and 'a positive insult to any sensitive adolescent from fifteen years upwards'.[155] In addition to providing an officious service, JEBs frequently carried the stigma, especially in the depressed areas, of being popularly known as the 'Juvenile Dole'. This led T. K. Cross to argue that they were simply part of 'a vast and impersonal administrative machine'.[156] In Manchester, as elsewhere, JEBs were responsible for administering the unemployment insurance scheme to the under-18 age group throughout this period and this work was conducted either in the same building as the placement work or in an adjacent one.[157] In the light of these problems and criticisms, how did the Manchester JEBs perform during this period?

During the war years, only a minority of local school-leavers bothered to register at the JEBs. In the eighteen-month period between January 1914 (when the first JEB was opened) and July 1915, the local service placed only 1,620 local school-leavers into employment; but 10,000 children each year left local schools during the war years.[158] By 1916, this figure had declined to 980 and only 772 local school-leavers were placed into employment by the service in 1917.[159] There was a turnaround in the JEBs' fortunes, however, immediately after the war. Section 22 of the 1918 Education Act extended their work. Henceforth, they were to deal not just with 14–16-year-olds but also 17-year-olds. In effect, this simply meant that more secondary school-leavers could now use the JEBs. The bureaux were also made responsible for administering the 'juvenile' section of the Government's 'Out of Work Donation' scheme. In addition, the local service found work for local juveniles and the staff gave talks to after-care workers, employers, welfare societies and student teachers, and visited schools.[160]

Despite this work, the local JEBs continued to place into employment only a minority of local juvenile wage-earners. In 1921, the number placed into employment locally (which now included anyone between the ages of 14 and 18) was only 2,112.[161] It was even fewer (1,871) the following year and had still not risen to 3,000 by 1928.[162] During the 1920s, between 9,000 and 10,000 14-year-olds entered the local labour market every year and there were 45,000 in the 14-18 age-group locally in 1925.[163] The Levenshulme JEB was even forced to close in October 1923 owing to a lack of local support.[164]

Slowly, however, the placement work of the local JEBs began to increase and by the end of the 1920s over three times as many local juveniles were being placed into employment by the service than in 1923.[165] By the early 1930s, between 8,000 and 9,000 14-18-year-olds every year were being found jobs. The number dealt with by the local service increased dramatically after 1934. Between 1935 and 1939, no fewer than 11,000 every year were placed into employment. In 1934, E. G. Greenwell, the supervisor at the city centre bureau, claimed that the service was finding jobs for 300 'children' a week. The number who registered themselves for employment at the bureau was a record-breaking 15,139 in 1934. 'This', argued the Director of Education in the city (W. O. Lester Smith), 'is a clear indication of the greater use that is being made of the advisory and placing service of the Department.'[166]

That the placement work of the local service increased quite dramatically over the two interwar decades is, then, indisputable. But it needs to be borne in mind that the number of local school-leavers who were placed into employment by the service was far fewer than the number who registered themselves for employment;[167] too much should not be read into W. O. Lester Smith's words, therefore. Also, in relation to the number of 14-18-year-olds in the city, the number placed into employment by the service, even in the 1930s, was no more than a third.[168]

The reasons why the service only attracted a minority of local teenage wage-earners are probably manifold. The austere, schoolroom atmosphere of the bureaux may have deterred some from attending, certainly more than once. But another reason undoubtedly lay in the bureaux' whole approach to juvenile employment. We have already mentioned the dichotomy between jobs the officials at JEBs deemed suitable for young wage-earners and young wage earners' (and their parents') own thoughts on this subject. This dichotomy is particularly apparent in the work of Manchester's juvenile employment service. During the post-war slump, the JEBs' officials urged parents to 'prolong their child's education rather than risk a deterioration in the child's character' through allowing their children to enter casual work. But this advice appears to have been rejected by many parents.[169] In 1936, the supervisor at the city centre JEB prepared a pamphlet on suitable occupations for school-leavers and sent this to all local schools. It instructed prospective school-leavers to 'give more serious attention to their choice of occupation' and to 'lessen the number who are indeterminate or even capricious about their first choice of a career'.[170] It appears the pamphlet did not achieve the desired effect since even by 1937: 'Many juveniles accepted the first job offered to them rather than first considering the whole field of employment.'[171] By 1939, although officials from the JEBs continued to visit local schools regularly in order to 'check too hasty entrance into employment', their advice was still being rejected by 'many juveniles'.[172]

There is also evidence that the relationship between the JEBs and local employers was far from reciprocal at this period. The supervisor at the headquarters bureau refused to place juveniles in certain occupations such as theatre work and billiard hall work or into any occupation that, because of long hours, prevented them from attending evening school.[173] In a radio broadcast to Manchester schools in 1925, he warned prospective school-leavers against accepting 'blind-alley' employment such as 'becoming an unskilled machine minder or labourer' and said that employers were only interested in them as labour.[174] In a second broadcast to school leavers he even instructed them not to waste time and money on visits to the cinema and to join a youth club.[175]

To some local employers it must have seemed as though the JEBs' officials were a perpetual thorn in their side. This is implicit in the comments of an early historian of the juvenile employment service: 'Juvenile Employment Officers sometimes visited employers to assist juveniles to overcome their employment difficulties and to acquaint employers of the law relating to the employment of juveniles.'[176] These periodic visits to local firms were still being undertaken at the end of the interwar period.[177]

To those juveniles who used the service its literature, circulated to all local schools, must have seemed incredibly patronising; particularly that which instructed them to spend their leisure time wisely. The following extract is from a pamphlet sent to Manchester schools in 1936:

> Remember, if you are not at school or at work you are not standing still, you are going backwards...Then, what about your leisure time?... There are people who do not know how to use it to the best advantage...the Officers of the Bureaux can assist you by introduction to some After-Care Committee, Club, Boys' Brigade, Scout Troop, Girls' Club, Girl Guides,...where you may usefully employ your time both in summer and winter.[178]

The after-care work of the bureaux was begun in 1925 when a team of voluntary workers were employed to visit the homes of all 14–18-year-olds locally in employment. The work was primarily intended to encourage them to join evening classes or youth movements, as well as inform them of the placement work of the bureaux. Some 24 district care committees were set up to administer the scheme; but, by 1937, only five of these were still functioning and only those considered by headmasters to be 'in special need of supervision and help' were visited.[179]

The placement work of the JEBs achieved greater success than their after-care schemes. But using the service to find work was both a lengthy exercise and an uncertain one. The following account illustrates how boys wishing to take up messenger work using the JEBs' service were recruited:

> Upon each occasion when candidates are required, an examination of the whole Waiting List is conducted by the Bureau...The results are sent to the employer, so that by this system each boy has an equal opportunity, and the employer enjoys the full benefits of the popularity of his vacancies by a wide and comprehensive selection.[180]

Many young workers at this period entered jobs not through using the JEBs, but by more informal means. As one former apprentice, who served his apprenticeship at an engineering firm in Trafford Park, Manchester, during the 1920s, commented, 'it was every father's ambition to get the sons to be an apprentice, so you, just as you're 14 somebody tells you...apply here, apply there, one of my neighbours told me dad for me to go and apply at the Westinghouse and they took me on...'[181] Precisely how many boys found jobs through either their own efforts or those of their parents is, of course, impossible to determine. Nevertheless, the evidence produced in this chapter suggests that a large number in their teens did use the official juvenile employment service. Reading between the lines of official reports, we observe that those who did use the service were highly selective in the type of employment they would accept: what the JEBs' officials considered suitable work did not always coincide with what the recipients of their service considered suitable or attractive employment.

Conclusion

Young wage-earners, especially in the cities, displayed a considerable degree of autonomy in their choice of work during the 1920s and 1930s. Those critics who argued that some young workers, those employed in so-called 'blind-alley' jobs, were trapped were alarmists out of touch with what many juveniles considered attractive employment. Van boy work, warehouse work, and other so-called 'blind-alley' work offered 14- and 15 year olds who might decide to take up apprenticeships at 16 attractive wages and ample opportunities for overtime work and thus even higher earnings. Many boys, it seems, deferred apprenticeships for two years in order to secure higher earnings in so-called 'blind-alley' jobs. Contemporaries such as William McG. Eagar, John Jewkes,

E. S. Griffith and R. A. Joseph seem to have overlooked this fact and certainly overstated the bleakness and apparent insecurity of blind-alley employment. Equally, they understated the buoyancy of the juvenile labour market which made movement from dead-end jobs into apprenticeships possible for large numbers of juveniles.

NOTES

1. W. McG. Eagar, 'The Next Step in Education', *Social Service Bulletin*, Vol.IX, No.8 (August 1928), p.139.
2. Jewkes and Jewkes, *The Juvenile Labour Market*, p.11; Appendix, Tables 1.1 and 1.2.
3. Stephen Humphries's study *Hooligans or Rebels?*, seriously neglects working-class youths' experiences in the labour market and at work. For the only historical work on this subject at this period see J. White, *The Worst Street in North London: Campbell Bunk, Islington, Between the Wars* (London 1986), pp.161–4, 188–92; E. Roberts, *A Woman's Place: An Oral History of Working-Class Women, 1890–1940* (1984 repr. Oxford, 1985), Ch. 2; D. Gittins, *Fair Sex: Family Size and Structure, 1900–39* (London, 1982), Ch. 3. The latter two studies, as will be obvious, only consider the working–class girl's labour market behaviour. For a discussion of their main conclusions see below, pp.24–5. For the debate about youth unemployment in interwar Britain see W. R. Garside, 'Juvenile Unemployment and Public Policy between the Wars', *Economic History Review*, Second Series, Vol.XXX, No.2 (May 1977), pp.322–39; D. K. Benjamin and L. A. Kochin, 'What went Right with Juvenile Unemployment Policy between the Wars: A Comment', *Economic History Review*, Vol.XXXII, No.4 (November 1979), pp.523–8; W. R. Garside, 'Juvenile Unemployment between the Wars: A Rejoinder', *Economic History Review*, Vol.XXXII, No.4 (November 1979), pp.529–32. See also M. A. Crowther, *British Social Policy 1914–1939* (London, 1988), pp.44–6.
4. E.S. Griffith and R.A. Joseph, 'The Unknown Years', *Social Service Bulletin*, Vol.IX, No.7 (July1928), p.114.
5. Ibid., pp.113–18.
6. J.L. Harley, 'Report of an enquiry into the occupations, further education and leisure inter ests of a number of girl wage–earners from elementary and central schools in the Manchester district, with special reference to the influence of school training on their use of leisure', unpublished MEd thesis, University of Manchester, 1937, p.36.
7. D. Caradog Jones (ed.), *The Social Survey of Merseyside*, Vol. 3 (London, 1934), pp.201–2.
8. J. Jewkes and A. Winterbottom, *Juvenile Unemployment* (London, 1933), pp.25–6.
9. See, in addition to the studies by Jewkes and Caradog Jones, Griffith and Joseph, 'Unknown Years'; and A. D. K. Owen, *A Survey of Juvenile Employment and Welfare in Sheffield* (Sheffield, 1933).
10. A. Winterbottom, *An Enquiry Into The Employment of Juveniles in Lancashire* (Manchester,1932), pp.6–7.
11. Ibid., pp.5–7, 22.
12. J. Hallsworth, *Protective Legislation for Shop and Office Employees* (3rd edn. London, 1939), p.135.
13. Jewkes and Winterbottom, *Juvenile Unemployment*, p.18. See also Garside, 'Rejoinder', pp.529–30, in which he makes the same point. See also the Unemployment Act 1934, 24 and 25 George V, Chapter 29, Section 1(1), on the entry of 14– and 15-year-olds into the unemployment insurance scheme, cited in *The Public General Acts* 24 and 25, Geo. V (London,1934), p.191.
14. Jewkes and Jewkes, *Juvenile Labour Market*, Introduction.
15. Harley, 'Report', Ch. II.

16   See Appendix, Tables 1.3 and 1.4, for the juvenile occupational structure at the Censuses of 1921 and 1931.

17.   Ibid.

18.   Census of England and Wales 1921, *County of Lancaster* (London, 1923), pp.3–13.

19.   Ibid.

20.   For example, Manchester's boundaries were extended quite dramatically between 1921 and 1931. See Census of England and Wales, 1931, *County of Lancaster*, Part I (London, 1932), p.23.

21.   See G. Stedman Jones, *Outcast London: A Study in the Relationship Between Classes in Victorian Society* (Oxford, 1971), Appendix 1 on this.

22.   Appendix, Table 1.3.

23.   Appendix, Table 1.4.

24.   Appendix, Table 1.3.

25.   Appendix, Table 1.4.

26.   S.P. Dobbs, *The Clothing Workers of Great Britain* (London, 1928), p.49.

27.   Ibid.

28.   Ibid.

29.   Ibid.

30.   Ibid., p.52.

31.   Census of 1921, op.cit., Table 18; Census of England and Wales 1931, *Occupation Tables* (London, 1934), Table 18.

32.   J. White, *Worst Street in North London*, p.163.

33.   Manchester Education Committee, Juvenile Employment Bureaux, *A Summary of Occupations Open to Boys and Girls in the City* (Manchester, 1936), p.3.

34.   Ibid.

35.   Ibid., pp.13–14.

36.   For this view see L. Davidoff and B. Westover, '"From Queen Victoria to the Jazz Age": Women's World in England 1880–1939' in idem (eds), *Our Work, Our Lives, Our Words: Women's History and Women's Work* (Hampshire, 1986), Ch. 1.

37.   Manchester Education Committee, Juvenile Employment Bureaux, *Occupations*, p.11.

38.   Ibid., p.7.

39.   Ibid., p.13.

40.   Ibid., p.1.

41.   Ibid., pp.1–2.

42.   Ibid., pp.2–3. See also Manchester Education Committee, Juvenile Employment Bureaux, *Annual Reports*, *passim*.

43.   Manchester Education Committee, Juvenile Employment Bureaux, *Occupations*, pp.4, 6, 7.

44.   *Manchester Evening News*, 24 July 1934.

45.   Manchester Education Committee, Juvenile Employment Bureaux, *Annual Report* 1933, pp.1, 10. These statistics and those cited below refer to the 'placements' by all the local Juvenile Employment Bureaux. There were four of these operating in Manchester during the 1930s: Deansgate JEB in the city centre; and Newton Heath, Openshaw, and Withington JEBs in the suburbs. See City of Manchester Education Committee, Juvenile Employment Bureaux, *Annual Report* 1935, pp.9–10.

46.   Manchester Education Committee, Juvenile Employment Bureaux, *Annual Report* 1935, p.9.

47.   Manchester Education Committee, Juvenile Employment Bureaux, *Annual Report* 1936, p.13.

48.   Ibid., p.5.

49.   Ibid.

50.   Manchester Education Committee, Juvenile Employment Bureaux, *Annual Report* 1938, p.1 cited in H.E. Canner, 'The Juvenile Employment Service in Manchester, 1910–1939', unpublished MEd thesis, University of Manchester, 1958, p.127.

51.   Canner, 'Juvenile Employment Service', p.128.

52.   Manchester Education Committee, Juvenile Employment Bureaux, *Annual Report* 1934, p.1.

53. Manchester Education Committee, Juvenile Employment Bureaux, *Annual Report* 1935, p.6.
54. Canner, 'Juvenile Employment Service', p.138.
55. Ibid, p.139.
56. Ibid.
57. See Ministry of Labour, *Memorandum on the Shortage, Surplus and Redistribution of Juvenile Labour during the Years 1928–1933* based on the views of Local Juvenile Employment Committees, Cmd 3327 (London, May 1929), p.4.
58. See Manchester Education Committee, Juvenile Employment Bureaux, *Annual Reports*, *passim*.
59. Manchester Education Committee, Juvenile Employment Bureaux, *Annual Report* 1936, p.16.
60. Canner, 'Juvenile Employment Service', p.141.
61. See Manchester Education Committee, Juvenile Employment Bureaux, *Annual Report* 1933, p.10; idem, *Annual Report* 1934, p.9; idem, *Annual Report* 1935, p.9; idem, *Annual Report* 1936, p.13.
62. Manchester Education Committee, Juvenile Employment Bureaux, *Annual Report* 1936, p.16.
63. Ibid.
64. Ibid.
65. See above, pp.8–10.
66. W.R. Garside, 'Juvenile Unemployment and Public Policy', pp.322, 332.
67. Ibid., pp.331–2. See also Ch. 3.
68. Jewkes and Winterbottom, *Juvenile Unemployment*, p.142.
69. Ibid.
70. Ibid.
71. Manchester Education Committee, Juvenile Employment Bureaux, *Annual Report* 1933, p.10; *Annual Report* 1935, p.9; *Annual Report* 1936, p.13.
72. Cited in E. Roberts, *Woman's Place*, p.38.
73. Harley, 'Report', p.3.
74. City of Manchester, *The Signpost: A Guide for Young People and their Elders* (Manchester, 1928), p.6.
75. E. Roberts, *Woman's Place*, p.39.
76. See Census 1921, op.cit., Table 18.
77. Ibid.
78. On the raising of the minimum school–leaving age to 14 under the Education Act of 1918 see Education Act, 1918, 8 and 9 George V Chapter 39, Section 8(1) cited in The Public General Acts 8 and 9, Geo.V (London, 1918), p.128. Elizabeth Roberts overstates the effectiveness of this legislation. See E. Roberts, *Woman's Place*, p.34.
79. J. Hallsworth, *Shop and Office Employees*, pp.113–14.
80. Ibid.
81. Ibid., p.115. See also Springhall, *Coming of Age*, Ch. 3 for a discussion of part–time paid employment in the major cities before 1914.
82. *The Signpost*, p.6.
83. Canner, 'Juvenile Employment Service', p.7.
84. Spurley Hey, *The School Leaving Age* (Manchester, 1928), p.32 cited in Canner, 'Juvenile Employment Service', p.7.
85. R. Roberts, *The Classic Slum: Salford Life in the First Quarter of the Century* (1971; repr. Middlesex, 1983), pp.157–8.
86. Cited in N. Gray, *The Worst of Times: An Oral History of the Great Depression in Britain* (London, 1985), pp.14–15.
87. Griffith and Joseph, 'Unknown Years', p.112.
88. Hendrick, focusing on an earlier period, makes the same point about the boy labour critics in Edwardian Britain. See Hendrick, *Images of Youth*, pp.4–5.
89. Caradog Jones (ed.), *Social Survey of Merseyside*, Vol.3, p.206.
90. Jewkes and Winterbottom, *Juvenile Unemployment*, pp.14, 146–7.
91. Ibid., p.14.

92. See the conflicting conclusions of Griffith and Joseph on Liverpool, op.cit; and a Birmingham Juvenile Employment Officer's inquiry outlined in *Social Service Review*, Vol.X, No.9 (September 1929), pp.175–8.

93. Caradog Jones (ed.), *Social Survey of Merseyside*, Vol.3, p.221. On the shift from 'unskilled' work to 'skilled' apprenticeships at 16 among boy labourers in Cambridge before the First World War see M.N. Keynes, *The Problem of Boy Labour in Cambridge* (Cambridge, 1911), p.8. On the same trend in Oxford before 1914 see C.V. Butler, *Social Conditions in Oxford* (Oxford, 1912), pp.52–60. Some of the errand boys in pre–war Oxford were the sons of artisans who wanted their sons to 'look around' before entering an apprenticeship. See also Springhall, *Coming of Age*, pp.85, 100–2.

94. Caradog Jones (ed.), *Social Survey of Merseyside*, Vol.3, p.206.

95. Of the 3,620 'Messengers and Porters' under 20 in 1921, 2,668 were under 16; only 787 were aged 16 and 17, and only 150 aged 18 and 19. The numbers in the respective age groups in 1931 were: 2,826 aged 14 and 15; 1,257 aged 16 and 17, and only 343 aged 18–20. See Census of 1921, op.cit., Table 18; Census of 1931, op.cit., Table 18.

96. There were 318 14- and 15-year-old apprentice fitters enumerated as 'Metal Workers' in 1921 and 716 16- and 17-year-olds. At the Census of 1931, the number in each age-group was 290 and 641 respectively. See Census of 1921, op.cit., Table 18; Census of 1931, op.cit., Table 18.

97. Ministry of Labour, *Report of an Enquiry into Apprenticeship and Training for the Skilled Occupations in Great Britain and Northern Ireland, 1925–6*, Vol. VII, General Report (London, 1928), p.4.

98. Ibid., pp.4, 81.

99. Griffith and Joseph, 'Unknown Years', p.113.

100. Ibid., pp.112, 114.

101. Ibid.

102. Cited in Canner, 'Juvenile Employment Service', p.136.

103. Ibid.

104. Ibid., p.139.

105. Ibid.

106. Harley, 'Report', Ch. V.

107. Ibid., p.43.

108. Ibid.

109. Ibid., p.44.

110. Ibid., pp.45, 53, 54.

111. Ibid., p.54.

112. Ibid. The author put this down to the fact that 'these girls are fairly new to factory life and have perhaps not yet had time to develop such ambitions'.

113. Ibid., pp.41, 48, 49, 51.

114. On the buoyancy of the youth labour market of London at this period see J. White, *Worst Street in North London*, Chs. 6 and 7.

115. See Jewkes and Jewkes, *Juvenile Labour Market*, pp.59–63. The unemployment rate among the 550 in the Jewkes' St. Helens sample never fell below 30 per cent between April and December 1934 and even by 1936 it had not fallen below 17 per cent. On a personal level, this meant that 200 juveniles in the Jewkes' sample experienced unemployment at some time over the two-year period of the inquiry. A fifth of these were unemployed for over 11 months during this two-year period and 32 had no employment at all during the two years.

116. Canner, 'Juvenile Employment Service', p.138. Canner wrote disapprovingly: 'It was considered that the shortage of juvenile workers encouraged some to "experiment" in different jobs rather than change employment in a serious attempt at improvement'.

117. Gittins, *Fair Sex*, Ch. 3; E. Roberts, *Woman's Place*, Ch. 2.

118. Gittins, *Fair Sex*, pp.69–71.

119. E. Roberts, *Woman's Place*, p.45.

120. Ibid.

121. Manchester Studies Oral History Archive, Manchester Metropolitan University, tape 250.

122. Idem, tape 780.

123. Ibid.
124. Letters From Packing Case Firms About Apprentices, 1913–1939, Manchester Central Reference Library, Archives Department, M308/4/3–8.
125. Ibid.
126. Ibid.
127. The testimony of Joseph Farrington who grew up in West Gorton, Manchester, during the Depression, cited in N. Gray, *Worst of Times*, p.25.
128. See the article 'A Day in a Juvenile Employment Officer's Life', *Human Factor*, Vol. XI, No.3 (March, 1937), pp.106–9.
129. See the article, 'Impressions and Animadversions by a Juvenile Bureaucrat', *Human Factor*, Vol. X, No.5 (May 1936).
130. Canner, 'Juvenile Employment Service', p.47.
131. Ibid., p.48.
132. J. White, *Worst Street in North London*, p.163.
133. Ibid.
134. Ibid., p.164.
135. E. L. Lewis, *The Children of the Unskilled: An Economic and Social Study* (London, 1924), p.xii. Lewis's study was based on a sample of 450 families (which included 2,000 children) in Glasgow, Middlesbrough, and the Welsh quarrying district of Blaenau Ffestiniog in North Wales.
136. Ibid.
137. Ibid., pp.15–16.
138. Ibid., pp.ix–x.
139. Manchester Education Committee, Juvenile Employment Bureaux, *Occupations*, p.3.
140. Ibid., p.6.
141. Ibid., pp.6–7.
142. Ibid., p.1.
143. Ibid., p.8.
144. On the latter see R. Roberts, *Classic Slum*, p.157.
145. 'A Day in a Juvenile Employment Officer's Life', pp.108–9.
146. Ministry of Labour, *Juvenile Labour*, p.2.
147. Ministry of Labour, *Report of the Committee on Education and Industry England and Wales*, First Part (London, 1926), p.16.
148. Ibid.
149. Caradog Jones (ed.), *Social Survey of Merseyside*, Vol.3, pp.202–4, 211–12.
150. Manchester Education Committee, Juvenile Employment Bureaux, *Annual Report 1914–15*, p.2.
151. Idem, *Annual Report 1935–36*, p.9.
152. *Manchester Evening News*, 24 July 1934.
153. Manchester Education Committee, Juvenile Employment Bureaux, *Annual Report 1934*, p.3.
154. See, in particular, 'Impressions and Animadversions, By a Juvenile Bureaucrat', op.cit.
155. Ibid., pp.192–3.
156. T. K. Cross, 'Social Service or Bureaucracy – A Problem for the Juvenile Employment Departments and Bureaux', *Human Factor*, Vol. X, No.10 (October 1936), p.348.
157. See below, pp.77–9.
158. Manchester Education Committee, Juvenile Employment Bureaux, *Annual Report 1914–15*, p.3.
159. Idem, *Annual Report 1916*, p.8; *Annual Report 1917*, p.17.
160. Idem, *Annual Report 1918–19*, p.6; *Annual Report 1920*, p.8; *Annual Report 1922*, p.1.
161. Canner, 'Juvenile Employment Service', p.229.
162. Ibid.
163. See Manchester Education Committee, *General Survey, 1914–1924* (Manchester, 1926), p.107.
164. Juvenile Employment Bureaux weekly report, 1/10/1923 cited in Canner, 'Juvenile Employment Service', p.51.
165. Ibid., p.229.

166. Ibid.; *Manchester Evening News*, 24 July 1934; Manchester Education Committee, Juvenile Employment Bureaux, *Annual Report* 1934, p.1.
167. See Appendix, Table 3.4.
168. Canner, 'Juvenile Employment Service', p.229.
169. Manchester Education Committee, Juvenile Employment Bureaux, *Annual Report* 1921, p.6. cited in Canner, 'Juvenile Employment Service', p.50. Canner comments: 'The Bureaux continued to stress the importance of future prospects. This advice was sometimes accepted but when parents were unemployed their children's earnings were vitally important and work was accepted, irrespective of conditions and prospects'.
170. Cited in Canner, 'Juvenile Employment Service', p.126.
171. Ibid., p.127.
172. Ibid., p.128.
173. Ibid., pp.39, 183.
174. Ibid., p.122.
175. Ibid.
176. Ibid., p.183.
177. Ibid., p.140.
178. Manchester Education Committee, Juvenile Employment Bureaux, *Advice To Boys and Girls About To Leave School* (Manchester, 1936), not paginated.
179. Canner, 'Juvenile Employment Service', p.184.
180. Manchester Education Committee, Juvenile Employment Bureaux, *Annual Report* 1934, pp.3–4.
181. Manchester Studies Oral History Archive, tape 780.

2
Deferential Workers?:
Young Wage-Earners And Their Work

'I am no longer interested in history, as I have never found anyone of my age who is,' a 16-year-old working girl told a research student from Manchester University in the mid-1930s.[1] But did young wage-earners derive any satisfaction from their work? This is an important issue because during the interwar years most 14–20-year-olds were either in full-time employment or seeking it.[2] Despite this fact, the young worker of this period has attracted very little comment from historians. Historians of work have attempted 'to reconstruct the working experiences of ordinary men and women', but important contributions to this debate have neglected even to mention young wage-earners.[3] Historians of 'youth' have assumed that work held little meaning for their subjects. Stephen Humphries argues, for example, that the street and gang life of the period provided working-class youth with a mechanism for escaping what the author terms 'the routine drudgery of work'. [4] In a similar vein, Jerry White has recently argued that the world of work held no attraction whatsoever for the boys of interwar Islington. Forced to suffer the 'disappointments of ill-paid, unstimulating work at long hours' during the day time, they sought consolation in the evenings in a culture organised around the street: in gambling, drinking, sport, and street theatre.[5] This street culture, White argues, offered male youths a status and recognition their work could not provide: 'The cultivation of physical strength and its display through aggression...the male-dominated underworld...all held some attractions for the young men of Campbell Road. Here was a world in which they could compctc and value themselves more highly if they won: it was hard to win in the work dominated world outside'.[6]

Robert Roberts's view of these male street cultures was a very different one. The gangs that met each evening in interwar Salford (the author was born in a Salford slum in 1905) spent most of the time, apparently, discussing their work:

During each nightly meeting the young worker, once fully

integrated, listened, questioned, argued and received unawares an informal education. Here work-a-day life beyond his personal ken came up for scrutiny. Jobs in factory, pit, mill, dock and wharf were mulled over and their skills explained. From first-hand experience youths compared wages, hours, conditions, considered labour prospects, were advised on whom to ask for when seeking a job and what to say. All this was bread and butter talk....[7]

It would appear that work was not simply regarded as 'routine drudgery', even by male youths who belonged to street gangs. It was a major topic of conversation and seems to have penetrated deeply the life of the street.

One of the few historians to begin to evaluate young workers' relationship with employers and their attitudes towards work is Elizabeth Roberts.[8] Her interviews with working-class women in Lancaster, Preston and Barrow strongly suggested that work had an intrinsic moral value, even to the young, at this period. Working-class children were, she claims:

> brought up in the belief that not only was hard work vitally necessary for the survival of both the individual and the family, but that work had an intrinsic moral value. Therefore those who did not work carried the stigma of being idlers, or good-for-nothings. Children learned too, from both home and school, that it was essential to do a job to the best of one's ability[9]

This seems a valid point, but its author can be accused of overlooking the extent to which young workers became disillusioned with their work and the various ways in which they expressed this. The majority of the young female workers in her study *A Woman's Place: An Oral History of Working-Class Women, 1890-1940* (1984) were deferential to the point of muteness in their relationship with their employers. ('Their basic deference, insecurity, their fear of losing respectability, but most of all their chronic poverty which drove them to work, all militated both against going on strike and remembering such an action even if they took part in it,' Roberts states.)[10] This is in line with her general thesis that obedience to authority, an attitude inculcated by parents,

43

was naturally extended to employers. 'It was unlikely', Roberts argues, 'that at any time in this period [c.1890-1940] working-class girls entered the world of work determined to challenge the authority of their employer.'[11]

This chapter focuses on the relationship between employers and their young workers and attempts to ascertain whether the latter were as deferential towards their employers as Elizabeth Roberts has suggested. It focuses on work environments in which employers were paternalistic and thus deferential young workers might be expected to be found. Roberts cites no examples of the young factory workers of north-east Lancashire ever clashing openly with their employers. There were cotton workers' strikes in Preston, for example, in the early 1930s, but whether young workers were involved in these disputes remains unclear. Strike action was not the only strategy available to young workers frustrated with their employment or employers. An option chosen by many, as Chapter 1 revealed, was a job change. There were, however, other less drastic ways of coping with oppressive working conditions.

The strategy most frequently adopted to relieve boredom with work was to engage a colleague or colleagues in conversation. Industrial psychologists, as we shall see, uncovered much information on workplace conversations, which they regarded as a deliberate attempt to interrupt production in some factories.[12] Another reliever of boredom, frequently deployed by young workers, was the impromptu break to smoke a cigarette.[13] Trade apprentices were also forever stopping work to subject new apprentices to a series of usually unpleasant ordeals.[14] Overt resistance to employers on the part of young workers was another option. At some firms, the teenage workforce would boycott the social and recreational facilities employers provided; or they would destroy them.[15] Some would deliberately miss evening classes and so on.[16] But before we can evaluate the extent of such practices and young workers' involvement in strikes, it is necessary first to consider the regimes employers established for training their young workers.

Employers' Regimes for Young Workers

A number of employers had set up works schools for their apprentices even before the President of the Board of Education, Herbert Fisher, recommended these in his Education Bill of 1917.[17]

Sir William Mather had opened a science and technical school for the apprentices at his Salford engineering firm in 1873 'for the purpose of enabling the apprentices of the Salford Iron Works to study technical subjects allied to their trade'.[18] This establishment remained in operation until 1905 after which all the apprentices at the firm were obliged to attend one of the technical schools in Manchester or Salford as a condition of their employment. The most able apprentices at the firm were excused work one day a week to attend these and the remainder were obliged to attend evening continuation classes. Mather was not unusual among employers – either nationally or locally – in insisting that apprentices should continue their education beyond elementary school. In 1907, Michael Sadler, Professor of Education at Manchester University, sent a questionnaire to 195 firms and received replies from 67 who either provided training schemes themselves for their adolescent workers, or utilised those organised by local education authorities.[19] A number of employers in Manchester and Salford completed the questionnaire. One Manchester engineering firm, Baxendale and Company, sent all their boy apprentices to evening classes. Likewise, Thomas Larmuth and Company (a Salford engineering firm) sent all their apprentices to evening classes and paid the costs. Meldrum Brothers Limited of Timperley (near Manchester) sent their apprentices to day classes in Manchester and some were sent to a technical school in Altrincham. Finally, Hans Renold Limited (a chain manufacturer) sent their best apprentices to a day class once a week at the Municipal School of Technology in Manchester, supplying the fees and the apprentices' normal daily wage. Other apprentices at the firm were encouraged, but not obliged, to attend evening classes. Those who did so were excused from overtime and if their attendance rate was high their fees were reimbursed by the firm at the end of each session.[20]

A number of employers followed William Mather's example and set up work schools. The Cadbury brothers, whose chocolate firm was situated at Bournville in Birmingham, reported in 1907 that they ran an evening school on the premises during the winter months for all the firm's employees who were under 16. They were obliged to attend the works school two evenings a week for two hours and young employees of 16 or older were 'encouraged' to attend technical classes. Information about the subjects taught at the school was not provided in the questionnaire the firm was asked to complete, but interesting details are provided on the array of social and recreational facilities on the firm's premises. Boys under 16, for instance, were obliged to attend physical training classes held at the works for two 30-minute periods every week. Girls under 15 were obliged to attend swimming classes (there was a swimming pool on the premises), or 'Swedish gymnastics' three times a week. The firm also ran gardening classes for its boy and girl employees; ambulance and sick nursing classes during the winter months, and also had its own boys' club.[21]

The regime Sir William Mather first set up in 1873 was adopted by one of Manchester's largest engineering firms, the British Westinghouse Company (later re-named Metropolitan Vickers) shortly before the First World War. In January 1914, 300 of the firm's boy employees competed for 100 places on the new apprentice training scheme operated from the firm's new 'Works School for Apprentices'. The cleverest boys were discarded as being well able to look after their own further education through evening schools and private study. The weakest academically were also discarded 'in order that the experiment should not be prejudiced by the introduction of poor material'. Those of average intelligence (100 boys of whom only 25 per cent were 'bound' apprentices) were chosen for the scheme.[22] Initially, they were taught, for one hour every day four mornings a week, four subjects: mathematics, mechanics, drawing and properties of materials. On the fifth day each week they were given a one-hour test on the week's work. Such regimes survived the Great War and were still very much in evidence twenty years later.[23] Moreover, from 1918 they were buttressed by a system of day continuation classes organised by LEAs and utilised by many employers.[24]

Works schools remained largely apprentices' preserves. In engineering establishments they were invariably exclusively for apprentices. William Mather established a new works school at his firm in 1918. Like its predecessor, it was exclusively for boy apprentices, all the firm's apprentices between 14 and 17 being obliged to attend for nine hours every week during working hours.[25] The ostensible purpose of the school was to provide work training, but Mather tried to make it the centre of the apprentices' entire existence and it appears that he succeeded. Most of the apparatus used in the school, for example, was constructed in the evenings and many of the boys gave up their free time to undertake this work.[26] The works school was also the centre of a number of social activities organised by the firm for its boy apprentices. These included a Boy Scout troop, a camping club, football and cricket teams, and a radio club.[27]

At the British Westinghouse engineering firm the apprentices' training scheme was so exclusive that it created tensions among the workforce. The foremen were not happy about the scheme because it meant releasing a number of boys from the shopfloor five times a week for five hours a week.[28] The majority of the workforce were, apparently, 'quite indifferent' towards the scheme; but nothing was said in the official account about how the non-apprenticed young workers reacted.[29] No doubt the 350 apprentices who attended in 1918 were as much a subject for ridicule as a source of envy among the 1,200 boys at the firm who were not permitted to attend.[30] Winifred Hindshaw, a Lecturer in Education at Manchester University, thoroughly approved of the scheme. She described the apprentices who were its recipients as 'young aristocrats of the labour world'.[31] This was a view the apprentices themselves shared. For instance, they published their own magazine, *The Trade Apprentice*, produced by a 'council' of 16 or 17 boys. Among its features were social events 'especially those of interest to the Trade Apprentices' Association', articles on technical subjects, and others on topics 'for the serious boy reader'.[32]

Boy apprentices at Hans Renold's engineering firm in Burnage, near Manchester, were regarded by their employer as 'an intellectual elite' and he was thoroughly opposed to the idea of allowing the unskilled members of his workforce to attend the firm's works school.[33] Apprentices at the firm spent one day a week at the school learning both vocational subjects (science, mathematics, drawing, and woodwork); English (where the emphasis was on lessons in 'citizenship'), and drill.[34] Around 120 boy apprentices at this firm were being educated at the works school in October 1917; but the 500 girls at the firm received no instruction whatsoever.[35]

During the interwar years, works schools continued to be reserved largely for apprentices. A number of employers who gave evidence before a government committee in 1917 were frankly opposed to the idea of providing instruction for non-apprenticed young workers.[36] A cotton manufacturer in Bolton argued that further education was less important in the case of young cotton spinners than in the engineering trades.[37] Neither was he in favour of the Committee's proposal to provide all young wage-earners over the age of 14 with part-time instruction of some kind, arguing that 'part-time day training is not necessary so far as the textile trades are concerned'. Such a system, he argued, 'would cause serious inconvenience, and even dislocation, in the cotton trade'.[38] Another cotton manufacturer who gave evidence shared this view. He argued that a system of part-time day classes for juveniles should not be introduced in the cotton trade 'if the supply of labour were thereby caused to be intermittent, as it is essential to keep the machinery going'.[39] He proceeded to argue that 'all part-time instruction is essentially scrappy and unsatisfactory, and...only a few profit by it. Whole-time education followed by whole-time employment is much to be preferred'.[40]

A boys' welfare officer at the Ministry of Munitions who gave evidence before the 1917 Committee had visited many firms, including several of the largest employers of boy labour in the country. He believed that 'on the whole the raising of the school age would be more acceptable to employers than the compulsory granting of facilities for time off'.[41] Employers in certain trades, particularly those providing employment for large numbers of unskilled boy labourers, regarded 'the suggestion that facilities should be given for general education...with suspicion'.[42] Employers in engineering works, however, proved the exception to this rule. He had visited a number of engineering firms which provided special classes for 'boys who intended to become tradesmen'. Employers who provided instruction were keen to preserve this state of affairs: 'Great stress was laid on the need for making provision for the supply of future skilled workers...certain firms deplored the constant poaching by neighbouring firms who took no trouble to produce their own skilled adult labour'.[43]

A. P. M. Fleming of the British Westinghouse engineering firm told the 1917 Committee that the works school at his own firm had brought apprentices into a closer relationship with the staff.[44] This was important in firms such as his own which were otherwise vast and impersonal institutions. Works schools established 'a close connection...between apprentices and the works staff', he argued, and 'can be utilised in replacing that personal touch between employer and employee which is not otherwise possible under modern industrial conditions'.[45] His own firm certainly attempted, through the works school, to cultivate a close relationship with their apprentices and to make them aware of their privileged status. The curriculum, for instance, included lessons on the 'rights, privileges and duties' of an apprentice; as well as arithmetic, mechanics and physics. Some senior trade apprentices were also trained as lecturers for the school.[46]

The outcome of the 1917 Committee's deliberations regarding the 14–18 age group was a proposal recommending the introduction of Day Continuation Schools (DCSs).[47] This was taken up by the President of the Board of Education, Herbert Fisher, and included in the Education Bill he presented to the House of Commons on 10 August 1917.[48] The DCS scheme finally implemented by the Education Act of 1918 has received little coverage from historians. D. W. Thoms considered the administrative background to the scheme and argued that Fisher's advisers were preoccupied with the question of national efficiency.[49] He largely ignored the implementation of the scheme and its effectiveness at a local level[50] for, he believed, good reasons. 'In essence', Thoms concluded, 'the future of the day continuation schools was in the balance by the end of 1919 and all but doomed by the close of the following year'.[51] The reasons for their apparent failure were, he argued, manifold. First, because of the economies forced upon the government immediately after the war and the operation of the Geddes 'axe', LEAs proved reluctant to build DCSs. Second, officials at the Board of Education adopted a 'somewhat casual approach to the matter'. Third, employers were opposed to a system which would have made DCSs compulsory for their young employees and preferred a system of evening classes which would have no adverse effects on production levels. Fourth, parents of working-class children were opposed to the scheme.[52]

Thoms, and more recently Hendrick,[53] clearly exaggerate the demise of the DCSs. Although a compulsory scheme was abandoned by central government in 1922,[54] local schemes, in operation in some areas even before the 1918 Education Act had been passed, survived on a voluntary basis into the 1930s. In Manchester, nine DCSs were opened between 1918 and 1922 and eight of these were still providing a range of part-time courses for young cotton workers, engineering apprentices, apprentice printers, grocers, and other young manual and clerical workers as late as

1935.[55] It seems worthwhile to consider briefly the operation of this scheme at a local level during the interwar years.

Day Continuation Schools: A Case Study

In Manchester, a number of DCSs were in the process of being established as early as 1917. In that year, Manchester Education Committee (MEC) undertook the task of providing some instruction for all juvenile employees (under 18s) in the city.[56] The first DCS was opened in January 1918; that is, before the 1918 Education Act was passed.[57] Over the next four years a number were opened across the city. Three of these were situated on the premises of individual firms; one was run from a building which at weekends served as a Sunday school, and the remainder were set up in buildings owned by MEC.[58] That body wholeheartedly supported the government's original idea to make attendance at DCSs compulsory but, because the government abandoned the scheme, the Manchester scheme was left to survive on a voluntary basis. That meant it was up to local employers whether they chose to send their young workers to the schools, but they were under no compulsion to do so.[59]

Edith A. Waterfall, an early historian of DCSs, argued that a number of employers in Manchester supported the scheme. Some 38 local firms sent their young workers to the Hulme DCS close to the city centre, for example, in the early 1920s.[60] However, others, owing to the high costs involved, proved reluctant to become involved in the scheme.[61] One Manchester firm estimated that it cost them £10 a year to send a single junior employee to a DCS.[62] Even Waterfall admitted that it was not really in the employer's interest to provide such a costly education when there was no guarantee that the young workers sent to a DCS would remain with the firm.[63] There was also some concern among local employers over the curriculum at the schools. There were obvious difficulties involved with administering a scheme for young employees from different trades and who therefore had different requirements. Waterfall hinted at the difficulties which had arisen at the Hulme DCS:

> In the case of the Hulme Day Continuation School, 38 firms are contributing, and this necessitates constant interchange of visits and much adjustment of school organisation to maintain interest and avoid friction.[64]

Since this DCS was largely dependent on the patronage of two big employers – Tootal, Broadhurst and Lee and Hans Renold – they tended to dictate the curriculum. Despite this, the 'headmaster' sent regular reports on each pupil's progress to all the employers who participated in the scheme and employers were also informed of each pupil's attendance rate.[65]

The local DCSs were clearly run as schools. Each had a 'headmaster' and a number of the 'pupils' were appointed 'prefects'. It was hoped that putting some students into positions of responsibility in the DCS would somehow improve their behaviour, and that of those below them, inside the factory: 'The influence of the elected prefects', Waterfall argued, 'extends, in practice, beyond the school and helps to raise the tone of the adolescent employees in the factory. The boys, or girls...will obey one of their number whom they know to be an elected leader in the school'.[66] The author provided no evidence that the DCSs did have this effect, however, and none of the evidence produced by anthropologists and industrial psychologists who studied the behaviour of young people at work offered support to this view.[67] The success of one of the scheme's main intentions must, therefore, be in some doubt.

Nevertheless, some of the pupils appear to have developed a genuine interest in the scheme. The boys who attended a DCS in Openshaw (mainly boys employed by the big engineering firm in the neighbourhood, Armstrong Whitworth) were so engrossed in the work of the school that they even attended evening classes in engineering theory there. 'Life is very serious to these boys,' Waterfall was told: 'They want to get on. They desire to study the theory that lies behind their work in the shops, and they are voluntarily attending evening classes run by the Lees School in Magnetism and Electricity; Handicrafts; Heat; and Machine Drawing. Recreative classes do not appeal to them.'[68] The girls who attended Oldham Road DCS in Manchester were also sent there by their firm; in this case, Tootal, Broadhurst and Lee. In the factory, the girls were employed on repetitive machine tasks, and they were sent to the school in order to experience a break from their work, rather than to receive further vocational training. The curriculum was, therefore, partly aimed at giving the girls a change of activity (there were singing classes, for instance, and reading and they also did physical exercises).[69] It also, however, prepared them for their probable future lives as wives and mothers (they studied hygiene, for instance, and 'homecraft' and also needlework).[70]

Hulme DCS, a mixed institution, illustrated some of the problems inherent in the scheme. First, it attracted pupils of widely differing abilities and backgrounds. Some of the boys who attended Hulme DCS had been educated at Manchester Grammar School; others were described by Waterfall as 'mentally subnormal'.[71] Consequently, the pupils required different types of instruction. A number of boys wanted further technical training; whereas others wanted a curriculum more geared towards hobbies.[72] A compromise arrangement seems to have prevailed, and E. Hulton and Company Limited, the printing and publishing firm which sent their boy and girl employees, were certainly satisfied with the scheme. In the firm's journal, *The Mat Box*, it was reported in July 1922 that the 'headmaster' at the school and his assistant: 'have made a tour through our works in order to become cognizant of the class of work undertaken by our juniors, and endeavour will be made to impart tuition especially suited to the departmental work of the scholar'.[73] Another feature in the firm's journal discussed the curriculum. The firm's boy and girl employees attended on the same day and even studied the same or similar subjects: mathematics and book-keeping (the girls studied 'domestic arithmetic' and book-keeping); physical exercises; English; and there was a special emphasis on hobbies. 'The idea is held here that every boy and girl is all the better for having a hobby', it was reported, 'and so one hour every day is called the "Hobby Hour"'.[74] During this hour, both boys and girls were taught wood carving. In addition, the girls were taught embroidery and fancy needlework and the boys light woodwork. The staff at Hulton's were extremely satisfied with the scheme, declaring: 'There is a delightful freedom about the place which all the boys and girls who are in attendance appreciate'.[75] Such praise led Edith Waterfall to single out the Manchester DCS scheme as one which was fulfilling the original purpose of the experiment. In her view, the DCS's principal function was 'to supply the educational needs of adolescent workers, and in so doing to enrich the community in good citizens and workers' and Manchester DCSs, she felt, were 'performing this function admirably'.[76]

Nevertheless, Manchester's DCSs did experience some problems. There was always a shortage of teachers, for instance.[77] Moreover, as W.E. Taylor pointed out in a local church magazine, the buildings in which the classes were held – invariably either a disused elementary school or one that at weekends doubled as a Sunday school – were quite unsuitable for young wage-earners, who no longer wished to be regarded as schoolchildren.[78] In some areas, notably Kent, West Sussex, and West Ham, DCSs had been given impressive-sounding names such as 'Institutes' and the Lever Brothers' soap manufacturing firm at Port Sunlight in Cheshire had christened its works school for adolescent employees 'The Staff Training College'.[79] But no such efforts were undertaken in Manchester before the Second World War.[80]

The attendance rate at DCSs fluctuated with movements in the trade cycle and demand for juvenile workers. When an employer ran into difficulties he frequently withdrew his adolescent workers from the scheme. Evidence of this is provided in the log book of one Manchester DCS covering the period from 1923 to 1937. An entry for 26 October 1923 records: 'The Belsize Motors Ltd. have discontinued sending their apprentices to School on account of trade depression in the Industry...The number of boys withdrawn is 40'.[81] In April 1925 it was disclosed that: 'The attendance during the last few weeks has been much below the normal on account of Armstrong Whitworth requiring their apprentices in certain departments to remain at work. This is likely to continue for a few weeks'.[82] The attendance rate at this DCS never recovered, however, and even entered a progressive decline.[83]

It was not only large firms that utilised DCSs. In Manchester, 260 local firms sent at least some of their young workers to DCSs during 1935.[84] It was the case, however, that moderately sized firms sent a limited number only of their junior employees during working hours; 152 of the 260 firms cited sent only one apprentice each in 1935. Large firms, on the other hand, sent up to 200 apprentices a week; seven local firms sent between 50 and 200 apprentices every week in 1935.[85]

The fact that so many firms participated in the scheme is significant. By participating, firms could establish a good reputation for producing highly skilled craftsmen. This was particularly important in the case of smaller firms that could not afford to build works schools for their adolescent employees and operated in difficult circumstances (there was a shortage of young workers in the labour market in the mid-1930s[86]), yet still wanted to attract apprentices of the highest standard. The Manchester scheme was thus utilised by employers small and large. This still did not guarantee the success of the scheme since employers, usually during periods of trade depression, sometimes withdrew their adolescent workers from the scheme. Manchester employers, praised by contemporaries[87] for their progressive attitudes to the education of their young workers, did not regard the DCSs as indispensable to their training. For those employers who maintained their support of the scheme, it served different purposes depending on which employers were involved. Some regarded the scheme as a useful means of improving the prestige of the firm and a good way of attracting adolescent workers of a high quality for the next generation of skilled workers. Engineering firms such as Armstrong Whitworth, who sent their boy apprentices to a DCS to learn the theory behind their work in the shops, probably held this view. Other employers, such as E. Hulton and Company Limited, seem to have regarded the scheme as a refreshing break from work for their boy and girl employees. But local employers as a group do not appear to have been entirely convinced of the intrinsic benefits of the scheme.

Few of the printed sources on DCSs and works schools convey young workers' feelings towards them. Undoubtedly, some apprentices developed a genuine interest in the classes since they gave up their free time in the evenings to attend them despite being under no obligation to do so.[88] Walter Greenwood found that the engineering apprentice he interviewed for his study *How the Other Man Lives* attended a technical class voluntarily in the evenings in order to learn how to repair the machinery in his engineering shop. He told Greenwood:

> Yes, I like what I'm learning now; it makes the work more interesting in the shop. They [the foreman and maintenance engineer at his works] let me try my hand at repairing one of the lathes that broke down...I made it go again.[89]

This apprentice was also able to use the knowledge he acquired in the evening class to repair motor cars in his spare time and to make models on the lathe he had set up in a shed at home.[90] In addition, he firmly believed that attending evening classes improved his future employment prospects. He told Greenwood: 'The engineer at the technical school says that there's nothing to stop me from getting letters after my name...That's what I'd like'.[91] He hoped eventually to be given a job in an aircraft factory, or with a firm of constructional engineers.[92]

Whether this apprentice was typical is difficult to say. From the above discussion it appears some found DCSs and evening classes rewarding because these complemented their work in the workshop. Perhaps, too, they were able to use the knowledge and skills they acquired in the classes to pursue hobbies related to their work.[93] But not all trade apprentices were as keen on the instruction as Greenwood's apprentice. This is apparent from Greenwood's own study. Only six boys at the firm his apprentice worked for attended technical classes in the evenings: 'a lot more started with us when we first began,' he told the author, 'but most of them stopped going. Some of them started going out with girls...to dances and the pictures.'[94] Some apprentices were never given the option of evening classes. Frank Wightman, who served an apprenticeship at a firm of millwrights in Gorton, Manchester, during the 1920s, recalled never having attended an evening class throughout his five-year training.[95] Joan L. Harley, who interviewed 169 girl wage-earners employed in a variety of trades in 1935-36, found: 'The direct appeal of evening schools and clubs is not a wide one: apart from the office workers and the few girls who have some active interest to pursue, evening classes may be said to have no appeal at all.'[96] DCSs, works schools and technical classes were intended mainly, it seems, for boy apprentices. Even among this group of young workers, however, there were some who quickly lost interest in the schools and ceased attending them.

Apprentices' Strikes
Though employers, particularly in the engineering industry, cultivated a special relationship with their boy apprentices via the mechanism of the works school, this relationship was a fragile one. On occasions, as during 1937, it was severely tested when thousands of boy apprentices throughout Britain undertook strike action against their employers. The significance of these disputes has not been debated by historians, though Richard Croucher has claimed that they were 'central to the development of trade union organisation...'.[97] Furthermore, Alan McKinlay, whose focus was the Clydeside apprentices' strike, has viewed this dispute as a symptom of tensions between apprentices and their employers

produced by changes in the structure of apprenticeship; most notably, the decline of indentured apprenticeships and the rise of non-indentured agreements.[98]

Little attention has been devoted to the apprentices' strikes in north-west England during September 1937 and their links, or lack of them, with the Scottish apprentices' strikes earlier in the year.[99] This is surprising given that over 13,000 boys participated in the north-west disputes; only slightly fewer than on Clydeside where 17,000 were involved.[100] The purpose of the following discussion is, therefore, twofold: first, to trace the origins, evolution, outcome and significance of the north-west strikes and, second, to place them in context.

The north-west strike began on 6 September 1937 when 40 apprentices at an engineering workshop in Salford went on strike in an effort to secure a three-shilling pay rise that had been awarded to the adult workers at the firm.[101] Two weeks later, over 13,000 engineering apprentices in Salford, Manchester, and the surrounding districts were also on strike; essentially, over the low wages they received for doing work they felt was highly skilled.[102] How did this situation arise?

The engineering apprentices' strike which affected most engineering firms in Manchester, Salford, and many firms in outlying districts in September 1937 was not the first large-scale strike organised by apprentices in Britain. What one contemporary described as 'the greatest youth strike movement the country has ever seen' had occurred five months earlier on Clydeside.[103] Around 17,000 engineering and shipbuilding apprentices participated in that strike and a further 23,000 adults organised a one-day strike in support of the Clydeside apprentices' demand for a wage rise.[104] This dispute dragged on into early May 1937, but the strike remained solid and employers on the Clyde were eventually forced to concede a wage rise for the apprentices amounting to between one and two shillings.[105] There were further apprentice strikes throughout Britain in 1937: in Edinburgh in the spring, which lasted two weeks; Stockton and Lincoln in May, and Aberdeen in May and June, which lasted over three weeks.[106] Only the Manchester apprentices' strike, however, was on the same scale as the Clydeside dispute in terms of the numbers involved.

On beginning their strike, the Salford apprentices immediately sought to draw into their dispute apprentices at neighbouring firms and their campaign soon attracted the attention of the local press. 'Throughout the day', wrote a reporter for the *Manchester Evening News* on 8 September, 'oily-faced lads in overalls have pedalled their bicycles along Salford side-streets from one rallying-point to another'.[107] Messages such as 'Support the Apprentice Strike' had also apparently been scrawled with chalk on walls throughout the city.[108] One of the strikers was interviewed by a local reporter on 8 September and he outlined very clearly the strike's purpose. 'Recently in one shop', he remarked, 'senior workers were given a 3s a week rise. Apprentices have not been included in that increase. The wage for 20-year-old apprentices is 22s. We think it should be 25s'.[109] At this stage, only about 100 apprentices from four local firms were on strike demanding the 3s wage rise;[110] but by 12 September almost 1,000 were.[111] On 13 September, 800 apprentices at a big engineering firm in Patricroft joined the strike demanding, in addition to the wage rise, holidays with pay.[112]

At this point, apprentices at a number of big engineering firms joined the strike: 250 at Metropolitan Vickers (formerly British Westinghouse); 180 at Ferranti's two plants; 200 at the Lancashire Dynamo and Crypto Limited engineering firm in Trafford Park; 700 at A.V. Roe's aircraft factory in Newton Heath, and apprentices at paternalistic firms such as Mather and Platt and Beyer Peacock.[113] Also, 60 girls at one Salford engineering workshop organised a sympathy strike in support of the apprentices on 16 September,[114] by which time, according to the *Manchester Guardian*, over 5,000 were out on strike and around 7,000 according to the *Manchester Evening News*.[115]

In an attempt to unify the strikers a small group of apprentices, on 16 September, set up a strike committee.[116] The degree of unity this body managed to impose on a dispute which eventually enveloped the whole of Greater Manchester, and beyond, was extremely impressive. It produced leaflets to try to persuade apprentices at big engineering firms who remained at work to join the strike; arranged mass meetings in Trafford Park attended by apprentices from as far afield as Miles Platting and Droylsden; published a Strike Bulletin which was sold for a halfpenny a copy at the mass meetings, and negotiated with trade union officials who acted as intermediaries in the dispute.[117]

Local employers were clearly worried by the scale of the strike and throughout its course sought to bring it rapidly to an end.[118] The management at Metropolitan Vickers utilised the national press to issue statements intended for the parents of apprentices involved. They also brought forward the firm's 'Parents' Day' by two weeks and used this occasion to denounce the strike.[119] When neither strategy produced results they began deploying apprentices who had remained at work as strike breakers. Members of the firm's Apprentices' Association 'were granted leave at certain times each day to infiltrate the body of strikers and 'to raise doubts among the strikers'.[120] This strategy eventually produced results for Metropolitan Vickers. All their apprentices had returned to work by 22 September.[121] Their removal from the strike force had no impact on the strength of the strike, however, which remained solid until 27 September when the apprentices agreed to return to work on the understanding that their employers would immediately address their wage demand.[122] The background to this wage demand requires elaboration.

Both the Manchester apprentices' strike and the Clydeside dispute were over pay. The apprentices were aggrieved, partly, because they felt their pay was low in relation to that of skilled workmen.[123] But there was a supplementary issue: apprentices' pay in relation to that of other workers of the same age.[124] The wage differentials between engineering apprentices and other young workers, particularly those employed in transport, were very considerable by the 1930s.[125] According to a comprehensive survey of young people's wages undertaken by the Ministry of Labour in October 1935, the average weekly wage of boy apprentices in general engineering was 21s. Boys who worked on trams, however, earned 31s 9d a week.[126] In certain branches of the engineering industry, boy apprentices earned less than 21s a week; those who built locomotives earned only 17s 3d.[127] In short, apprentices in the engineering industry were by the mid-1930s among the lowest paid young industrial workers in the country.

A trade union official in the industry was genuinely worried that, owing to the low wages paid, fewer boys were entering engineering apprenticeships by the mid-1930s. W. F. Watson, a skilled mechanic and a branch secretary of the Amalgamated Engineering Union (AEU), argued in January 1936: 'Can one expect youths who have been reared in an atmosphere of cinemas...and dance-halls...to go to the trouble of learning a craft and entering an industry which will return to them a very precarious £3 a week?'[128] John Gollan, the 25-

year-old Secretary of the Young Communist League (YCL), who had served an apprenticeship in the engineering industry, endorsed this view. According to him, 'the mass of [engineering] apprentices in Britain' received a mere 8s to 12s a week in their first year (i.e. at 16) and only 16s to 20s in their final year (i.e. at 20). 'Can it be wondered at', Gollan wrote in 1937, 'that boys of 23 years object to being paid a pound a week for doing the finest skilled job?'[129] He went on to point out that up to two-thirds of an apprentice's weekly wage was soaked up by travel fares to and from work, insurance contributions and the like and all that was left for the apprentice was 4d or 'a double Woodbine'.[130]

In Manchester and Salford, engineering apprentices were paid more than Gollan estimated for engineering apprentices nationally. In September 1937, a 16-year-old engineering apprentice locally earned 14s 6d a week and a 20-year-old apprentice 22s.[131] Doubtless apprentices felt aggrieved at earning such low wages before 1937. What brought their grievance to the surface, however, was the fact that adult engineers received a wage rise that year while apprentices in the same industry received nothing.

The Manchester apprentices' achieved a successful outcome in their three-week strike. As a result almost entirely of their own efforts, they received a 2s wage rise from their employers.[132] The trade union movement only belatedly declared its support for the strike. Moreover, it soon became clear that the unions were less interested in the apprentices' wage claim than in the opportunity the strike presented for enhanced apprentice recruitment into the unions. The local AEU branch tried to tempt more apprentices into their movement by offering them the prospect of strike pay. A statement by the local AEU Organiser printed in the *Daily Worker* could not have been clearer on that union's pragmatic interest in the dispute:

> If any of the strikers will join our organisation they will have their strike pay given special consideration. Normally, a new member does not become entitled to strike pay for 12 months, but we will treat this as an emergency case.[133]

This offer of financial support to the strikers had not, however, materialised for apprentices in the union. None of the striking apprentices who belonged to the union had received any strike pay by 22 September.[134] Instead they had been maintained by donations from adult workers distributed through a strike fund set up and administered by the apprentices out on strike.[135]

The local trade union movement's tactical support for the apprentices is further revealed by meetings between the two. A meeting convened on 24 September, towards the end of the strike, was concerned ostensibly to discuss whether the apprentices should return to work. The union officials, however, were preoccupied with the question of how they could recruit more apprentices into the unions. Immediately following the apprentices' return to work, Manchester and Salford Trades Council launched a publicity campaign targeted at apprentices. A report in the *Daily Worker* noted: 'Factories are being flooded with leaflets, meetings are taking place in all districts, and many striking posters setting out the need and value of trades unionism are displayed on the hoardings'.[136]

It is clear, however, that not all local trade unionists supported the strike out of self-interest. The Secretary of Manchester and Salford Trades Council, acting independently of the union movement, helped the apprentices raise funds through sending letters to firms requesting works collections and individual donations.[137] These generated £263 4s 8d for the strikers.[138] This official also helped the strike committee conduct their meetings in an efficient manner.[139] The trade union rank-and-file, meanwhile, provided generous financial assistance for those out on strike as did non-unionised adult workers and fellow apprentices around the country. A donation of £3, for example, was sent to the Manchester apprentices from an apprentice engineer in Edinburgh.[140] In addition, numerous donations were received from the Leagues of Youth around the country and from Young Communist League branches in Stoke Newington (5s) and Ealing (5s 3d).[141]

The role of the Young Communist League in the Manchester apprentices' strike was seen as crucial by an ex-member of the organisation who participated in the dispute. In handwritten correspondence drafted during the strike this individual even claimed that the Young Communist League 'was responsible for the action taken at Larmuths' where the strike began.[142] This is impossible to demonstrate, but it does appear from the newspaper coverage of the strike, even in left-wing papers, that the Young Communist League's role was not central to the evolution of the dispute in contrast to events on Clydeside. There the apprentices' strike committee was chaired by a member of the Young Communist League;[143] but the Manchester apprentices' strike committee wanted nothing to do with the Young Communist League or other political movements. These were denounced at the public meetings. At a meeting held on 17 September, in the middle of the dispute, the following statement was read: 'We will have no outside interference from Communism, Fascism or any other political party'.[144] When, on 20 September, the Manchester apprentices' strike committee agreed to merge with the committee co-ordinating the Salford strike, the members agreed not to allow any member of a political organisation to sit on the new committee. The agreement was aimed at bringing an end to the Young Communist League's involvement in the strike.[145]

As to the strike's significance, the left-wing press at the time – the *Daily Worker*, *Challenge* (the Young Communist League's paper) and *Militant* ('Organ of the Militant Group in the Labour Party') – all felt the dispute was a class struggle. 'Out of their strike,' one correspondent wrote retrospectively in the *Daily Worker*, 'organisation has arisen binding youths from different factories and shops together in what for many of them is their first elementary organisation as part of a class fighting against part of another hostile class.'[146] But this is not how the leaders of the strike viewed their dispute. From the beginning, they campaigned merely for a wage rise that in their opinion was 'correct and just' and their conduct during the dispute was in no sense a struggle. On the contrary, their behaviour was exemplary: always peaceable (there were no arrests at any point during the strike); even respectful (the apprentices at most firms presented their wage demands in the form of deputations to the management).[147]

A further problem with the class-struggle interpretation of events is that it overlooks divisions which clearly existed within the apprentice workforce. From the very first week of the strike, these were revealed. When the apprentices at W.H. Bailey's Albion Works were asked to join the Salford apprentices' strike they refused.[148] The apprentices at Thomas Matthews's Salford engineering firm returned to work early in the dispute.[149] The majority of apprentices at Metropolitan Vickers' engineering firm were indentured and not prepared to risk their long-term contracts for the sake of participation in the strike and thus remained at work.[150] Apprentices who secured a wage settlement with their employers early on simply deserted the strike. Those at Ferranti's, for example, who had joined the strike decided to accept their employer's offer of a shilling wage rise for apprentices under 18 and 1s 6d for those 18 and older. They returned to work in the middle of the strike.[151] These divisions within the apprentice workforce never seriously jeopardised the Manchester and Salford strike, but they existed nevertheless; a point not acknowledged since either by contemporary chroniclers of the disputes, such as John Gollan, or by historians.[152]

There is no evidence that the Manchester apprentices' strike was central to the development of trade unionism. As revealed, the trade union movement played only a limited, intermediary role in the dispute and the momentum of the strike was generated solely by the apprentices. There were no sympathy strikes by adult workers, organised by the unions, as happened on Clydeside. Political activists in Manchester were clearly disappointed by the lack of initiative shown by the union movement. One wrote to the *Daily Worker* explaining his frustration with the unions thus: 'A feature...which would have made the strike as solid as a rock would have been the holding of factory gate meetings addressed by trade union officials, but this was neglected and had the effect of allowing false statements concerning the support of the AEU to circulate.'[153]

There were lessons in the strike for employers as well as the unions. The former could, as a number of Manchester employers had done, construct work regimes for their apprentices but these did not quell the apprentices' autonomous feelings and behaviour. Apprentices at paternalistic firms – Mather and Platt's, Metropolitan Vickers, Hans Renold and so on – were involved in the strike and, because of their numbers, central to its successful outcome.[154] Clearly, the scale and outcome of the strike calls into question the notion of young workers at this period being deferential towards their employers and the involvement of girls in sympathy strikes appears to highlight that deference did not depend on one's gender. Finally, this episode reveals that the apprentices who participated in the strike were interested in their work – interested enough to go without wages for three weeks – and were, in fact, strongly attached to their work, believing they were performing highly skilled tasks for which they were underpaid. As we saw earlier, some apprentices were so involved in their work they sacrificed their free time to pursue work-related interests.[155]

Girls' Attitudes Towards Work

The study of work behaviour and attitudes towards work and employers was in its infancy at this period. The social historian Ross McKibbin remarked in his 1983 article on work and hobbies in Britain between 1880 and 1950: 'we know little enough of people's attitudes to work at the best of times and have almost no accurate knowledge for the period before the 1930s. As for how people see the relation between work and leisure...we can only proceed by the most delicate inference.'[156] Nevertheless, social investigators and industrial psychologists did begin to address these issues during the 1930s and, increasingly, by the 1940s.[157] Their studies need to be read with care since their authors often asked loaded questions and tended to be middle-class outsiders entirely dependent on the information their working-class subjects chose to disclose. For these reasons, they are somewhat problematic. Some of these problems were overcome, however, by the devious technique of unobserved observation, a strategy the independent organisation Mass Observation used extensively.[158]

Joan L. Harley, a research student at Manchester University during the 1930s, undertook a detailed study of the girl wage-earner's attitude towards work and her leisure interests. The girls she interviewed were all based in Manchester, though a variety of ages (14–19), and employed in a range of jobs (manual and white-collar).[159] She discovered that the majority of the girls in her sample found their work 'interesting'; even those whose occupations appeared to Harley to be 'rather dull and unattractive'.[160] The office workers gave a variety of reasons for liking their work, ranging from interest in the goods dealt with by their firms to gratitude for being allowed a long lunch hour.[161] Many girls employed as machinists in Manchester's sewing trades told Harley they liked their jobs because they were interested in clothes and fashions.[162] A number stated that they liked finding out about new styles before they were put on sale in the shops.[163] Others said they liked the work because it taught them how to make their own clothes.[164] Harley spoke to other girls who liked their work because it was lively. A girl employed as a boxmaker told her: 'I like my work because you are always on the go. It is very quick.'[165] Another who worked in a warehouse derived satisfaction from her work for the same reason.

'My work', she told Harley, 'is to go to the stockroom with mistakes. When busy I do more running about than work and I like the walking about.'[166]

Very few of the girls featured in Harley's study derived no satisfaction from their work. Those who did dislike their jobs tended to be girls who worked alone and were isolated from the rest of their age-group, such as domestic servants.[167] But for the vast majority work, even when it was not intrinsically interesting, was still enjoyable in some way. Most girls in Manchester worked either in a factory or a workshop and, as Harley pointed out, these establishments were attractive to girls partly because of the social contacts they provided. 'There is no doubt,' she wrote, 'many of the girls regard their workroom as a kind of club. Nearly all of them like their workmates...Very often their best friend of the moment is the girl who sits next to them at work.'[168]

This troubled other investigators, especially industrial psychologists who were hired by employers to suggest ways of improving workers' productivity. A study undertaken by an official from the Industrial Health Research Board, the results of which were published in 1934, focused on girl operatives of 15 and 16 employed in a chocolate factory.[169] The author observed 10 girls in their work environment over a twelve-month period. During this time, they were under continuous observation and every aspect of their behaviour was noted.[170] The study revealed how girls overcame boredom with work. They resorted either to conversation or day-dreaming. The first strategy was the most widespread one; only one of the girls (described as 'an introvert') resorted to day-dreaming.[171] The official was at pains to point out how a conversation between two of the girls could quickly spread and have an extremely disruptive effect on the work-rate of all the girls. Most of the girls chosen were described as 'quiet and industrious', but on one occasion Worker D started a conversation about film heroes with her partner C and the observer recorded the following scene:

> As a result there was an immediate fall in the rate of working of these two operatives. It was evident that D wanted to involve the whole group in the discussion for she began to address questions to the adjoining pair (I and J) who readily responded to her remarks. A little later the next pair (G and

H) were drawn into the conversation, and the disturbance then spread to the more remote pair (A and B). The last to be affected were E and F, who were employed in weighing and wrapping at a separate bench.[172]

The official subsequently calculated that when Worker D was absent from work the productivity of the girls increased by, on average, 12½ per cent.[173]

Mass Observation, whose technique for gauging attitudes to work (unobserved observation) was in many ways the best, sent a Cambridge graduate to study the behaviour of young female factory workers in a machine-tool factory.[174] Moments of boredom, the subsequent report revealed, were once again relieved by conversation which, it was felt, helped the time to pass more quickly. The following conversation between two girls was recorded verbatim by the Mass Observer:

It [time] went quick this morning, didn't it?

Yes, it went lovely and quick between eleven and twelve, but it dragged after that, I thought.

Yes, just after the twelve o'clock buzzer. It started to drag then.

Funny, wasn't it? It usually goes so quick after the twelve o'clock buzzer. I hope it will go as quick this afternoon.

Hope so, you can always tell, can't you? If it goes quick up to half-past two, then it's going to go quick all the afternoon.

It's funny that.[175]

Pearl Jephcott was intrigued by the question: what made dull jobs bearable to girls? She asked a number of working girls in various parts of England and Wales to write about their work and to indicate what interested them about it.[176] She received mixed replies. Jean, for instance, who sat at a bench (packing soups) from 8am to 5pm felt her work was very boring, but not devoid of interest. She recorded: 'the foreman's nice, the boss is nice, you can have an hour and a half for dinner and you can talk and eat.'[177] Another girl, Maud, had a more instrumental attitude towards her work (separating perfect from imperfect cigarettes in a factory). In her account of what she found interesting in her work, she hedged the question and declared instead that she was earning 'good money' and, because the work was piecework, could work at a more relaxed pace some days.[178]

Jephcott's most significant finding was that the girls who wrote to her, and the 103 she subsequently interviewed for a follow-up study, were much less prepared to talk about their work than about their leisure interests. 'It was difficult to unearth much information about their working life', the author recorded, 'because they seldom referred to their jobs spontaneously and were impatient at the idea of wasting time by talking of such a distasteful topic.'[179] This led her to argue that girls were interested in their work only as a means to an end; namely, 'the money it brought in'.[180] This, however, seems too simplistic. Jephcott, it needs to be borne in mind, interviewed girls at their homes, or in the neighbourhood of their homes.[181] It does not seem particularly surprising that in these circumstances the girls she interviewed were unwilling to talk about their work. The industrial psychologist, mentioned earlier, who observed girls at work in a chocolate factory found that although the girls in his study were employed on repetitive work it was unthinkable that their attitude towards work could have been purely instrumental: 'The weekly wage was too remote to act as a complete antidote to the monotonous conditions of work and failed to satisfy immediate aims and desires.'[182] These were satisfied instead, principally, through conversation. Moreover, as Harley found, repetition work was not always regarded by the girls who performed it as monotonous. Such a judgement was merely the view of the investigators who studied them.

It appears, therefore, that young wage-earners of both sexes were far more interested in their work than either contemporaries believed could be possible in so-called blind-alley jobs, or historians since have given credit for. The enjoyment young wage-earners derived from work was not simply related to the degree of skill involved, as contemporary commentators mistakenly believed. It was also to do with the relationships and social contacts work made possible; in short, to the companionship work offered. Proof that this was as crucial to some as the type of work they did was provided by investigators and by unemployed young people interviewed during the 1930s.[183] What they tended to miss most about work was the social life and the social contacts associated with it.[184]

NOTES

1. Harley, 'Report', p.17.
2. Appendix, Tables 2.1 and 2.2.
3. See, for example, P. Joyce's essay, 'Work' in F. M. L. Thompson (ed.), *The Cambridge Social History of Britain, 1750–1950, Vol.2* (Cambridge, 1990) Ch. 3; P. Joyce (ed.), *The Historical Meanings of Work* (Cambridge, 1987); and J. Benson's essay, 'Work' in idem (ed.), *The Working Class in England, 1875–1914* (Kent, 1985), Ch. 3; (ibid., p.64 for the quotation). For a recent study of women workers that considers single women at the workplace see M. Glucksmann, *Women Assemble: Women Workers and the New Industries in inter-war Britain* (London, 1990), pp.35–6, 39–40, 61–2, 94, 217–18, 259–60. See also E. Roberts, *Woman's Place*, Ch. 2. On young women's involvement in strikes at an earlier period see E. Gordon, *Women and the Labour Movement in Scotland 1850–1914* (Oxford, 1991), pp.118, 122–4, 126, 134. For a sectoral study that mentions girls, though without systematically analysing their workplace experience, see J.A. Jowitt and A.J. McIvor (eds), *Employers and Labour in the English Textile Industries, 1850–1939* (London, 1988).
4. Humphries, *Hooligans or Rebels?*, p.138. For a similar view of girls' work at this period (described as 'a dreary routine') see L. Davidoff and B. Westover, '"From Queen Victoria to the Jazz Age": Women's World in England, 1880–1939' in Davidoff and Westover (eds), *Our Work, Our Lives, Our Words: Women's History and Women's Work*, p.28.
5. J. White, *Worst Street in North London*, pp.161, 164, 197.
6. Ibid., p.164.
7. R. Roberts, *Classic Slum*, p.157.
8. E. Roberts, *Woman's Place*, Ch. 2.
9. Ibid., p.51.
10. Ibid., p.49.
11. Ibid., p.46.
12. See below, pp.64–5.
13. The engineering apprentices at Marlowe's, the engineering firm in Walter Greenwood's novel *Love on the Dole* (1933 repr. Middlesex, 1981), frequently broke off work to smoke cigarettes. Marlowe's was, apparently, based on the Metropolitan Vickers engineering firm in Trafford Park, Manchester. See E. Frow and R. Frow, *Manchester's Big House in Trafford Park: Class Conflict and Collaboration at Metro-Vicks* (Manchester, 1983), p.31.
14. For the particularly unpleasant ordeals suffered by T.R. Dennis, who served his apprenticeship in a cabinet-maker's shop in Preston during the 1920s, see J. Burnett (ed.), *Useful Toil: Autobiographies of Working People from the 1820s to the 1920s* (London, 1974), pp.347–55. See also Robert Roberts, *A Ragged Schooling: Growing up in the Classic Slum* (1976 repr. London, 1984), pp.158–68.
15. Cora Tenen found, in interviews with 14- to 18-year-olds employed at a clothing factory in Lancashire during the Second World War, that the extensive welfare services provided by the firm – which included free medical, sun-ray, dental and optical services; sick funds; a sports club; a library, and a canteen service – were 'largely ignored in practice by the young workers' owing to their strong feelings of resentment towards the management. She was in contact with young workers at the firm over a three-month period. During that time, its sports room was 'completely wrecked by boys in the factory' on two occasions known to the author. See C. Tenen, 'Adolescent Attitudes to Authority at Work', unpublished MA thesis, University of Manchester, 1945, pp.134, 143.

16. See Walter Greenwood's interview with an apprentice in idem, *How the Other Man Lives* (London, 1939?), Ch. XVII.
17. House of Commons Debates, Fifth Series, Vol.XCVII, 1917, col.807.
18. See M.E. Sadler (ed.), *Continuation Schools in England and Elsewhere* (Manchester, 1907), pp.282–3, 307.
19. Ibid., p.265.
20. Ibid., pp.274–5, 280–1, 284–5.
21. Ibid., pp.282–3, 294–5.
22 A. P. M. Fleming and J.G. Pearce, *The Principles of Apprentice Training* (London, 1916), pp.141–4, 155.
23 See, for example, R.W. Ferguson and A. Abbott, *Day Continuation Schools* (London, 1935), pp.44–7. See also *Our Journal: The Magazine of the Employees of Mather and Platt Ltd*, January 1939, pp.46, 49.
24. See below, pp.49–55.
25. Ferguson and Abbott, *Day Continuation Schools*, pp.23, 46, 47.
26. Ibid., p.47.
27. Ibid.
28. Fleming and Pearce, *Principles of Apprentice Training*, p.152.
29 .Ibid.
30. For details of the numbers involved in the scheme see Winifred Hindshaw, 'Works Schools for Engineers' in J.J. Findlay (ed.), *The Young Wage-Earner and the Problem of his Education* (London, 1918), pp.162–74.
31. Ibid., p.172.
32. Ibid., p.171.
33. Ibid., p.167. This impression also receives support in C.G. Renolds's history of the firm, *Joint Consultation Over Thirty Years: A Case Study* (London, 1950). The author points out, for instance, that before the First World War the firm's founder would present 'deserving' apprentices with special treats. These included invitations to tea at his home; flowers from his greenhouse and, occasionally, he would take 'his' apprentices on a trip to a neighbouring firm. See, especially, p.95.
34. Hindshaw, 'Works Schools', p.166.
35. Ibid.
36. See the Final Report of the Departmental Committee on *Juvenile Education in relation to employment after the War*, Vol. II, Summaries of Evidence and Appendices, *Cd.*8577 (London, 1917), pp.20–2.
37. Ibid., p.21.
38. Ibid.
39. Ibid., p.22.
40. Ibid.
41. Ibid., p.76.
42. Ibid.
43. Ibid.
44. Ibid., p.14.
45. Ibid.
46. Ibid.
47. Final Report of the Departmental Committee on *Juvenile Education in relation to employment after the War,* Vol.1, Report, Cd.8512 (London, 1917), pp.8, 12, 14.
48. House of Commons Debates, Fifth Series, Vol.XCVII, 1917, cols. 795–852.
49. D.W. Thoms, 'The Emergence and Failure of the Day Continuation School Experiment', *History of Education*, Vol.4, No.1 (Spring 1975), pp.36–50.
50. Ibid., pp.42–3, for some discussion of DCSs in London.
51. Ibid., p.45.
52. Ibid., pp.47–8.
53. Hendrick, *Images of Youth*, p.220.
54. Thoms, 'Day Continuation School Experiment', pp.36–7.
55. Manchester Education Committee, *General Survey*, p.105; Ferguson and Abbott, *Day Continuation Schools*, pp.vii, 22–3, 44–7.

56. Manchester Education Committee, *General Survey*, p.112.
57. Ibid.
58. Ibid., p.105; Grey Mare Lane Day Continuation School, Openshaw, Log Book, 1923–1937, Manchester Central Library, Archives Department, M66/32 additional/Box 1. Entry for 15 March 1923.
59. Manchester Education Committee, *General Survey*, pp.28, 122; idem, *Education in Manchester: A Survey of Progress, 1924–1934* (Manchester, 1935), p.77.
60. E.A. Waterfall, *The Day Continuation School in England: Its Function and Future* (London, 1923), Ch. VII.
61. Ibid, p.193.
62. Ibid.
63. Ibid., pp.193–4.
64. Ibid., p.193.
65. Ibid., p.198. See also Grey Mare Lane Day Continuation School, Log Book, *passim*, for the same pattern.
66. Waterfall, *Day Continuation School*, p.194.
67. Tenen, 'Adolescent Attitudes to Authority', *passim*; see also below, pp.64–5.
68. Waterfall, *Day Continuation School*, p.196.
69. Ibid., p.197.
70. Ibid.
71. Ibid., p.198. The same was noted of Day Continuation School pupils in Bristol and Coventry. See Ibid., pp.87–8.
72. Ibid.
73. *The Mat Box, the staff magazine of E. Hulton and Co., Ltd*, July 1922, cited in Waterfall, *Day Continuation School*, p.200.
74. Ibid., p.201.
75. Ibid., pp.201–2.
76. Ibid., pp.202–3.
77. Manchester Education Committee., *General Survey*, p.114; W.E. Taylor, 'Educational Opportunities', *Odds and Ends: A Manuscript Magazine*, Vol. LXXXVI (1946), p.190. The latter source was produced by St. Paul's Church in Manchester and is held at Manchester Central Library, Archives Department.
78. Taylor, 'Educational Opportunities', p.192.
79. Waterfall, *Day Continuation School*, p.105.
80. See, for instance, Grey Mare Lane Day Continuation School, Log Book, *passim*; Manchester Education Committee, *General Survey*, pp.28, 114; idem, *Education in Manchester*, p.77; Taylor, 'Educational Opportunities', pp.190–2. Taylor notes that Manchester's Day Continuation Schools were being re-christened 'County Colleges' in 1946 (ibid., p.193).
81. Grey Mare Lane Day Continuation School, Log Book, 26 Oct. 1923. For other examples see idem, 7 Jan. 1924; 25 April 1924; 25 April 1927; Manchester Education Committee, *General Survey*, pp.28, 112, 114; idem, *Education in Manchester*, p.77.
82. Grey Mare Lane Day Continuation School, Log Book, 25 April 1925.
83. Ibid., *passim*.
84. Ferguson and Abbott, *Day Continuation Schools*, p.60.
85. Ibid.
86. See Ch. 1.
87. Waterfall, for instance, praised Manchester employers for supporting Day Continuation Schools. See idem, *Day Continuation School*, p.193.
88. Ibid., p.196.
89. Greenwood, *How The Other Man Lives*, p.119.
90. Ibid, pp.119–20.
91. Ibid, p.119.
92. Ibid.
93. On the relationship between work and hobbies see R. McKibbin, 'Work and Hobbies in Britain, 1880–1950' in J. Winter (ed.), *The Working Class in Modern British History: Essays in Honour of Henry Pelling* (Cambridge, 1983), Ch. 7.

94. Greenwood, *How The Other Man Lives*, p.120.
95. *Manchester Evening News*, 6 Dec. 1976.
96. Harley, 'Report', p.2.
97. R. Croucher, *Engineers At War, 1939–1945* (London, 1982), p.47.
98. A. McKinlay, 'From Industrial Serf to Wage-Labourer: The 1937 Apprentice Revolt in Britain', *International Review of Social History*, Vol.XXXI (1986), Pt.I, pp.1–18. For a study which locates these changes in the late nineteenth century see W. Knox, 'Apprenticeship and De-Skilling In Britain, 1850–1914', *International Review of Social History*, Vol.XXXI (1986), Pt.2, pp.166–184. For brief narrative accounts of the strikes see N. Branson, *History of the Communist Party of Great Britain, 1927–1941* (London, 1985), pp.180–2; N. Branson and M. Heinemann, *Britain in the Nineteen Thirties* (London, 1971), pp.114–15; J.E. Cronin, *Labour and Society in Britain, 1918–1979* (London, 1984), pp.108–9.
99. McKinlay, 'Apprentice Revolt', p.16; Croucher, *Engineers At War*, p.54; Cronin, *Labour and Society in Britain*, pp.108–9.
100. *Manchester Evening News*, 21 Sept. 1937; *Manchester Guardian*, 22 Sept. 1937; McKinlay, 'Apprentice Revolt', p.14.
101. *Manchester Evening News*, 8 Sept. 1937; *Manchester Guardian*, 9 Sept. 1937. For a brief account of the Manchester and Salford engineering apprentices' strike of 1937 see E. Frow and R. Frow, *Manchester's Big House in Trafford Park: Class Conflict and Collaboration at Metro–Vicks*, p.32.
102. *Manchester Evening News*, 21 Sept. 1937; *Manchester Guardian*, 22 Sept. 1937.
103. J. Gollan, *Youth in British Industry: A survey of labour conditions today* (London, 1937), p.311.
104. Croucher, *Engineers At War*, pp.49–53; McKinlay, 'Apprentice Revolt', p.14.
105. McKinlay, 'Apprentice Revolt', pp.7, 8, 14, 15.
106. Croucher, *Engineers at War*, p.53.
107. *Manchester Evening News*, 8 Sept. 1937.
108. Ibid.
109. Ibid.
110. Ibid; *Manchester Guardian*, 9 Sept. 1937.
111. *Manchester Evening News*, 13 Sept. 1937.
112. Ibid.
113. *Manchester Evening News*, 16 and 17 Sept. 1937; *Manchester Guardian*, 17 and 18 Sept. 1937.
114. *Manchester Evening News*, 17 Sept. 1937.
115. *Manchester Guardian*, 16 Sept. 1937; *Manchester Evening News*, 16 Sept. 1937. The strike was even mentioned in *The Times* on 16 Sept. 1937.
116. *Manchester Evening News*, 16 Sept. 1937.
117. *Daily Worker*, 16 Sept. 1937; *Manchester Guardian*, 17, 18, 20 and 25 Sept. 1937.
118. *Manchester Evening News*, 7 and 8 Oct. 1937; *Manchester Guardian*, 2 Oct. 1937. On the disruption the strike caused to production targets see *Manchester Guardian*, 17 and 22 Sept. 1937; *Manchester Evening News*, 17 Sept. 1937; *Daily Worker*, 16 and 30 Sept. 1937; *Daily Herald*, 18 and 20 Sept. 1937; *Daily Express*, 17 Sept. 1937.
119. *Daily Worker*, 21 Sept. 1937.
120. *Daily Worker*, 22 Sept. 1937.
121. *Manchester Guardian*, 22 Sept. 1937.
122. *Manchester Guardian*, 25 Sept. 1937.
123. On the Clydeside apprentices' grievance see Gollan, *Youth in British Industry*, p.312; McKinlay, 'Apprentice Revolt', p.14; on the Manchester and Salford apprentices' grievance see *Manchester Evening News*, 8 Sept. 1937; *Manchester Guardian*, 9 Sept. 1937.
124. See, for example, W.F. Watson, 'Is There a Shortage of Skilled Craftsmen?', *Human Factor*, Vol.X, No.1 (January 1936), p.32.
125. See Appendix, Table 2.1.
126. Ibid.
127. Ibid.
128. Watson, 'Is There a Shortage of Skilled Craftsmen?', p.32.

129. Gollan, *Youth in British Industry*, p.312.
130. Ibid.
131. *Manchester Guardian*, 9 Sept. 1937.
132. The Manchester and Salford apprentices were offered the 2s wage rise on 2 October 1937, following a meeting of the Engineering Employers' Federation and the engineering unions in London. The apprentices did not accept the offer immediately. Their strike committee first considered the proposal (on 6 October) and contemplated prolonging their strike for a 3s wage rise. See *Manchester Guardian*, 2 and 6 Oct. 1937; *Manchester Evening News*, 8 Oct. 1937.
133. *Daily Worker*, 22 Sept. 1937.
134. Ibid.
135. *Manchester Guardian*, 11, 21 and 22 Sept. 1937.
136. *Manchester Guardian*, 25 Sept. 1937; *Daily Worker*, 30 Sept. 1937.
137. *Manchester Guardian*, 21 Sept. 1937; *Daily Worker*, 21 Sept. 1937.
138. Manchester and Salford Trades Council, *Annual Report*, 1938, pp.18–19.
139. *Daily Worker*, 21 Sept. 1937.
140. Manchester and Salford Trades Council, *Annual Report*, 1938, pp.18–19.
141. Ibid.
142. E. Frow, 'The Apprentice Strike And Our New Tasks: How The Strike Started And Developed' (handwritten notes dated 1937), Working-Class Movement Archive, Salford.
143. Cronin, *Labour and Society in Britain*, p.108; Croucher, *Engineers At War*, p.50.
144. *Manchester Guardian*, 18 Sept. 1937.
145. *Manchester Guardian*, 21 Sept. 1937.
146. *Daily Worker*, 30 Sept. 1937. See also *The Militant*, October 1937, which described the apprentices' strikes as: 'A heartening sign of the growth of militancy...among the youth' (p.4); *Challenge*, 16 Sept. 1937.
147. *Manchester Guardian*, 9 and 17 Sept. 1937.
148. *Manchester Guardian*, 9 Sept. 1937.
149. *Manchester Guardian*, 10 Sept. 1937.
150. *Manchester Guardian*, 17 Sept. 1937.
151. *Manchester Evening News*, 16 Sept. 1937.
152. Gollan, *Youth in British Industry*, pp.311–16; Croucher, *Engineers At War*, pp.45–57; Cronin, *Labour and Society in Britain*, pp.108–9; McKinlay, 'Apprentice Revolt', *passim*.
153. *Daily Worker*, 30 Sept. 1937.
154. *Manchester Evening News*, 23 Sept. 1937; *Manchester Guardian*, 18 Sept. 1937.
155. See above, pp.46–7, 51.
156. McKibbin, 'Work and Hobbies in Britain', pp.133–4.
157. Harley, 'Report', *passim*; S. Wyatt, *Incentives in Repetitive Work: A Practical Experiment in a Factory* (London, 1934); P. Jephcott, *Girls Growing Up* (London, 1942); idem, *Rising Twenty: Notes On Some Ordinary Girls* (London, 1948); Mass Observation, *War Factory* (London, 1943).
158. Mass Observation, *War Factory*, p.10.
159. Harley, 'Report', pp.1–5, 39.
160. Ibid., p.46.
161. Ibid., p.47.
162. Ibid.
163. Ibid.
164. Ibid.
165. Ibid., p.48.
166. Ibid.
167. Ibid., p.49.
168. Ibid., pp.45–6. Springhall makes the same point about factory work for girls before 1914. See Springhall, *Coming of Age*, pp.90–1.
169. Wyatt, *Incentives in Repetitive Work*, p.2.
170. Ibid., pp.2, 20.
171. Ibid., pp. 23, 36, 45, 48.
172. Ibid., p.36.

173. Ibid., p.37.
174. Mass Observation, *War Factory*, pp. 6, 8, 9, 10, 49.
175. Ibid., p.42.
176. Jephcott, *Girls Growing Up*, p.86.
177. Ibid.
178. Ibid.
179. Jephcott, *Rising Twenty*, p.16.
180. Ibid.
181. Ibid., p.22.
182. Wyatt, *Incentives in Repetitive Work*, p.54.
183. Harley, 'Report', pp.45–6. See also C. Cameron, A. Lush and G. Meara, *Disinherited Youth: A Report On The 18+ Age–Group Enquiry Prepared for the Trustees of the Carnegie United Kingdom Trust* (Edinburgh, 1943), pp.67, 69.
184. Ibid.

3

Youth Unemployment in Interwar Britain: A Case Study

> One of the most pernicious and socially disturbing aspects of British unemployment between the Wars was the enforced idleness suffered by thousands of youngsters under the age of 18. With ambitions quashed and its independence and morale noticeably weakened, the army of unemployed youth represented an economic and social problem of alarming proportions...

Thus did the economic historian W. R. Garside depict the scale and seriousness of the youth unemployment 'problem' in interwar Britain in his pioneering article on the subject.[1] In that article, Garside cited five cities where youth unemployment apparently reached serious levels at this period: Liverpool, Glasgow, Bristol, Manchester, and Newcastle.[2] One of these, Manchester, forms the focus of this chapter.[3] A range of sources not used by Garside – the records of the Juvenile Employment Bureaux (JEBs) that administered the unemployment insurance scheme for 14-18-year-olds, in addition to finding employment for unemployed juveniles; social surveys; police records; youth movement records, and the records of voluntary groups active in the alleviation of unemployment – cast much light on this issue. Such sources highlight, among other things, the scale of youth unemployment in one provincial city; its structure (an issue Garside and his critics, Benjamin and Kochin, say little about), and its impact upon the teenage population.[4] They, in fact, enable judgements to be made not simply on the volume of youth unemployment at this period, the focus of the debate between Garside and his critics, but also on its distribution across occupations and age groups; the duration of bouts of unemployment; its impact upon morale, health, and lifestyles, and the relationship between unemployment and crime.[5]

The data referred to, and utilised in this chapter, also make possible an evaluation of whether there were, as contemporaries believed, merely 'progressive' and 'blind-alley' occupations for juveniles. The former, embracing apprenticeships and clerical work, were thought to insulate young workers from bouts of unemployment; the latter, which included van boy and messenger work, to expose them to it at the dangerous ages of 16 or 18.[6] Other issues that perplexed contemporaries who studied the juvenile labour market are also discussed. For example, whether the 14–16 age group, absent from the unemployment statistics before 1934, experienced bouts of unemployment; whether those juveniles apparently thrown out of 'blind-alley' jobs were restricted to casual, intermittent employment as adults, and whether unemployed juveniles were more likely to commit crime than those in employment.[7]

The Scale of the 'Problem'
As Table 3.1 (see page 176) demonstrates, the unemployment rate among 14- to 18-year-olds in Manchester was significantly lower than in other major cities at this period. In November 1927, when only 3.4 per cent of the under- 18s of Manchester were unemployed, 17.5 per cent were in Liverpool; 11.2 per cent in Sheffield, and 10.8 per cent in Salford. A year later, when the Manchester figure was still under five per cent, the youth unemployment figures in Liverpool, Sheffield and Salford were still over 10 per cent. This pattern of low youth unemployment in Manchester compared with other major cities (with the single exception of London) is also apparent during the depression years of the early 1930s and subsequently. While the number of 14–18s unemployed in Manchester never reached 10 per cent of the insured juvenile population during the 1930s, it never fell below this figure in Glasgow, Liverpool and Newcastle.

Manchester juveniles were also far less afflicted by unemployment than those in other parts of Lancashire. The unemployment rate among 'insured juveniles' (16- and 17-year-olds) was only 5.2 per cent in Manchester in the depression year of 1932. With the exception of Lancaster, where the unemployment rate among 16- and 17-year-olds was four per cent, this was the lowest rate in the entire county.[8] This favourable unemployment situation for the under-18s of Manchester was reflected in the high migration rates of 14- to 18-year-olds into the city. Unable to find work in their own areas, many juveniles from other parts of the country were placed in employment locally by the

JEBs active in the city.[9] The number of young migrants averaged 300 a year during the 1920s, but this figure increased markedly to around 500 during the 1930s.[10] The migrants included boys and girls from towns bordering on Manchester such as Altrincham, Ashton-under-Lyne and Glossop, but also a number who had travelled from as far afield as Jarrow, Stockton-on-Tees and Sunderland in order to take up work in Manchester.[11] Some local youngsters were found work in other towns and cities, but always significantly fewer than the number from outside placed into employment locally.

Furthermore, the policy of the city's juvenile employment service was always to offer local youngsters jobs before those from outside.[12] Thus, given the high migration rates of juveniles into employment in Manchester and the fact that in every interwar year for which placement statistics are available the number of juveniles placed into employment locally fell short of the number of jobs advertised at the bureaux, it might be concluded that Manchester did not have a youth unemployment problem during these years; that the insatiable demand for juvenile labour far outstripped the supply and rendered the juvenile unemployment that existed merely frictional. At a macro level, this appears to have been the case. Furthermore, Garside's argument that the bureaux' statistics seriously underrecord the true level of juvenile unemployment because they ignore 14- and 15-year-olds is not applicable in the Manchester context since many in this age group used the bureaux' placement service and attended juvenile unemployment centres voluntarily because of the opportunities provided for job search.[13]

At a micro level, however, many juveniles experienced bouts of unemployment, though at any one time they constituted only a small minority of their age group. This much is clear from two sources: the 1931 Census, which enumerated the 14–21-year-olds in the city 'out of work' on census day (27 April 1931) and the annual reports of the city's JEBs. The census figures (reproduced in Tables 3.2 and 3.3, see pp. 177 and 178) reveal that, although the unemployment rate among girls locally was not high in 1931 (6.4 per cent), a significant number of girls, 2,579, were 'out of work' on census day. Moreover, twice as many boys were unemployed: 4,851, representing 12.4 per cent of the boy labour force. But how accurate are these statistics? What do they measure? They were obtained by census investigators who visited every household in

Manchester and collected information on the employment circumstances of every member of each household on census day. Since they include all 14–21-year-olds who were out of work on census day, regardless of whether they were claiming unemployment benefit, they provide the only absolutely accurate account of the true extent of youth unemployment on one particular day.[14]

Much is revealed in the census tables (reproduced in condensed form in Tables 3.2, 3.3 and 3.5 (see page 180)) about the young unemployed of a typical provincial city. Three points require emphasis. First, the young unemployed were from a variety of occupational backgrounds; white-collar workers, for example, were experiencing unemployment as well as blue-collar workers. Second, juveniles normally employed in the so-called 'blind-alley' occupations were no more affected by unemployment than those normally in 'progressive' employment; in fact, less so.[15] The boys most affected by unemployment were metal workers who were thought to be insulated from it.[16] Third, the alarmist views of contemporaries regarding the prospects for juveniles employed in the 'blind-alley occupations' are not borne out. Not only did such occupations return the lowest unemployment rates for juveniles, they also provided work for many juveniles over 16 and over 18 who contemporaries felt would inevitably be thrown out of employment at 16 or 18. Of the 971 van boys in Manchester in 1931, 73 per cent were 16 or older, as Table 3.5 makes clear. It appears, therefore, that the distinction contemporaries drew between 'blind-alley' and 'progressive' employment is not a meaningful one for one provincial city. There is no way of discovering whether it had more meaning at other times during the period because in no other interwar year was the actual number of 14–21-year-olds, along with their employment circumstances, enumerated. The Census of 1921 only classified juveniles as either 'occupied' or 'unoccupied', and those 'occupied' were not necessarily in work. The census authorities felt that those who were out of work but looking for it were also 'occupied' in seeking work.[17]

Even in Manchester, juvenile unemployment was regarded by the authorities as a problem before 1931. This can be demonstrated in two ways. First, the records of the JEBs active locally give some impression of the volume of juvenile unemployment in the city. Second, a more effective way of showing that youth unemployment was regarded as a problem is to demonstrate that measures were undertaken to cater for unemployed 14–18-year-olds. State-sponsored and voluntary schemes for unemployed youngsters, and for others who were working short-time, were introduced in depressed regions such as north-east Lancashire and south Wales during this period.[18] Such schemes were not, however, confined to these areas. In Manchester, not considered either a depressed area or a 'Special Area', a number of centres for unemployed juveniles were opened by Manchester Education Committee (MEC) in co-operation with the Ministry of Labour between December 1918 and February 1919 and day classes of this kind remained a permanent feature in the city until 1939.[19] The official state scheme was entirely unique. The only organisations that had bothered to cater for the young unemployed of Manchester before December 1918 were voluntary bodies such as lads' and girls' clubs. They only provided instruction for their members or former members.[20] The focus here will be mainly on the official state scheme of Juvenile Unemployment Centres (JUCs) – renamed Junior Instruction Centres (JICs) in 1929 – since voluntary provision in Manchester affected very few unemployed 14–18-year-olds.[21]

The Work of the Juvenile Employment Bureaux

Youth unemployment on quite a large scale first hit Manchester in the transition period from wartime economic conditions to peacetime ones between December 1918 and July 1919. In this eight-month period 4,449 juvenile workers, split equally between boys and girls, 'signed on' at the local JEBs in order to claim the government's 'Out of Work Donation' and almost £8,600 was paid out in benefits to unemployed juveniles locally.[22] The 'Out of Work Donation' was originally intended simply as a temporary measure to assist 15–18-year-olds who had been employed on war work until they found alternative employment. The Manchester scheme, however, remained in operation for almost a year and, from 1920, 16–18-year-olds who found themselves unemployed could claim unemployment benefit providing they 'signed on' every day at their local JEB, if they lived within two miles of the bureau, and every other day if they lived between two and four miles from it.[23] The officials at the local JEBs complained that they had to administer the unemployment insurance scheme for 16–18-year-olds from 1920, as well as find 14–18-year-olds 'suitable' jobs.[24] During the early 1920s, in fact, the placement work of the bureaux was pushed into the background and the officials were forced to concentrate on their unemployment insurance duties under the Unemployment Insurance Act of 1920. Those at one of the city's four JEBs – the Openshaw bureau – bore the brunt of this extra responsibility. In April 1921, when nearly 5,000 under-18s locally were claiming unemployment benefit, over 2,000 were registered at the Openshaw bureau. A high proportion of the under-18s in the district worked in the engineering and cotton trades, particularly badly hit by the post-war depression.[25]

By 1923, the number of unemployed under-18s throughout the city had begun to fall, but the JEBs' unemployment insurance work held up placement work throughout 1923 and 1924. The number of 16- and 17-year-olds claiming benefit did not begin to rise again until 1930, but in the following year, 1931, it reached a post-war peak: 4,049 'fresh claims' for benefit were made at the local JEBs and a record £13,652 was paid out in benefits to the under-18s. Trade in the city was described as 'very poor' in the JEBs' annual report for 1932 and, in December of that year, 3,200 under-18s locally were registered as unemployed.[26]

Employment prospects for the under-18s improved, however, after 1932 partly as a result of the sharp decline in the number entering the labour market between 1933 and 1937 (a consequence of the decline in the birth rate during the war), but largely to the revival of local industries and the increased demand for juvenile labour. The JEBs' annual reports clearly reflect the economic upturn. During the 1930s, the JEBs were informed of more vacancies for juveniles than at any time in the past, and in certain local industries (cotton, clothing, engineering, and wireless assembly) there were not enough juveniles to fill the vacancies available.[27]

This did not mean that juvenile workers in the city no longer experienced unemployment after 1932. There were, for example, 2,554 'fresh claims' for unemployment benefit during 1934. Furthermore, the unemployment insurance work of the JEBs increased after 1934 because 14- and 15-year-olds were brought within the scheme under the Unemployment Act of that year.

Although they were still not entitled to claim benefit, they were now required to register themselves at their local JEB if they were unemployed and were also obliged to attend one of the centres for unemployed juveniles daily.[28] The administrative work of the JEBs thus increased enormously after 1934. In 1935, for example, nearly 10,000 letters were sent to local juveniles understood to be unemployed who had not registered at the JEBs.[29] Recalcitrant juveniles were brought before a board of assessors, a sub-committee of Manchester Education Committee, and informed of their legal obligation to attend a centre. Meetings of the board were held once a month and the number of cases investigated each month varied from six to sixteen. At each meeting legal proceedings were invariably taken out on a number of juveniles. In the case of an individual under 16 this could mean a fine of up to twenty shillings which parents were liable to pay after appearing in court. Those aged 16 or older could be summoned to appear in court themselves and risked forfeiting their unemployment benefit if they did not do so. The threat of legal proceedings against young workers, or their parents, proved extremely effective in the short term. By 1938, only 36 cases of non-attendance at a JIC were investigated and in only three cases were legal proceedings recommended.[30]

The officials who administered the unemployment insurance scheme for the under-18s of Manchester were, then, clearly concerned about the issue of juvenile unemployment, during both the 1920s and 1930s. Whether these concerns were justified will become clearer in the remainder of this chapter. To address this question it is necessary to consider, first, the structure of youth unemployment in Manchester.

The Structure of Youth Unemployment
The clientele at the unemployment centres for juveniles was extremely heterogeneous. Boys and girls from a range of occupational backgrounds, both manual and non-manual, were in attendance. Among the boys there were unemployed boiler-makers, carters, dyers and finishers, labourers, mill workers, warehouse workers, and office boys. Among the girls were machinists, mill workers, warehouse workers, wire weavers, and office workers.[31] Not all the juveniles that attended these centres were 'wholly unemployed'; a number were only 'partially unemployed' which meant they were unemployed for at least three days a week and

employed the rest of the time.[32] This group were still entitled to the 'Out of Work Donation', however; and, in order to qualify for this, they and the 'wholly unemployed' group had to attend a centre every day that they were unemployed otherwise they would risk forfeiting their benefit. Another group in attendance were those who had been temporarily 'stopped' for a specified period; invariably, no more than two weeks.[33] Only a section of the young unemployed of Manchester, therefore, were actually without work. Many had jobs and were working short-time. Exactly how many were in this category is unclear for the early 1920s, but in 1928 one and a half times as many young workers who were working short-time were claiming unemployment benefit than young workers who were 'wholly unemployed'.[34]

How long were the juveniles of interwar Manchester unemployed? The average stay of juveniles who attended the JUC in the city centre between December 1918 and April 1919 was only three and a half weeks.[35] This pattern was repeated at centres in other districts. At the Newton Heath JUC, boys were in attendance, on average, four weeks in April 1919. Girls who attended this centre stayed, on average, three weeks. At the Openshaw JUC, the average stay for boys and girls in 1919 was just under five weeks.[36]

Juveniles locally continued to experience short bouts of unemployment after 1919. Boys who attended the Deansgate JUC in 1928, the only centre operating in the city during that year, were in attendance for less than four weeks, on average, and the girls only three weeks.[37] When an official from the Ministry of Labour visited this centre, in October 1929, she was told that the personnel was 'continually changing' and in her subsequent report on the centre she pointed out that those who were attending voluntarily (that is, 14- and 15-year-olds) were finding clerical jobs 'rather quickly'.[38] When the same official visited the centre the following year, in March 1930, a number of girls in attendance were working short-time in the local cotton industry and attending the centre in their 'play' week. The JIC in Newton Heath was set up specifically for the short-time workers of the district.[39]

It is quite certain, therefore, that a number of the young unemployed of Manchester during this period were short-time workers rather than wholly unemployed ones, though the official juvenile unemployment statistics – whether those cited in census reports, the Ministry of Labour's records, or the JEBs' annual reports – do not separate the two. Furthermore, even wholly unemployed juveniles in Manchester tended to experience short spells of unemployment lasting not longer than three or four weeks usually and not more than a few days by the mid-1930s. In April 1937, for instance, 60 per cent of all the under-18s in the city who had been dismissed from their jobs in the previous three months had found employment within three days.[40] In view of this, it seems unlikely that unemployment had a catastrophic effect on the majority of juveniles locally who experienced it.

As regards the age profile of the young unemployed, no single age-group under 18 was hit more severely than others by unemployment. During one week in April 1919, for example, a more or less equal proportion of 15-, 16-, and 17-year-old girls were in attendance at the local JUCs; 128, 168, and 181 respectively. A higher proportion of the boys were 16- and 17-year-olds but there were still a significant number of 15-year-olds in attendance; 90 in all out of 396 during one week. In March 1924, the superintendent of one local JUC reported that almost 200 14- and 15-year-old boys and over 100 14- and 15-year-old girls had attended his centre over the preceding twelve months. It is clear from this that 14- and 15-year-olds definitely experienced bouts of unemployment and voluntarily attended unemployment centres.[41]

The Juvenile Unemployment Centres

Provision for unemployed juveniles was a permanent feature during this period and not simply apparent during periods of severe economic depression. By the mid-1920s, there were five JUCs active in Manchester. Four of these were still in existence in 1935.[42] They were financed, initially, mainly by the Ministry of Labour, but its grant fluctuated from 75 per cent of 'approved costs' to 50 per cent and, on occasions, the Ministry withdrew its contribution entirely. On such occasions Manchester Education Committee became solely responsible for the continued existence of the centres and had to provide all the finance. The centres were kept open during such periods.[43] According to the officials who administered the JUCs in Manchester, the purpose of the classes was 'to prevent demoralisation and degradation resulting from enforced prolonged idleness'.[44] The JUCs were not, therefore, set up to retrain unemployed juveniles for specific jobs, as two recent commentators have argued.[45] Their function, in Manchester and elsewhere, was simply to buoy up the spirits of unemployed juveniles.[46] The methods deployed to achieve this purpose varied depending on the particular centre in question. JUCs in Manchester quickly acquired a reputation for being either 'scholastic centres' or 'recreation centres' similar to lads' and girls' clubs.[47] At one centre the emphasis was clearly on cultural provision: English and Welsh folk songs were sung and classical music by Rubenstein, Schumann, Handel, Schubert, Giordani and Gluck was played.[48] At all the centres the curriculum was strictly non-vocational: arithmetic, English composition, recreative reading, drawing, general knowledge, physical training and music were the principal subjects.

Girls were taught the same subjects as boys, the one exception being sewing. The two sexes attended the centres at different times, however; boys in the mornings one week and girls in the afternoons, and this system would alternate each week. The reasoning behind this system of half-daily instruction was that it allowed those in attendance some time every day to look for work. This proved a successful policy because, as has been shown, most of those who attended the JUCs were in attendance for less than a month and many for just a few days.[49] The potentially demoralising effects of unemployment on the under-18s of Manchester were thus largely mitigated, partly by the work of the JUCs and partly by the fact that most of those who experienced bouts of unemployment were only unemployed for extremely short intervals between leaving one job and starting the next. A number also, as we have seen, already had jobs and were working short-time for a limited period.

The staff at the JUCs went to great lengths to vary the curriculum and prevent youngsters from becoming bored and inactive. The boys at Ancoats JUC, for instance, built a wireless set and produced their own magazine, in addition to doing the core subjects of arithmetic, English, general knowledge, drawing, drill and organised games. They also paid a weekly visit to the local swimming baths for which there was no charge and listened to classical music some afternoons.[50] One boy who attended a JUC in Manchester during the 1920s recorded his impressions of the experience in an essay:

The JUC is really a blessing in disguise for how many people know the truthfulness of the old proverbial saying 'Idleness Breeds Discontent' ...the centres all over the country prevent the idleness breeding discontent, and harness the time that would otherwise be wasted, to some useful practical purpose.[51]

Girls also appear to have derived at least some satisfaction from the experience. One girl who attended a centre during the 1920s and then went to work in a factory wrote to the superintendent saying how much she missed the centre. 'I am getting along very nicely thank you', she confided: 'but I don't like it. I would much rather be back at school...I will do all I can to live up to your ideas regarding my painting. I want you to be proud of me and I hope you will be some day.'[52] Another girl who attended a centre and then went to work in a shop asked the superintendent if it would still be possible for her to attend the centre on Wednesday afternoons (her half-day holiday) to allow her to continue her education.[53]

It is not suggested that all those who attended JUCs derived satisfaction from the experience. For some, the work was tedious. One woman who attended a centre in Staffordshire commented: 'The boys were all right, they got woodwork and what-have-you, but us women had either to do the laundry or cooking – there was nothing else for us to do. It was very boring, I thought.'[54] Such evidence clearly indicates that juveniles' responses to the centres varied. It cannot be argued, therefore, that the centres simply produced a feeling of 'alienation' in their clientele, as Pope suggests.[55] The superintendent of the Openshaw JUC would certainly have disagreed with this view. His centre, he believed, provided the unemployed youngsters of his district with a worthwhile alternative to the streets. He described it colourfully as 'an oasis in the desert of their drab life'.[56]

In Manchester, the JUCs were run as improving institutions. Spurley Hey, the city's Director of Education, felt that they promoted 'healthy competition' and prevented juveniles, especially boys, from mixing with 'undesirable acquaintances' on the street. Boys, he felt, would be prevented from mixing with 'itinerant vendors of merchandise' and from becoming runners for street bookmakers.[57] It is clear, however, that the centres performed a number of functions: they kept unemployed juveniles in good spirits; were vehicles for influencing juveniles' labour market behaviour (a Ministry of Labour official drew attention, for instance, in 1928 to 'the assistance they render in preventing unemployed juveniles from...taking casual...work, such as helping in garage work'); for encouraging juveniles to continue their education, and for inculcating an appreciation of culture.[58]

The staff at the Manchester JUCs obviously had no control over the high turnover, which was a product of the buoyant demand for juvenile labour in the city. Also, they managed to provide an effective service in spite of fluctuations in the Ministry of Labour's financial support for the scheme. Meanwhile, they were not in a particularly enviable occupation. They enjoyed far less job security than schoolteachers and were not entitled to certain pensions schoolteachers were entitled to. They also worked in extremely cramped and dingy rooms and there was a lack of basic facilities. At the Ancoats centre, for example, there was a gymnasium but no wash basins and showers.[59] The work of the local JUCs does not appear to have suffered much as a consequence of these problems.

Little information is available on individual teachers, but the superintendent at one Manchester centre apparently tried desperately hard to channel the skills of boys who could 'calculate accurately a betting slip containing a dozen entries' into solving mathematical problems.[60] This man had no sympathy for unemployed boys who idled away their time standing on street corners. Such behaviour led, inevitably he believed, to 'a serious deterioration in character and eventually to drunkenness or prison'.[61] Other contemporaries shared this view. An after-care officer in Salford was moved to write to the *Manchester Guardian* on the social consequences of youth unemployment:

> The rot of unemployment is eating into the morale of the young people...there are unmistakable signs that the enforced idleness is having a bad effect on these young people. A good proportion of their leisure is spent in the kinemas and other amusements. It has been found difficult to induce them to consider education and interest themselves in social activities when they are unemployed.[62]

The JUCs, operating in difficult circumstances, achieved some successes. Is this to overlook, however, that unemployment still lowered the morale of some young people?

The Impact of Unemployment on Juveniles

How did bouts of unemployment affect juveniles? William McG. Eagar and Herbert Secretan sought to answer this question in a study of the effects of unemployment on boys in Bermondsey, published in 1925. They concluded that it had a profound effect on boys who held positions of responsibility in a boys' club. 'All of us who have direct practical experience in the management of Boys' Clubs', they remarked, 'are disappointed again and again by the inability of boy officers to stand the strain of unemployment.'[63] Boys who experienced unemployment, they believed, displayed certain symptoms. They tended to become 'slack, irregular, unthoughtful, self-centred and incapable either of initiative or sustained effort'.[64] If they were unemployed continuously for a few months they were also likely to become bad citizens:

> If a boy is a good Club officer he is fairly certain to be a good employee, a good sportsman, and a good member of society in all its relations. A boy who goes to bits as a Club officer is gravely unlikely to fulfil the promise of good citizenship he showed before the process of disintegration began.[65]

Another symptom among those who experienced unemployment at regular intervals over a period of three to four years was what the authors termed 'lasting deterioration'. This took a number of forms: cynicism, coarseness, uncleanliness, a loss of interest in football stars, a lack of ambition, and so on. 'The outward signs are clear enough,' wrote McG. Eagar and Secretan:

> The boys are no longer young hopefuls; they are premature cynics....The sense of humour persists, but it is coarsening. Their wit is getting bitter and self-destructive. Cleanliness, achieved earlier by a series of miracles in bathless homes, is neglected. Hero-worship...of...football professionals, is dead. Ambition is obviously absurd. Physique varies...[66]

McG. Eagar and Secretan produced, on their own admission, nothing more than a 'subjective' analysis of the effects of unemployment on boys.[67] They eschewed scientific techniques for recording such matters as the deterioration in physique and instead simply recorded their impressions of the direct effects of unemployment on an undefined number of boys whom they knew.[68] This is not to suggest that their conclusions are invalid; but since they conflated the two quite separate issues of unemployment and what they termed 'misemployment' (meaning employment in so-called 'blind-alley' jobs) it is difficult to say whether the adverse effects they attributed to unemployment were specific effects of unemployment or of certain types of employment. Certain types of factory employment, for example, were known to have a deleterious effect on physique.[69] This being the case, it is far from clear whether the poor physique of some of the juveniles who attended JUCs in Manchester was the direct result of unemployment. Since juvenile unemployment was short-term the poor physique of some juveniles was, presumably, the consequence of family poverty during their childhoods.[70]

To be fair to McG. Eagar and Secretan, they argued that boys who experienced unemployment suffered mentally rather than physically from it. In suggesting, however, that boys who became unemployed displayed certain negative characteristics they ended up arguing that there were employed and unemployed 'types' among the boys of Bermondsey.[71] Those who showed all the symptoms of unemployment were seen to be the most delinquent. This argument was founded, however, on the progress of one individual labelled 'H.J.'. Described at 14 by his headmaster as 'an honest and industrious boy', over the next two years 'H.J.' secured employment only intermittently. Shortly before his 17th birthday, he was convicted for breaking into a warehouse and sent to a reformatory. 'Possibly, even probably,' McG. Eagar and Secretan remarked, 'H.J. would not now be detained in a Reformatory at the public expense if he had been able to obtain steady work.'[72] This simply reveals, however, that their assessment of the effects of unemployment was flawed. It is unclear, for example, whether 'H.J.' was driven to crime by his experience of unemployment, his experience of 'dead-end' employment, or for other reasons.

The relationship between unemployment and crime in the case of juveniles is extremely difficult to untangle. Whether unemployed juveniles were more likely to commit criminal acts than those in employment cannot be gleaned from juvenile crime statistics which do not supply information on the employment circumstances of individual juveniles. Furthermore, they only record the amount of crime detected; the proportion of undetected crimes committed by juveniles is, obviously, impossible to gauge. In the absence of solid statistical evidence on the relationship between unemployment and crime, the focus must necessarily be on contemporary perceptions of the relationship. The chief constable of Manchester, in his annual reports, frequently outlined his views on the causes of juvenile crime. While juvenile unemployment was undoubtedly a problem in the city during the 1920s, the level of juvenile crime was not considered a problem at all by the chief constable. 'Juvenile crime is as low now as at any time for which records can be produced', he remarked in 1927.[73] Furthermore, he placed the blame for much of the juvenile crime committed in the city on parents. Unemployment was not seen as a major cause of juvenile crime in 1927 or subsequently.[74]

It is difficult to say whether unemployment had any other adverse effects on 14–18-year-olds either in Manchester, or in other cities. There is some evidence that a period of unemployment could have a drastic effect on young people; two unemployed girls tried to commit suicide together by throwing themselves into the Rochdale canal near Manchester's city centre in May 1922. When they appeared in court afterwards, they threatened to attempt suicide again if they did not find work.[75] These girls were not, however, typical. Joan Harley found in interviews with 56 unemployed girls locally in 1935–36 that their lifestyles were not altered by unemployment. They visited cinemas and dance halls as frequently, in fact more so, than girls who were in employment.[76] This was largely because of the short-term nature of juvenile unemployment in the city; but there were other reasons. Cinemas offered cut-price matinée performances for the unemployed and girls were frequently treated to cinema visits by boyfriends.[77]

In Cardiff, where juvenile unemployment was more serious than in Manchester during the 1930s, it was reported that girls who were experiencing periodic bouts of unemployment because they had been put on short-time were reluctant to give up their jobs in shops, factories, and workshops despite the fact that these employments were severely affected by short-time working. A survey undertaken by the Save The Children Fund of Great Britain into the effects of unemployment on children and young people showed that such girls were prepared to accept short spells of unemployment and were unwilling to change jobs:

> The money which they can earn when employed, together with the benefit they can draw when unemployed, appear to be sufficient to enable them to carry on. Consequently it is seldom that they can be induced to accept an alternative employment such as domestic service, in which they can be assured of constant work...[78]

Another reason young workers who had been put on short-time work may have been reluctant to change jobs was that their employers were seen to be doing them a service in not putting them on short-time until they qualified for unemployment benefit. It was reported that the Cardiff employer, for instance, was

> a careful student of Unemployment Insurance regulations and divides up the work which he is able to give among as many juveniles as possible, standing his juvenile employees off in rotation when each has qualified for Unemployment Insurance.[79]

Given the short-term nature of much juvenile unemployment around the country during this period, it seems that few 14–18-year-olds actually suffered from it. The day centres that were set up in the areas where juvenile unemployment was regarded as a 'problem' – Manchester was one such despite the lack of attention it has received from historians – specifically aimed at checking a deterioration in morale and they achieved this limited aim, not just in Manchester, but in areas where juveniles were continuously unemployed for longer such as in south Wales. The same cannot be said of the centres run by voluntary societies. Manchester University Settlement opened a day centre for the unemployed boys of Ancoats in May 1931, but few boys attended it. 'The fruit of a hundred visits of boys on the lists of the Juvenile Employment Bureau might be an actual appearance of ten boys,' a Settlement officer remarked in 1932.[80] Between September 1932 and May 1933 the average attendance at this centre was only 25 boys.[81] It was finally forced to close in 1934, partly owing to lack of money, but mainly because most of the boys who had been in attendance had found work.[82] From 1934, 14–17-year-olds in the Ancoats district who found themselves unemployed were encouraged to attend the Settlement's day club for unemployed men. Few, if any, did: the Settlement's annual report for 1936–37 stated that the membership of the club was 'sharply divided' between 'young men' of 18–25 and 'older men' in the 40–55 age-group.[83]

Before 1934, unemployed 14- and 15-year-olds were not obliged to attend unemployment centres and, as a consequence, a number of critics felt this age-group were more likely than 16- and 17-year-olds to indulge in questionable pursuits. Gwynne Meara was convinced that 14- and 15-year-olds in south Wales did not attend unemployment centres. They instead

> drag out monotonous hours lounging on the streets, going to 'the pictures' and to 'the dogs', snatching a feverish enjoyment at 'twopenny hops', waking from their listless apathy only occasionally.[84]

In Manchester, it was civic leaders such as Spurley Hey who expressed such fears. He believed that unemployed youngsters who roamed the streets would inevitably turn to crime. This prognosis was not, however, borne out in the juvenile crime statistics produced annually by the chief constable of the city. One possible reason unemployed 14- and 15-year-olds locally did not turn to crime is that, as we saw earlier, a number attended JUCs voluntarily. Unemployment among the under-18s of Manchester was not, then, 'an economic and social problem of alarming proportions' and, with very few exceptions, it had no perceptible impact either on their behaviour, or on their lifestyles.

NOTES

1. Garside, 'Juvenile Unemployment and Public Policy', p. 322.
2. Ibid., p. 332; also cited in idem, *British Unemployment, 1919–1939: A Study in Public Policy* (Cambridge, 1990), p. 104.
3. For a closer analysis see D.M. Fowler, 'The Lifestyles of the Young Wage–Earner in Interwar Manchester, 1919–1939,' unpublished PhD thesis, University of Manchester, 1988, Ch. 3.
4. For the debate see Benjamin and Kochin, 'What Went Right with Juvenile Unemployment Policy'; and Garside's 'Juvenile Unemployment, Rejoinder'. See above, p.36, n.3.
5. A recent contribution to the debate by B. Eichengreen throws interesting light on the structure of youth unemployment in interwar London (short-term, frictional, voluntary (and involuntary) but ignores its impact. See idem, 'Juvenile Unemployment in Twentieth-Century Britain: The Emergence of a Problem,' *Social Research*, 54 (1987), pp.273–301.
6. Those who argued that the juvenile labour market was stratified in this way included the economists John Jewkes and Alan Winterbottom; the social scientist and social investigator David Caradog Jones, and the social workers E. S. Griffith and R. A. Joseph. See Jewkes and Winterbottom, *Juvenile Unemployment*, pp.25–6; Caradog Jones (ed.), *Social Survey of Merseyside*, Vol.3, p. 206; Griffith and Joseph, 'Unknown Years', pp.113–18. This view was, of course, deeply entrenched. Edwardian critics of boy labour such as R. H. Tawney held the same view. See, for example, R.H. Tawney, 'The Economics of Boy Labour', *Economic Journal*, Vol.XIX (1909), pp.517–37.
7. On 'blind–alley' employment see also Ch.1.
8. Jewkes and Winterbottom, *Juvenile Unemployment*, p.142.
9. See Appendix, Table 3.4.
10. Ibid.
11. Manchester Education Committee, Juvenile Employment Bureaux, *Annual Report*, 1935–36, p.16.
12. Ibid. 'In all cases where young people have been brought from other areas, it has been impossible to fill the vacancy by the introduction of local candidates'.
13. Garside, *British Unemployment*, pp.95–6. On the opportunities the Juvenile Unemployment Centres provided for job search see below, pp.81–2.
14. Census of England and Wales 1931, *Occupation Tables*, pp. iv, vi, vii.
15. Garside argues that the former were far more likely to become unemployed in their teens than the latter. See idem, 'Juvenile Unemployment and Public Policy', pp.324, 335–6.
16. See note 6 above.
17. Census of England and Wales 1931, *Occupation Tables*, pp. iv, vi, vii. For clarification of the 'occupied'and 'unoccupied' in the census tables see also Carr-Saunders, Caradog Jones and Moser, *Survey of Social Conditions in England and Wales*, p.104.
18. See, for instance, R. Pope, '"Dole Schools"'; idem, 'Education and the Young Unemployed: A Pre-War Experiment', *Journal of Further and Higher Education*, 2 (1978), pp.15–20. G. Meara, *Juvenile Unemployment in South Wales* (Cardiff, 1936); V. A. Bell, *Junior Instruction Centres and their Future: A Report to the Carnegie U.K. Trust* (Edinburgh, 1934) and W. Hannington, *The Problem of the Distressed Areas* (1937; repr. Wakefield, 1976).
19. Canner, 'Juvenile Employment Service', pp.64, 67, 103–5, 107, 109–12, 173, 180.
20. Ibid., pp.12–21.
21. For an analysis of the activities of one voluntary body in the alleviation of juvenile unemployment see below, pp.88–9.
22. Canner, 'Juvenile Employment Service', p.64.
23. Ibid., pp. 63–4, 90.
24. On the latter see Ch. 1.
25. Canner, 'Juvenile Employment Service', p.96.
26. Ibid., pp. 96–7; Manchester Education Committee, Juvenile Employment Bureaux, Annual Report, 1932–33, pp.1–3.
27. Manchester Education Committee, Juvenile Employment Bureaux, *Annual Report*, 1934–35, pp. 6–7.
28. Idem, *Annual Report*, 1933–34, pp.3–4; *Annual Report*, 1934–35, pp.4–5.
29. Canner, 'Juvenile Employment Service', p.99.

30. Ibid., pp.99, 171, 179.
31. Ibid., p.67.
32. Ibid., p.65.
33. Ibid.
34. Ibid., p.97.
35. Ibid., p.66.
36. Ibid.
37. Ibid., pp.109–10.
38. PRO, LAB 2/1078. Juvenile Unemployment Centres – Manchester Education Authority Centre at Byrom Street Course 1929–30 (typescript).
39. Ibid.
40. Canner, 'Juvenile Employment Service', p.138.
41. Ibid., pp.66, 105–6.
42. Ibid., pp.105, 173.
43. Ibid., pp.103–4; Bell, *Junior Instruction Centres*, p. 2.
44. Manchester Education Committee, Juvenile Employment Bureaux, *Annual Report*, 1918–19, p.16 cited in Canner, 'Juvenile Employment Service', p.65.
45. See G. Rees and T. L. Rees, 'Juvenile Unemployment and the State Between The Wars' in T. L. Rees and P. Atkinson (eds), *Youth Unemployment and State Intervention* (London, 1982), p.20.
46. The chief purpose of the centres that were set up in South Wales was the same. See Meara, *Juvenile Unemployment in South Wales*, pp. 87–8.
47. Canner, 'Juvenile Employment Service', p. 65.
48. Ibid., p.66.
49. Ibid., pp.65–6.
50. Ibid., pp.102–4.
51. Ibid., p.110.
52. Ibid., p.106.
53. Ibid.
54. Cited in J. Horne, 'Continuity and Change in the State Regulation and Schooling of Unemployed Youth' in S. Walker and L. Barton (eds), *Youth, Unemployment and Schooling* (Milton Keynes, 1986), p.21.
55. Pope, 'Education and the Young Unemployed', p.18.
56. Cited in Canner, 'Juvenile Employment Service', p. 106.
57. PRO, LAB 2/1311/EDJ 525/4/1928. National Advisory Committee on Juvenile Employment – Inquiry into the Usefulness of Juvenile Unemployment Centres, 1928 (typescript).
58. Ibid.; Canner, 'Juvenile Employment Service', pp.68, 110, 113.
59. Canner, 'Juvenile Employment Service', pp.109, 174; PRO, LAB 2/1078. 'Juvenile Unemployment Centres – Manchester'; Garside, *British Unemployment*, p.96.
60. Canner, 'Juvenile Employment Service', p.106.
61. Ibid.
62. *Manchester Guardian*, 21 Jan. 1922.
63. W. McG. Eagar and H. A. Secretan, *Unemployment Among Boys* (London, 1925), pp.60–1.
64. Ibid., p.60.
65. Ibid., p.65.
66. Ibid., p.67.
67. Ibid., pp.61–2. They acknowledged, for instance, that 'most evidence of the effects of unemployment must be generic and largely subjective'.
68. Ibid., pp.57, 62, 64.
69. On this see D. J. Collier, *The Girl in Industry* (London, 1918), *passim*.
70. For observations on the poor physiques of some juveniles in attendance at Manchester's JUCs see PRO, LAB 2/1078. 'Juvenile Unemployment Centres, Manchester'; Canner, 'Juvenile Employment Service', p.175.
71. Eagar and Secretan, *Unemployment Among Boys*, pp.62–3.
72. Ibid., p.62.
73. City of Manchester Watch Committee, Chief Constable's *Annual Report* 1927, p.v.

74. Idem, *Annual Reports* 1927–1939, *passim*.
75. *Manchester Guardian*, 10 May 1922.
76. See below, Ch. 5.
77. See below, Ch. 4.
78. Save The Children Fund, *Unemployment and the Child: The Report on an Enquiry into the Effects of Unemployment on the Children of the Unemployed and on Unemployed Young Workers in Great Britain* (London, 1933), p.73.
79. Ibid., pp.72–3.
80. Manchester University Settlement, *Day Clubs for Men and Boys, An Experiment And An Appeal For Volunteers* (Manchester, 1932), not paginated.
81. Manchester University Settlement, *Annual Report* 1932–33, pp.12–13.
82. Idem, *Annual Report* 1933–34, p.16.
83. Idem, *Annual Report* 1936–37, p.7.
84. Meara, *Juvenile Unemployment in South Wales*, p.106.

4

The Teenage Consumer in Interwar Britain[1]

The teenager who had a significant amount of money to spend on consumer products and leisure generally – be it on cosmetics, clothes, magazines, motor cycles, cinemas or dance halls – is still thought to have suddenly appeared in Britain, along with the products that were allegedly aimed at the teenager, in the decade and a half after 1945. Economic and social historians, and sociologists, seem to agree that the phenomenon Mark Abrams first identified and described in his pamphlet study *The Teenage Consumer* (1959) was a by-product of the economic climate of postwar Britain.[2] It was only after the Second World War, Abrams argued, that working-class teenagers especially (who constituted 90 per cent of teenage consumers in 1959) found themselves with a high disposable income owing to two developments: the improvement in their earnings and the decline of youth unemployment. Moreover, it was only in the 1950s that manufacturers became interested in teenagers as a viable market for particular leisure products and services.[3]

Abrams was the first market researcher in Britain to analyse the spending patterns of teenagers; but he defined them loosely as young people 'from the time they leave school to the age at which they marry'. He had in mind all those between the ages of 14 and 25.[4] Besides being working-class and single, the teenage consumers he described were in work. Many were in highly paid factory occupations. The money wages of teenage wage-earners as a whole during the 1950s had increased by 400 per cent from their pre-war levels.[5]

All of this was true, however, of the teenage group in interwar Britain. Money wages for boy and girl wage-earners, in a range of industries, had increased by between 300 and 500 per cent since the pre-First World War period. For girls, increases were of the order of between 100 and 500 per cent and for boys between 100 and 300 per cent.[6] Youth unemployment averaged five per cent between 1920 and 1939; and, as regards marital status, a higher proportion of the teenage population and a higher proportionof 20–24 year olds were single during the interwar years than during the 1950s.[7] Moreover, the age profile of the population was similar at both dates. In fact, as Table 4.1 (see page 000) reveals, there were more 15–24-year-olds in the population during the 1920s and 1930s than during the 1950s and 1960s.[8] Thus the economic and demographic conditions for a youth market to emerge were extremely favourable in interwar Britain. This chapter will examine whether this in fact happened.

The Disposable Income of Young Wage-Earners

It seems by no means remarkable that the teenage consumer should have emerged between the wars. The social surveys of the 1920s and 1930s all stressed that the period between starting work and marriage was the one point during the life-cycle when a person was least likely to be experiencing poverty. Seebohm Rowntree, the author of one of the most exhaustive social surveys of the working-class between the wars (based on information obtained from 16,362 families comprising 55,206 persons living in York in 1936), identified the three major periods of economic stress in working-class families as occurring in early childhood, old age and, for more than a quarter of the working-class population of York, in early middle life (between the ages of 25 and 44).[9] He also showed that once children became wage-earners, in most cases they rose out of poverty. Thus 76.3 per cent of the 15–25-year-olds in Rowntree's survey were above his poverty line; but only 60.9 per cent of 5–14-year-olds, 50.3 per cent of 1–4-year-olds, and less than half (47.5 per cent) of those less than twelve months old.[10]

Herbert Tout, the author of a survey of Bristol conducted in 1937, reached the same conclusion as Rowntree on the age distribution of poverty. Those most likely to be experiencing poverty in Bristol were children under 14. One in five children under 14 there in 1937 was below even the spartan standards of the George poverty line.[11] Once children reached 14 or 15, however, their living standard improved dramatically. Thus, while 20.6 per cent of the 10-14 age-group (sample: 1,350 persons) in Tout's survey were experiencing poverty, thereafter there was a dramatic improvement. Only 9.6 per cent of 15–19-year-olds (sample: 1,276 persons) and only 4.1 per cent of 20–24-year-olds (sample: 1,029 persons) fell below Tout's minimum standard.[12] While his survey of Bristol exposed 'the appalling fact that one working-class child in every five comes from a home where income is inadequate to provide a bare minimum standard'[13] and Rowntree's survey that 52.5 per cent of all children under a year old in York in 1936 were born into poverty,[14] the evidence assembled on young people at the other end of the childhood cycle revealed a quite different picture.

Such evidence suggests that, even among working-class families experiencing poverty, young wage-earners invariably enjoyed a standard of living higher than that of the rest of the family; a fact which was made clear to the authors of a social survey of Ancoats, a slum area of Manchester, conducted in 1937.[15] They assumed, for instance, that young wage-earners in working-class families 'would have holidays and outings and new clothes, while probably the parents, the mother certainly, stayed at home and wore old clothes'.[16] They also assumed that wage-earning sons and daughters living in the district 'quite certainly would not contribute the whole of their wages to the household exchequer'[17] and, therefore, that the standard of living of the family as a whole would be lower than its total income level suggested.

Rowntree calculated that in York supplementary earners aged 16 and older (who constituted 15 per cent of the working-class population of that city) retained 13 per cent of the total weekly income of the working-class.[18] A distinction therefore had to be made, he argued, between a family's total weekly income and its available weekly income (that available to the mother); the amount retained by young wage-earners being, apparently, determined by the material circumstances of the family. He substantiated this theory to some extent, demonstrating that in families below his poverty line supplementary earners retained less than 13 per cent of the total weekly income (only five per cent in the poorest families) and more than 13 per cent in families above it (15 per cent in the most prosperous families).[19] Case studies he cites reveal, however, that there seems in some cases to have been no relationship between the financial circumstances of the family and the discretionary income retained by its young wage-earners. In one such, a family of man, wife and four children (three of whom were wage-earners) living marginally above Rowntree's poverty line, the total weekly income of the family was £6 13s 3d; but its available weekly income only amounted to £3 15s. The young wage-earners in the family, in other words, retained almost 50 per cent of the weekly income.[20] In another family comprising man, wife and six children (five of whom were wage-earners) the male head was unemployed and received no benefit either for himself or his wife. The family's total weekly income was £13 16s 10d. The children retained 60 per cent of this figure and only £5 4s was available to the family.[21] Finally, in another family of man, wife and six children (four of these being wage-earners) the male head was in temporary employment and his wife did not work. The total weekly income of the family was £9 18s, its available income only £5 5s.[22] Such evidence led Rowntree to admit that a wage-earning boy or girl's standard of living 'may be, and often is, higher than that of the rest of [the] family'.[23]

The spending money retained by young wage-earners seems to have depended not only on the material circumstances of the family, but also on the ages of young wage-earning dependants. Rowntree found that in York only the youngest wage-earners (14- and 15-year-olds) handed over the whole of their earnings to parents and received back a limited amount for pocket money. Among those aged 16 and older, however, he found: 'It is the general custom...to pay to their parents such portion of their wages as they would have to pay for board and lodgings if not living at home'.[24] The case studies he cites reveal that boy and girl wage-earners frequently retained 50 per cent or more of their earnings. For example, a boy of 19 in a 'Class C' family, which was only marginally above the Rowntree poverty line, earned 30s. He paid 18s 'keep' and retained 12s.[25] In another 'Class C' family of widow, son aged 20, and daughter aged 18, the mother received a pension of 10s; the son, an apprentice electrician, earned 35s, gave his mother 18s and kept 17s; and the daughter, who earned 29s in a factory, paid 15s board and kept 14s.[26] In one 'Class E' family, at the highest point above Rowntree's poverty line, one of the boy wage-earners earned 88s as a factory worker, but surrendered only 25s to the family purse.[27] In another such family a girl of 19 earned 36s 11d in a factory, paid 15s board and retained 21s 11d.[28] Even within poor working-class families, therefore, but more so within better-off ones, young wage-earning dependants were, not infrequently, an affluent group compared with other members of the family.

Other social investigators who studied the household budgets of working-class families found this to be the case. A.L. Bowley and M.H. Hogg studied working-class families in five towns (Reading, Northampton, Warrington, Bolton and Stanley) during the 1920s.

They concluded: '[I]t is assumed that the incomes of all the members of the family are pooled. In fact, of course, grown children assert the right to their own money and only make a fixed payment to the household.'[29] After investigating the household budgets of a number of working-class families in Liverpool in the early 1930s, the authors of *The Social Survey of Merseyside* noted:

> It is a matter of common experience that the husband and other earning members of the family usually hand over to the wife and mother only a part of their earnings for housekeeping: what they retain may be spent on 'necessaries' or on 'luxuries' according to their own choice.[30]

In 1931, Percy Ford gathered data on the weekly income and expenditure of 559 working-class families living in Southampton, reaching the conclusion that:

> ...the amount and proportion [of his or her earnings] reserved by the child...tend to increase as he grows older, that there are 'good' children, and 'bad' children who refuse even to pay for any of their keep, are common knowledge. It is also true that some parents seem to be as ignorant of their children's earnings...as many wives are of their husband's.[31]

Ford even implied that young wage-earners who kept a substantial portion of their wages for personal expenditure were contributing to the poverty experienced by some families.[32]

All the social investigators who studied the income and expenditure of working-class families were agreed, then, that the young wage-earners in such families retained around 50 per cent of their earnings, and some an even higher percentage. What determined the size of their disposable income? The evidence cited suggests that the degree of poverty in a family was not always crucial. One's gender was even less important. Many girls, as we shall see, had as much disposable income as boys. Joan Harley, for example, was startled at the amount of money girl wage-earners in Manchester spent on themselves and on leisure each week. Most of the girls she spoke to

> seem to spend their money on amusements, cosmetics and

hairdressing. The majority go to the cinema and buy magazines. One or two may occasionally buy themselves a pair of stockings, a scarf or a handbag, but as a general rule...their parents pay their travelling expenses to work and provide their clothes.[33]

Age, it seems, was the most important determinant of disposable income. As revealed in the studies of Rowntree and other social investigators, while 14- and 15-year-olds might hand over their wage packets to their mothers and receive only a few coppers back, those of 16 and older insisted on keeping much more of their earnings.

Young Wage-Earners and their Families
The argument developed so far goes against the grain of existing historical research on the working-class family; most notably, the work of Elizabeth Roberts.[34] She regards the 'youth' phase in the three towns she studied over the period from 1890 to 1940 (Lancaster, Preston and Barrow) as being, if anything, a period of extended dependence on parents. Her interviews with 160 people in north-west England led her to conclude: '...in view of their early conditioning about the importance of obeying parents and of making their contribution to the family's well-being, it would be unusual to find much real independence, still less youthful rebellion.'[35] Young wage-earners, she argues, certainly did not become financially independent automatically on starting work. In fact, there was a 'tradition' in Lancaster for all the wage-earners in a family to hand over their wage packets, unopened, to their mothers 'who then decided how the income should be spent'. Usually, young workers in Lancaster would be given pocket money by the mother at the rate of 1d in the shilling and 1s in the pound.[36]

The questions raised by this research relate to its typicality and perhaps its atypicality. In the first place, compared with Rowntree's survey of 16,362 families (comprising 55,206 persons) Roberts's research is based on a relatively small sample (160 persons). Second, and more important, the evidence on wage-earners in Lancaster conflicts with Rowntree's on wage-earners in York and that produced by other social investigators, who found that only the youngest wage-earners handed over the whole of their earnings to their mothers.[37] A third point is that Roberts does not consider age differences among young wage-earners. Important questions are thus overlooked. At what age, for instance, did young workers become financially independent? What implications did this have for the hitherto unassailable moral authority of working-class parents? Roberts seems to argue that the conformist and deferential young workers of the north-west never became truly independent. At home, autonomy was denied them by the tremendous moral authority of their parents; at work, by the industrial discipline of the factory floor, combined with the likelihood of working either with another member of the family or with some friend of the family. 'Even marriage', she argues, 'did not necessarily bring complete independence', many young couples being forced to live with in-laws if they had few savings.[38]

The view that young wage-earners' lives were governed totally by the needs of the family ignores much that was important to this group. Those in their teens, as we have seen an affluent group within working-class families, did not see their lives in terms of struggle. Conversations at work invariably centred on activities pursued outside the workplace and outside the family.[39] Moreover, as will become clearer later in this chapter, teenage wage-earners spent most of their free time during the evenings and at weekends outside their homes and, it appears, were the principal beneficiaries of developments in commercialised leisure provision at this period.[40] It is now necessary to review some of the evidence that suggests this to have been the case.

The Leisure Behaviour of Young Wage-Earners

Cinemagoing was indisputably the most popular form of commercial recreation among young people during the interwar period. The first statistical survey of cinemagoing was not undertaken until 1934, and it did not distinguish in sufficient detail the age structure of the cinema audience.[41] Virtually all the social investigators of the interwar years, however, pointed out that the most habitual cinemagoers were young people in their teens.[42] Furthermore, the Carnegie UK Trust's study of unemployed youths in Glasgow, Cardiff and Liverpool conducted between 1936 and 1939 showed that cinemagoing was not simply confined to young people in employment. About 80 per cent of unemployed youths in these cities attended the cinema at least once a week and 25 per cent more frequently.[43]

Of the girls Joan Harley spoke to about their leisure, the vast majority (90 per cent of her sample) visited the cinema at least once a week and apparently regardless of the film being shown. Some went to cinemas as often as six times a week and a number also found time to visit dance halls.[44] Harley was extremely concerned about such undiscriminating and, as she judged, unbeneficial use of leisure time, declaring:

> The big field of leisure for...girls is out of doors in...the adjuncts of the cinema and the dance hall. While it would be idle to criticise these ways of spending leisure....it is clear that in so far as young girl wage-earners cannot discriminate between excess and moderation, these activities are to say the least of it not beneficial to them.[45]

She was concerned about the growing influence of cinemas and dance halls in the lives of teenage girls of the 1930s, for two reasons. First, she felt that these entertainments were drawing girl wage-earners away from their homes and families.[46] Given the habitual nature of attendance, it is difficult to argue against this. She also felt that many of the films girl wage-earners watched glorified materialism and wealth. She was convinced, for instance, that the Hollywood musicals were having an effect on the girls. Some girls she spoke to, she claimed, had adopted a 'Hollywood accent' and a number of others copied the dress styles, hairstyles, and mannerisms of their favourite film actresses to a ludicrous degree. '[T]he influence of a popular star', Harley remarked, 'is easily traceable in quite a number of girls in the angle of a hat, the way a scarf is worn, the style of hairdressing and even the way of entering a room, shaking hands and sitting in a chair'.[47] Copycat behaviour of this sort was also noticed in other parts of the country. The authors of *The New Survey of London Life and Labour* commented:

> The influence of films can be traced in the clothes and appearance of the women...girls copy the fashions of their favourite film star. At the time of writing, girls in all classes of society wear 'Garbo' coats and wave their hair à la Norma Shearer or Lilian Harvey.[48]

A shop girl from Leeds, in a letter to a weekly film magazine, confirmed such impressions:

> I wonder whether people realize how very strong is [the] effect [of the cinema] on the lives of hundreds of girls in similar positions to myself. Here is my weekly budget: Wages 32s – Board and lodging 25s – Saturday visit to cinema 1d – Monday visit 7d – Thursday visit 7d – That makes 27s 2d. Then there is threepence for *Film Weekly* and three shillings for dress allowance...People consider me smartly dressed, but this is undoubtedly because I copy the clothes I have seen in films. Powders, soap and odds and ends are those used by my favourite film stars. When I get a rise in salary, I shall be able to afford another night at the pictures.[49]

When girls in Manchester were not 'at the pictures' they were, it seems, either talking about films or reading about them. The following account of a typical Monday evening was written by a girl from Hulme, Manchester, in the summer of 1939:

Monday	
4 p.m.	Left school with girl friend, talked about school and film stars...
6.10 p.m.	Girl friend called for me. Walked to pictures.
6.30 p.m.	Saw 'It's in the Air'.
9 p.m.	Left pictures, talked about picture, met two girl friends on the way home.
9.15 p.m.	Stood talking at corner with two girls about clothes, holidays and boys...
10 p.m.	Arrived home, had supper, listened to dance music, talked to family about pictures...[50]

This girl was not exceptional. In Hulme, girls spent between a third and a half of their free time each weekday evening (excluding Saturdays) inside a cinema, from the age of 12 to the age of 21;[51] so, too, did the boys of the district.[52]

There were some differences according to status. The 'working boys' and 'working girls' of Hulme, for example, visited cinemas as frequently as other adolescents, but also found time to visit dance halls on weekday evenings. For both sexes, weekday visits to dance halls began at the relatively young age of 15. Young wage-earners, of both sexes, continued to attend dances on weekday evenings until at least the age of 21.[53] None of the schoolboys or schoolgirls of the district visited dance halls during the week; presumably because they could not afford to on a disposable income that must have been extremely limited.[54] Those still at school visited cinemas regularly, however, since admission prices could be as low as 1d during the 1930s and the average price of a ticket in Manchester was only 6d.[55] Thus, although wage-earners alone had access to dance halls, schoolboys and schoolgirls spent some money on cheaper forms of commercialised entertainment, notably cinema visits. Young wage-earners were, however, a more lucrative market for entertainment entrepreneurs and manufacturers than schoolchildren and such people, as will become clear, were beginning to aim their products and services at young wage-earners by the 1930s.

Leisure Entrepreneurs and the Emergence of a Youth Market

A plethora of magazines aimed at young wage-earners first appeared during the interwar years. Among those in circulation by the 1930s were the following: *Boys' Cinema*, a 2d weekly launched in 1919; *Boys' Broadcast*, a 2d weekly started in 1934; *The Motor Cycle Book for Boys*, a fortnightly magazine launched in 1927; *Girls' Cinema*, a 2d weekly launched in 1920; *Peg's Paper*, a 2d weekly aimed at the 'mill-girl', and a host of others.[56]

Some magazines were not as specialist as their titles imply. They included features on a range of topics of interest to the boy or girl wage-earner. *Boys' Cinema*, for example, included features for 'intelligent young men (17½ to 25)' on careers; features on 'How to Become Strong'; 'How to Catch Roach', and a regular column on young female film stars such as Mabel Normand, 'the popular and dashing film comedienne', Colleen Moore, a 'dainty little maiden [of] eighteen', and Pearl White, 'the peerless, fearless girl of the movies...'.[57]

Magazines were also vehicles for manufacturers and the proprietors of other magazines. A single issue of *Boys' Cinema* (in December 1920) included advertisements for: *The Picture Show* magazine; a holiday annual for boys and girls (price 6s); *Girls' Cinema*; a treatment for increasing height (5s); an air rifle (7s 9d); a potion for curling hair ('Summers' Curlit', 1s 5d); boxing gloves (8s 6d); a gramophone (no price given); a hair treatment for girls

(1s); a violin (52s 6d); a model railway set and a watch (2s).[58] Girls' magazines brimmed with advertisements. *Peg's Paper* publicised shampoo; make-up; potions for curing obesity; others for removing body hair and increasing bust measurements; creams; soaps; clothes and chocolate. It also included free song-sheets comprising the notes and music of the most popular songs of the day.[59] Such evidence clearly points to the existence of a hard-sell market aimed at the young wage-earners of interwar Britain. The editors of certain magazines even conducted market research on their readers' preferences for features.[60] Either that or they included free gifts with the magazines in an effort to establish a stable readership in a highly competitive environment.[61]

Film titles are further evidence of an emerging youth market. A number of films screened in Manchester during the 1920s were firmly pitched at youth judging by the titles. In January 1920, the Tower Picturedrome in Broughton screened *The Echo of Youth* and *Blindness of Youth* during the same week. The same month the Temple Pictorium in Manchester screened *Jazz Mania*. In November 1929, Manchester Hippodrome screened *Movietone Follies of 1929*, described in a local film programme as a song and dance talking film about a 'jazz mad flapper', the theme of which was 'Youth with a capital Y'.[62] Nationally, during 1938 a number of films featuring boy gangsters were shown around the country: *Boy of the Streets*, a film about juvenile criminals in New York; *Youth on Parole*; *Fire Fighters*, a film about a youthful arson gang; *The Boy From Barnardo's*, about a juvenile criminal sent to a school for waifs and strays; *The Devil's Party*, about young gangsters in New York; *Crime School*, starring Humphrey Bogart, about juvenile delinquency in New York; *Young Fugitives*, about a young crook and his gangster associates; and *Boys' Town*, about a colony of delinquent boys.[63]

The dance halls that began to open in working-class districts of cities during the 1920s catered exclusively for young wage-earners. Robert Roberts remarked of dance halls in Salford:

> In the explosive dancing boom after the war, the young from sixteen to twenty-five flocked into the dance halls by the hundred thousand: some went 'jigging' as often as six times a week. The great 'barn' we patronised as apprentices held at least a thousand....at 6d per head (1s on Saturdays) youth at

every level of the manual working-class, from the bound apprentice to the 'scum of the slum', fox-trotted through the new bliss in each other's arms.[64]

Oral evidence gives the same impression. Speaking of the immediate post-war period, a former apprentice of Trafford Park, Manchester, recalled:

the 16 years of ages was going then oh and they were going there in clean collars...every Saturday night and...when you went to work on a Monday morning you was thinking about it, next Saturday night the dance will be on...and that was your thoughts all the way through the week, waiting for Saturday night for the dance to be on.[65]

When a local band began playing regularly at the dances in Trafford Park young people from adjacent districts began to attend them: 'that was when it developed when the band was there, and then it turned into a real Saturday night, all the people used to come along – the teenagers – from Salford and Gorse Hill and Stretford'.[66]

Dance halls were invariably supervised by an 'MC'. This did not, however, prevent the clientele from using the halls for a number of purposes. 'Most of us', Roberts recalled, 'went to the Crown to dance and to find a girl to dally with on Sunday evening – sex night Number One – down some local lovers' lane'.[67] Manchester's Jewish youths visited halls where they were likely to meet English girls.[68] Dance halls also served as meeting places for gangs of youths, who were as obsessed with fashion and the film world as girls. The Napoo gang, for instance, which regularly met at a dance hall in Belle Vue, Manchester, wore a uniform borrowed from American gangster films. Each member wore a navy blue suit, a trilby, and a pink neckerchief. The fear the gang aroused among the population of Ancoats, where its members lived and worked, suggests that it should be viewed as a pre-Teddy boy youth cult. There is evidence, for instance, that its members even pulled up cinema seats in the Cosy Corner picture house in Ancoats.[69]

Young wage-earners were thus not passive recipients of commercialised leisure. In fact, they used the ephemera sold to them and cinemas and dance halls for distinct ends. Moreover, certain types of consumerism required considerable effort from the consumers. Boys who bought the 2d weekly *Hobbies* were encouraged to build models and toys 'for little brothers or young friends'; to make beads and necklaces 'for young lady friends', and cigarette boxes, pipe racks, and match holders for 'fathers and uncles'. In July 1931, the magazine encouraged its readers to enter a competition involving the construction of a model of MV *Britannic* using cardboard. (The first prize was a 2 horsepower motorcycle.) The same issue included features on how to make gramophone records; a bathing buoy and air cushion for non-swimmers; a useful cabinet for the coin collector, and how to keep fish in a marine aquarium.[70] *Hobbies* readers were encouraged to use their spare time constructively, but many of the activities recommended required them to spend money. Readers were encouraged to purchase fretsaws and other tools and raw materials such as wood at regular intervals: 'Arrange...to put away a certain sum... each week for the purchase of more materials, or extra tools,' they were told in November 1931.[71] Alongside young wage-earners who spent their disposable income on cinemas and dance halls, therefore, were others who did so on hobbies. In other words, teenage spending and culture was not restricted to the public domain. There was a home-based, private culture also.[72]

A Distinctive Youth Culture?
Contemporaries writing during the 1920s and 1930s believed that the youth culture of these years was novel in the sense of being, for the first time, quite distinct from adult leisure pursuits. This culture was organised not only around cinemas and dance halls but also around a love of jazz music. 'By its vigour and cleverness jazz', R.W.S. Mendl remarked in the first book on the subject to be published in Britain, 'is felt to have knocked out the sentimental ballad of a bygone age, and thus it makes its appeal to the most modern – or ultra modern – members of the younger generation.'[73] After visiting a number of dance halls in Bolton during 1937-38 Tom Harrisson of Mass Observation concluded: 'Jazz has become or is becoming the religious ritual of post-war youth, and these songs of hope and happiness...are the hymns of young England.'[74] Jazz music certainly, as we have seen, figured prominently in the films young wage-earners watched and at the dance halls they frequented. But whether the market for jazz records was dominated by young people requires further research.[75]

Journalists were as convinced as social investigators of the novelty of the youth culture they observed. A Miss Pat Sykes drew attention to a 'Modern Craze for Leisure' which she proceeded to define as a craze for dancing at dance halls. She argued that old adult dances such as the Lancers and the foxtrot were 'doomed' and implied that dance halls were being patronised by the younger generation only.[76] A correspondent for the *Manchester Guardian* implied that young wage-earners were the beneficiaries of all post-war commercialised entertainment:

> Grandmothers and bishops, preaching from their armchairs and pulpits, insist that this is the Age of Luxury...short skirts, lipsticks, vulgar films...sex novels, jazz, the Eton crop...There is almost no end to the list of abominations...Before the war and in the uneasy years which immediately followed it, luxury was mainly a matter of means. Now any young typist from Manchester or Kensington can keep her hair trimmed and waved and her busy feet in fine silk stockings and pale kid shoes.[77]

In January 1929, someone who described himself as 'an Ordinary Man' wrote to the *Manchester Evening News* urging the fathers of wage-earning boys to take more interest in their son's leisure behaviour. 'How many fathers', he asked, 'know what kind of cinemas their sons attend, or where they spend their hours of recreation?'[78] Having reminded them of their responsibilities towards their sons he then instructed them to: 'Tell your boy what a wonderful age this is for the youth. Never was there an age when youth had such advantages and opportunities.'[79] Journalists echoed this judgement. Robert Blatchford, a regular columnist for the *Manchester Evening News* at this period, argued that wage-earning boys were the principal beneficiaries of recent developments in commercialised leisure provision and certainly of the 'talkies' and motor cycles. He had no objections to the advent of the motor cycle. But he violently objected to the influence American films were having on the way youths spoke. English youths, he noted in 1937, were resorting to 'a sorry mess of lubberly slang' frequently using terms borrowed from the films such as 'Sez yous' and 'OK'.[80] Sir Alfred Yarrow was less critical than Blatchford. He pointed to the new opportunities opening up to boy wage-earners and their girlfriends to escape the claustrophobic world of the cities and venture into the countryside on bicycles.[81] But how accurate were these impressions of the apparent novelty of interwar youth culture?

It appears from social surveys conducted in Victorian and Edwardian Britain that the young wage-earners of these years were much less distinct from their elders than those of the 1920s and 1930s. In Edwardian Manchester, girl wage-earners and married women participated in the same activities. The wives and daughters of 'the artisan class' were, E.A. Hadden noted, 'entirely dependent' on Sunday schools for their recreation; both working girls and married women attending tea-parties, singing classes, and amateur theatricals organised by the church.[82] The audience at commercialised entertainments was also characterised by its heterogeneity. In Victorian London, the 'penny gaff' or cheap theatre was, according to one contemporary who visited a number of these establishments, patronised by mothers with babies, schoolboys and schoolgirls, youths 'from sixteen to twenty', and 'broken-down old men'.[83] The cheap theatres in Edwardian Manchester were patronised by adults (men and women) and children.[84] According to Charles Russell, the same was true of the music hall audiences in the north of England. Meanwhile, the audiences at Edwardian picture theatres comprised adults in the main, especially women.[85]

Rowntree was well qualified to observe changes in young wage-earners' leisure behaviour over time, being the author of two social surveys separated by almost forty years. At the time of his second social survey of York, conducted between 1936 and 1939, young wage-earners' lives bore little resemblance to those of their predecessors. In 1899, the year Rowntree's first social survey of York was conducted, young wage-earners spent most evenings 'lounging about in the neighbourhood of their houses or promenading up and down certain streets in the city'.[86] By the late 1930s, this was no longer true. According to Rowntree: 'the promenading of streets has almost ceased...young people... for the most part...are in cinemas, the theatre, the music hall or dancing....At weekends and on summer evenings many of them are bicycling in the country....'[87] He even claimed that 'hundreds of young men have motor-bicycles'.[88]

In other cities, the streets had not altogether ceased to serve as meeting places for young wage-earners; but the centres of youth culture were elsewhere – in the cinemas, dance halls, and increasingly soft drinks bars.[89] Moreover, the street activity was frequently merely an extension of the ethos of dance halls. Frank Findley recalled of promenading in Harpurhey, Manchester, in the late 1930s:

> The boys dressed in their thirty bob suits with 22 inch trouser bottoms, would stroll along emulating the screen tough guys of the day...James Cagney and George Raft. They would flirt with and chat up the girls in their coats or frocks with the padded shoulder look, sporting the feminine hairstyles of the day.[90]

One of Findley's friends would spend up to £6 on suits for the Sunday evening parades.[91] Though usually restricted to Sundays, parading was held throughout the year. Occasionally, on cold winter evenings, it would be called off; but those involved would pursue some other activity that involved spending money. 'If the weather was cold', Findley recalled, 'we could always go and fortify ourselves in Turner's temperance bar or Gottelli's ice cream shop with a good, hot, highly potent drink of VIMTO at two-pence a shot.'[92] The 'monkey parade' in Harpurhey only survived as an adjunct to cinemas and dance halls as long as these institutions remained closed on Sundays. When local cinemas finally opened on Sundays, during the Second World War, the 'monkey parade' disappeared.[93]

Work and Leisure

The only obstacle that prevented a minority of teenage wage-earners attending cinemas or dance halls regularly was work. When Joan Harley interviewed 169 girl wage-earners about their work and 'use' of leisure in 1935–36, she found that most of the girls she spoke to finished work before 6pm; 73 per cent of her sample, in fact, worked between 8am and 6pm. Her sample included girls who worked in a range of manual occupations; some who worked in the service sector either as shop assistants or domestic servants, and a number of office workers. Virtually all Harley's respondents (95 per cent) had finished work by 7pm on weekday evenings. This meant the vast majority had between three and three and a half hours' free time every evening.[94]

Young workers in certain occupations did work long hours during the 1930s; notably van boys, page boys in cinemas, and cinema usherettes. A report by Manchester University Settlement into the hours worked by local van boys in 1937 revealed a working week of between 46 and 70 hours. As part of the same enquiry, the hours worked by seven local cinema page boys were also investigated; five were found to be working 60 hours or more a week and one boy was working 84 hours a week.[95]

Such long hours were not the norm, however, among teenage workers. The authors of a survey of adolescent leisure in Hulme, Manchester, conducted in 1939, reached the same conclusion as Harley. They found that the 'working boys' and 'working girls' of the district had between four and five hours' leisure time each weekday evening, although this did include time for meals and travel and also time spent performing household duties.[96] Nevertheless, only 'working girls' between 14 and 17 were found to be spending a large amount of their free time performing such duties.[97] 'Working girls' aged 17 and older spent hardly any of their free time performing domestic duties and these ceased altogether for boys when they started work at 14.[98] 'Working boys' of 14–17, therefore, had marginally more leisure time (one hour) than 'working girls' of the same age. But 17–21-year-olds of both sexes spent the same amount of time each evening pursuing leisure activities.[99] In Hulme, their interests were almost identical. Boys and girls spent approximately 50 per cent of their free time talking; 30 per cent inside a cinema, and the remainder of the time at dance halls, clubs, reading, and listening to the radio.[100] This survey, it needs to be remembered, only took into account leisure activities pursued between Monday and Friday. The amount of time spent at cinemas and dance halls would undoubtedly have been greater had Saturday evening been included.

The Young Unemployed and Leisure
One of Harley's most intriguing findings was that unemployed girls also spent money on leisure interests. In fact, their interests did not differ from those of girls in employment. She interviewed 56 girls who were unemployed and all of these visited the cinema at least once a week; 25 did so, on average, twice a week and a further 11 girls between three and six times a week. In addition, 13 unemployed girls went dancing regularly.[101] Harley was clearly

astounded by this discovery. 'A question which comes to mind at once', she pointed out, 'is how they can afford to go to the pictures so often, since they are earning no wages and, in many cases, come from homes where the financial position is bad...Presumably they are given money for amusements by their parents.'[102] It is conceivable that unemployed girls shared the same attitude as girls in employment; they may have handed over to their mothers only a certain amount of their unemployment benefit. A more plausible theory, suggested by oral evidence, is that girls – whether employed or unemployed – were treated to cinema visits by their boyfriends; sometimes in return for sexual favours. One of Stephen Humphries' interviewees remarked: 'We'd either go promenading or get them to take us to the pictures an' get 'em to pay as well....We'd give 'em a kiss an' let 'em do a bit of smooching....' [103]

Whatever the correct explanation, it is clear that the lifestyle of a girl wage-earner did not change if she became unemployed. Possibly the principal reason for this lies in the short-term nature of youth unemployment at this period. In Manchester, as revealed in Chapter 3, it was exceptional for a teenage girl or boy of 14–18 to be unemployed more than three to four weeks.[104] Even in cities where youth unemployment was more long-term, unemployed youths still visited cinemas regularly; making use of reduced admission prices for matinée performances.[105]

Conclusion

It thus appears that a distinctive teenage culture, based largely upon access to commercialised leisure and the conspicuous consumption of leisure products and services aimed at the young, was in evidence in British towns and cities by the 1930s. Neither the teenager who had money to spend on leisure, nor the manufacturer or leisure entrepreneur interested in exploiting the teenage market, was a post-war development as the market researcher Mark Abrams claimed in 1959 and historians and sociologists writing since have been prepared to accept. Those who benefited most from these developments were young wage-earners in working-class families. They were also chiefly responsible for what Robert Roberts called 'the new permissiveness' after 1918.[106] His father testified to this. During the dancing boom of the 1920s, he strove to maintain a 'respectable household' (the new dancing rooms, he believed, catered for 'the scum of the nation'). But his teenage daughter and teenage son were defiant. Janie went dancing until 11pm some evenings and Robert found a 'den' well away from home and 'joined the dancing millions of the time'.[107]

All the social investigators who studied the income and expenditure of working-class families at this period emphasised that teenage wage-earners possessed the disposable income and time for commercialised entertainments. Some young wage-earners who kept a substantial portion of their earnings, it appears, were contributing to the poverty in certain families. Those families with teenage wage-earners, however, were unlikely to be in dire poverty and, as the case studies cited earlier suggest, were certainly better-off than families dependent on a single adult earner. In such families, therefore, young wage-earners found themselves with a high disposable income, especially those in their late teens.[108] But even in families where the chief wage-earner was unemployed, teenage wage-earners were shielded from having to support the family. The unemployment insurance scheme, radically extended in 1920 to include most manual workers, provided a safety net for families who before the First World War would have been entirely dependent on the income of supplementary wage-earners.[109] The interwar years, therefore, saw the emergence of a substantial group of young wage-earners with a significant disposable income and leisure entrepreneurs intent upon tapping this market.

NOTES

1. Earlier versions of this chapter have been presented at research seminars in the Department of History, University of Lancaster; the Institute of Historical Research, University of London; the Department of Economics and Related Studies, University of York, and the Centre for the Study of Social History, University of Warwick. I am grateful to the participants for their comments. I would also like to thank the Economic History Society of the UK for allowing me to present preliminary findings at the Society's annual conference in Cheltenham during 1986. I would particularly like to thank Professor Michael Rose, Dr Alastair Reid and Dr Bernard Harris for their helpful suggestions.

2. M. Abrams, *The Teenage Consumer* (London, 1959); see also Introduction, note 3.

3. Abrams, *Teenage Consumer*, pp.1, 3, 5, 9, 10, 13.

4. Ibid., p.3.

5. See the wages information Abrams made available to a government committee investigating the youth service of England and Wales in 1958. Ministry of Education, *The Youth Service in England and Wales*, Report of the Committee Appointed by the Minister of Education in November, 1958, Cmnd 929 (London, 1960), pp.23–4.

6. Appendix, Table 4.3. The cost of entertainment goods and services consumed by teenage wage-earners, meanwhile, fell by approximately one third over the interwar period; from a price index of 336.4 in 1920 to 262.5 in 1938. See R. Stone and D.A. Rowe, *The Measurement of Consumers' Expenditure and Behaviour in the United Kingdom, 1920–1938, Vol. II* (Cambridge, 1966), Table 40, p.93. On the fall in cinema ticket prices see below, pp.117–18.

7. Benjamin and Kochin, 'What went Right with Juvenile Unemployment', p. 523; Appendix, Table 4.2.
8. Appendix, Table 4.1.
9. B.S. Rowntree, *Poverty and Progress: A Second Social Survey of York* (London, 1941), pp.156,160.
10. Ibid., p.156.
11. H. Tout, *The Standard of Living in Bristol* (Bristol, 1938), pp.16, 37. For details of R.F. George's poverty line see idem, 'A New Calculation of the Poverty Line', *Journal of the Royal Statistical Society* Vol.C, Pt.I (1937), p.74. The George poverty line, which was eschewed by Rowntree for being too spartan a standard but used by Tout in Bristol, covered only the bare necessities of life: shelter, food, warmth, light, clothes, etc. It omitted many items including furniture, replacement of household goods, and even allowances for travel, newspapers, and recreation (Rowntree's 'personal sundries'). It was, therefore, a theoretical standard of bare subsistence which denied the poorest even a modicum of domestic comforts.
12. Tout, *Bristol*, Table VII, p.37. See also A.L. Bowley and M.H. Hogg, *Has Poverty Diminished?* (London, 1925), a follow-up survey of five towns – Northampton, Warrington, Reading, Bolton and Stanley – conducted in 1924. This study showed that not only was poverty less widespread among young wage–earners than among children, but also that it had diminished considerably among young wage–earners of both sexes since their earlier survey in 1913–14. See especially pp.102, 125, 156, 195.
13. Tout, *Bristol*, p.36.
14. Rowntree, *Poverty and Progress*, p.156.
15. Manchester University Settlement, *Ancoats: A Study of a Clearance Area*, Report of a survey made in 1937–38 (Manchester, 1945), p.15.
16. Ibid., p.21. On the wives of the long–term unemployed bearing the 'burden of want' in a family see The Pilgrim Trust's survey, *Men Without Work* (Cambridge, 1938), p.112.
17. Manchester University Settlement, *Ancoats*, p.21.
18. Rowntree, *Poverty and Progress*, Table, p.125.
19. Ibid.
20. Ibid., p.135.
21. Ibid., p.142.
22. Ibid., p.141.
23. Ibid., p.125.
24. Ibid., p.27.
25. Ibid., p.130.
26. Ibid., p.134.
27. Ibid., p.141.
28. Ibid., p.142.
29. Bowley and Hogg, *Has Poverty Diminished?*, p.16.
30. D. Caradog Jones (ed.), *The Social Survey of Merseyside*, Vol.1 (London, 1934), p.148.
31. P. Ford, *Work and Wealth In A Modern Port: An Economic Survey of Southampton* (London, 1934), p.136.
32. Ibid., p.137.
33. Harley, 'Report', p.101.
34. E. Roberts, *Woman's Place*; idem, 'The Family' in J. Benson (ed.), *The Working Class In England, 1875–1914* (Kent, 1985), pp.1–35.
35. E. Roberts, 'Family', p.26.
36. Ibid.
37. See, for example, Bowley and Hogg's comments on working–class families in Reading, Northampton, Warrington, Bolton and Stanley in their 1925 survey *Has Poverty Diminished?* in which they state (p. 16): 'As in the previous investigation it is assumed that the incomes of all the members of the family are pooled. In fact, of course, grown children assert the right to their own money and only make a fixed payment to the household...' For the same pattern in Liverpool see Caradog Jones, *Social Survey of Merseyside*, Vol.1, p.148; and in Southampton, Ford, *Work and Wealth In A Modern Port*, p.136.
38. E. Roberts, 'Family', pp.26–7.

39. Jephcott, *Rising Twenty*, p.118.
40. See below, *passim*.
41. S. Rowson, 'A Statistical Survey of the Cinema Industry in Great Britain in 1934', *Journal of the Royal Statistical Society*, Vol.XCIX, Pt.I (1936), pp.115–18.
42. Ibid.; National Council of Public Morals, *The Cinema: Its Present Position and Future Possibilities* (London, 1917), p.xxiv; Caradog Jones, *Social Survey of Merseyside*, Vol.3, p.281; Rowntree, *Poverty and Progress*, p.413; Cameron, Lush and Meara, *Disinherited Youth*, pp.104–5.
43. Cameron, Lush and Meara, *Disinherited Youth*, p.104.
44. Harley, 'Report', pp.96–7, 100–1, 107, 111, 157.
45. Ibid., p.101.
46. Ibid., pp.107, 112.
47. Ibid., p.109.
48. H. Llewellyn Smith *et al.* (eds), *The New Survey of London Life and Labour*, Vol.IX (London, 1934), p.47.
49. *Film Weekly*, 3 Nov. 1933, cited in S.C. Schafer, '"Enter the Dream House": The British Film Industry And The Working Classes In Depression England, 1929–1939', unpublished PhD thesis, University of Illinois at Urbana-Champaign, 1982, p.54.
50. Cited in H. E. O. James and F.T. Moore, 'Adolescent Leisure in a Working-Class District', *Occupational Psychology*, Vol.XIV (July 1940), p.135.
51. Ibid., pp.140, 138–9. James and Moore's survey was based on information provided by 535 'working-class adolescents' of Hulme between the ages of 12 and 21. The sample comprised 165 'adolescents' attending elementary schools; 210 central and secondary school pupils, and 160 who were working. Each individual was asked to keep a diary recording for one week the leisure activities pursued during that week and the time spent pursuing them. The data for the survey were collected during June and July of 1939. See ibid., pp.134–6.
52. Ibid., p.139.
53. Ibid., pp.139–40.
54. Ibid.
55. See Les Sutton's autobiography, *Mainly About Ardwick*, I (Manchester, 1975), pp.2–3. See also Harley, 'Report', p.111. Cinema tickets invariably cost less than tickets for dance halls. A dance hall ticket could cost as much as 2s, but a cinema ticket rarely exceeded 1s [ibid].
56. British Library Newspaper Section, Colindale, General Index.
57. *Boys' Cinema*, 3 and 31 July 1920, 14 and 21 Aug. 1920, 4 Dec. 1920, 25 Feb. 1939. Interwar issues of this paper and *Peg's Paper* (referred to below) are held at the British Library, the former at Colindale, the latter at Great Russell Street.
58. *Boys' Cinema*, 4 Dec. 1920.
59. *Peg's Paper*, 15 and 29 May 1919; 26 June 1919; 24 July 1919.
60. See K. Drotner, 'Schoolgirls, Madcaps and Air Aces: English Girls and their Magazine Reading between the Wars', *Feminist Studies*, Vol.9, No.1 (Spring 1983), pp.42–3. See also idem, *English Children and Their Magazines, 1751–1945* (Yale, 1988), p.207.
61. Early issues of *Peg's Paper*, for example, included free Tarot cards and free song-sheets comprising the words and music of popular songs. See *Peg's Paper*, 29 May 1919; 26 June 1919; 3 and 17 July 1919.
62. *The Manchester Programme: Entertainments and Pleasures*, 5 and 26 Jan. 1920; 11 Nov. 1929. Held at Manchester Central Library, Arts Library Collection.
63. *Boys' Cinema*, 12 March 1938; 23 April 1938; 16 July 1938; 1 Oct. 1938; 17 and 24 Dec. 1938.
64. R. Roberts, *Classic Slum*, p.188. Young wage–earners between 16 and 25 also monopolised the dance halls of Bolton at this period. See, for instance, Tom Harrisson's report on his visits to the palais at Bolton, 'Whistle While You Work' in J. Lehmann (ed.), *New Writing*, 1 (Autumn 1938), pp.47–67. 'They are all young folks from fifteen and sixteen to twenty-five...' (p.54). This age group also predominated at dance halls in Blackpool. See, for instance, G. Cross (ed.), *Worktowners At Blackpool: Mass–Observation and popular leisure in the 1930s* (London, 1990), Ch. 16.
65. Manchester Studies Oral History Archive, tape 780.

66. Ibid.
67. R. Roberts, *Classic Slum*, p.190.
68. Manchester Studies Oral History Archive, tapes J43 and 189. All tapes with the prefix 'J' are held at Manchester Jewish Museum.
69. Idem, tapes J124, J214 and 486.
70. *Hobbies*, 4 and 11 July 1931; 28 Nov. 1931. Held at British Library Newspaper Section, Colindale, London.
71. *Hobbies*, 28 Nov. 1931.
72. By the early 1930s, a plethora of specialist magazines aimed at boys, girls, young men and young women had appeared in Britain. Among those in circulation in 1930 were the following: *Home Topics*, a weekly for boys and girls; *The Motor Cycle Book for Boys*, a fortnightly; *Motor Cycle*, a weekly with the largest circulation of any specialist paper 'in the world' (160,000); *Stamp Collecting*, a weekly; *Stamp Collectors' Fortnightly*; *The Stamp Lover*, a monthly; *Home Fashions*, a monthly; *Leach's Home Dressmaker*, a monthly; *Leach's Sixpenny Knitting and Handcraft Series*, a monthly; and *Welldon's Home Dressmaker*, a monthly. For those cited and others, see *The Advertiser's Annual and Convention Year Book* (London, 1930).
73. R. W. S. Mendl, *The Appeal of Jazz* (London, 1927), p.110. On the appearance of a distinctive youth culture see the reports on youth dance crazes in London *c*.1920, in *Daily Herald*, 2, 5, 8 and 26 Jan. 1920; 16 Feb. 1920. On the emergence of teenage fashions and behaviour in Manchester see *Manchester Guardian*, 2 Oct. 1926; *Manchester Evening News*, 1 Jan. 1929. The early twentieth-century origins of modern youth culture and the important role students played in its development in Britain are discussed in D. M. Fowler, *Youth Culture in the Twentieth Century* (London: Macmillan, forthcoming).
74. Harrisson, 'Whistle While You Work', p.66.
75. On the music industry of the 1920s and 1930s see S. Frith, *Music for Pleasure: Essays in the Sociology of Pop* (Cambridge, 1988), pp.45–63; C. Ehrlich, *The Music Profession in Britain since the Eighteenth Century: A Social History* (Oxford, 1985), Chs. IX and X; D.L. Le Mahieu, *A Culture for Democracy: Mass Communication and the Cultivated Mind in Britain Between the Wars* (Oxford, 1988), Ch. 2.
76. *Manchester Evening News*, 1 Jan. 1929.
77. *Manchester Guardian*, 2 Oct. 1926.
78. *Manchester Evening News*, 7 Jan. 1929.
79. Ibid.
80. *Manchester Evening News*, 5 Jan. 1929; *Manchester Evening News*, 10 Sept. 1937. The same criticism was made in a later generation. See R. Hoggart, *The Uses of Literacy: Aspects of working-class life with special reference to publications and entertainments* (Middlesex, 1957), Ch. 8(A).
81. *Manchester Evening News*, 14 Jan. 1929.
82. See E.A. Hadden, 'Women's Recreations in Ancoats', *Odds and Ends*, L (1904), pp.305–22.
83. See G. Godwin, *Town Swamps and Social Bridges* (1859 repr. Leicester, 1972), p.95.
84. See the first-hand account of J.H. Hobbins, 'From the Threepenny Gallery: Some Impressions of the Cheap Theatre', *Odds and Ends*, XLIX (1903), pp.365–82.
85. See C. E. B. Russell, *Social Problems of the North* (1913 repr. London, 1980), pp.96–7.
86. Rowntree, *Poverty and Progress*, p.469.
87. Ibid., p.470.
88. Ibid., p.475.
89. On the growth of milk bars and their young clientele see *The Milk Trade Gazette*, 1936–8, *passim*. Hoggart viewed the milk bars of the 1950s as symptomatic of a new Americanised youth culture; see *The Uses of Literacy*, pp.247–8. These were, however, an interwar development. There were over 1,000 milk bars in Britain (chiefly in towns and cities) by 1938. London was best served with 250; but Lancashire was also well served with 120, and Yorkshire with 90. There were 18 milk bars in Manchester in 1938. See, for example, *The Milk Trade Gazette*, 16 April 1938, p.3; C. Chisholm (ed.), *Marketing Survey of the United Kingdom, 1938* (London, 1939), p.210.
90. F.T. Findley, 'Days That Used To Be' (Manchester, 1976), p.22; the unpublished memoirs

of Frank Findley, born in August 1922 in Harpurhey, Manchester. This working-class auto-biography is held at Manchester Central Library, Local History Department. For a contrasting picture of 'monkey parades' during the 1920s see E. Roberts, *Woman's Place*, p.72.

91. Findley, 'Days That Used To Be', p.22. See also D. Thompson, 'Courtship and Marriage in Preston between the Wars', *Oral History*, Vol.3, No.2 (1975), pp.39–44. Young wage-earners in interwar Preston also spent substantial amounts on clothes for 'the parade'. 'They used to put their new suits on.. and walk up and down Fishergate...it were a mass...wi' young people. No owd uns were there' (ibid., p.42).

92. Findley, 'Days That Used To Be', p.23.

93. Ibid.

94. Harley, 'Report', p.59.

95. See the Report of the Departmental Committee on the *Hours of Employment of Young Persons in Certain Unregulated Occupations*, March 1937, Cmd 5394 (London, 1937), Section IV, pp.12, 20.

96. James and Moore, 'Adolescent Leisure', pp.139–40.

97. Ibid., p.140.

98. Ibid., pp.139–40.

99. Ibid.

100. Ibid.

101. Harley, 'Report', pp.151–7.

102. Ibid., p.157.

103. Humphries, *Hooligans or Rebels?*, p.140.

104. See above, Ch. 3.

105. See Cameron, Lush and Meara, *Disinherited Youth*, pp.104–5.

106. R. Roberts, *Classic Slum*, pp.181–2. See also Rowntree, *Poverty and Progress*, Chs. XIII and XV.

107. R. Roberts, *Classic Slum*, pp.188–92; idem, *Ragged Schooling*, pp.209–10.

108. See the case studies in Rowntree, *Poverty and Progress*, Ch. XIII.

109. For an essay which adds support to this view see W. Seccombe, 'Patriarchy Stabilised: the construction of the male bread-winner wage norm in nineteenth century Britain', *Social History*, XI (January, 1986), pp.53–76. On the safety net provided by the unemployment insurance scheme after 1920 see P. Johnson, *Saving and Spending: The Working-Class Economy in Britain, 1870–1939* (Oxford, 1985), p.193.

5

The Younger Generation's 'Unhappy Craze for Excitement': Young Wage-Earners and the Cinema

Authority figures' anxieties over affluent youth were well established in Britain by the time the Teddy boy made his appearance in the capital during 1953.[1] In the interwar years, most attention was directed at the role of cinema within youth culture and a protracted public debate emerged over its so-called 'deleterious' influence on the minds, physiques and behaviour of the young.[2] Prominent among the cinema's critics at this period were youth leaders and clergymen. Precisely why this was so is considered below.[3] It will become apparent that tensions were emerging between the various providers of leisure for young people which the cinema debate exposed. A second issue addressed is the cinema's role in juvenile crime, a subject on which the views of contemporaries have been documented but the merits of their arguments not analysed in detail; for example, with reference to crime trends.[4] A third aim of the chapter is to consider the cinema's role within youth culture, a subject on which research is sadly lacking.[5]

Young Wage-Earners and the Cinema Habit

Although contemporaries were struck by the large numbers of children and young people in the cinema audiences of the interwar years,[6] the most habitual cinemagoers appear to have been young wage-earners. In Manchester, they visited cinemas in far greater numbers, and more frequently, than school children. A survey of 'adolescents' and the cinema undertaken in 1932 revealed that 64 per cent of boy apprentices in Manchester and 65 per cent of female apprentices visited cinemas up to three times every week. By contrast, only 38 per cent of secondary school boys and 26 per cent of secondary school girls did so.[7] Joan L. Harley's study of the leisure interests of girl wage-earners in Manchester confirmed that visiting cinemas was so frequent among such girls that it had taken on the force of a habit. She interviewed 169 girls. Of these, 159 (90 per cent) visited cinemas at least once a week; a third went at least twice a week, and she even cited the case of a girl who made six trips every week.[8] The majority of girl wage-earners, Harley found, 'go at least once a week as a matter of course and apparently regardless of the film that is being shown'.[9]

This pattern was further confirmed, for working boys as well as working girls, by H. E. O. James and F. T. Moore in their study of adolescent leisure in Hulme, a working-class district of Manchester. Their survey, undertaken in the summer of 1939, found that young wage-earners of both sexes spent a third of their leisure time on weekday evenings (excluding Saturday) inside a cinema.[10] Had Saturday been included this statistic would undoubtedly have been higher; in effect, increasing from almost two nights in the cinema each week to three since Saturday evening was the busiest as regards cinema and dance hall visits.[11]

Unemployed youths also visited cinemas regularly, a fact confirmed by a study of the young unemployed in three British cities – Glasgow, Liverpool and Cardiff – undertaken in 1936.[12] The authors, in their final report on their findings, concluded: 'Attendance at cinemas was the most important single activity of the young men of the Enquiry. About 80% attended at least once a week and 25% of these attended more often.'[13] This study was, moreover, a comprehensive one. Under the supervision of D. Caradog Jones of the University of Liverpool three research officers, using interviewing techniques, investigated the leisure interests of 1,821 young men (predominantly 18–23-year-olds) over a three-year period.[14] Unemployed girls were also habitual cinemagoers.[15]

It is not difficult to determine why the young, and especially young wage-earners, frequented cinemas every week. The reasons were partly cultural (discussed below);[16] there was also an economic rationale, and there were practical considerations. In the first place, a cinema visit could be extremely cheap; as little as 1d for admission to some suburban cinemas (the notorious 'fleapits') during the 1930s.[17] In Manchester, ticket prices averaged only 6d in 1937.[18] Nationally, the average ticket cost 10d in the mid-1930s, though there was significant variation around this mean figure.[19] Around 50 per cent of all the tickets purchased in 1934 cost 7d or less each and 60 per cent 9d or less. Less than one third of the tickets sold were at the other end of the price range (1s to 2s 6d).

Young wage-earners, nationally, benefited from these low admission prices and from the fact that admission prices fell during the 1930s; from 1s, on average, in 1930 to 10½d in 1938.[20] The practical benefits to be reaped from visiting cinemas included the possibility of meeting someone of the opposite sex[21] and the fact that, for courting couples, the cinema provided a warm, dark haven well away from overcrowded homes and interfering parents.[22] In York, there were cinemas that catered specifically for courting couples by means of double seats on the back row. One local resident recalled: 'We used to walk, when we were courting, all the way to the Grand and sit in the double seats.'[23] Such provision was also available in other cities.[24]

The cinema supply also favoured frequent visits by young wage-earners. Britain's towns and cities were crammed with cinemas by the 1930s and working-class districts of cities especially so.[25] Manchester was among the best served in terms of both the number of cinemas and the number in relation to the resident population. There were, as early as 1914, 138 cinemas in the city and, despite the emergence in the early 1930s of the huge 'super cinemas', still over 100 by 1937.[26] The seating capacity of Manchester's cinemas was 107,401 in 1937 when the resident population was c.700,000. In other words, there were seven people in theory competing for each seat.[27] London's young wage-earners were nothing like as well served. There were many more cinemas in the capital (401 in 1934) than in Manchester, but twice as many people competing for a seat.[28] Nationally, the best cinema provision was in Lancashire and Scotland (nine persons per seat); northern England and south Wales (10 persons per seat), and Yorkshire (11 persons per seat). The worst provision was in London (14 persons per seat) and the eastern counties (19 persons per seat).[29]

The Cinema's Critics

One of the earliest critics to point to the British cinema's harmful influence on children and young people was Charles Russell, Chief Inspector of Reformatory and Industrial Schools at the Home Office between 1913 and 1917 and formerly a youth leader in Manchester.[30] He argued, in a lecture delivered in Oxford in 1917 (and subsequently published), that cinemas were indirectly responsible for boys committing certain crimes. 'The harm done [by the cinema] is', he noted, 'indisputable...the picture-theatre has so irresistible an attraction for children that some of them will go to the length of stealing money to provide the price of admission...'[31] He further observed: 'Thoughts of burglary are, without doubt, put into boys' minds and in some places gangs of juvenile thieves try to emulate the exploits of their cinema heroes.'[32] He also believed that boys who visited cinemas frequently suffered physically from the experience; first, from eye strain and, second, from what he termed 'undue excitement', both of which, he felt, undermined their health.[33] Cinemas also, he claimed, had an insidious impact upon most boys. As he put it: 'whilst I believe there is little that is actually immoral in most of the pictures...their vulgarity and silliness, and the distorted, unreal, Americanised (in the worst sense) view of life presented must have a deteriorating effect, and lead, at the best, to the formation of false ideals.'[34]

Russell may have been echoing the views of his Home Secretary, Herbert Samuel. In a letter to a local licensing committee in Hornsea, sent in November 1916, Samuel pointed out that information obtained from chief constables and other authorities at a conference held at the Home Office earlier in the year 'suggests that not infrequently children are led to commit offences as a result of seeing detailed representations of crimes on the cinematograph'.[35] Throughout 1916, in fact, the Home Secretary met numerous groups concerned about 'the objectional nature of some of the cinematograph films...exhibited to the public' and especially those watched by children and adolescents.[36] In May 1916, he told the House of Commons: 'From information obtained from the principal towns, it appears that there has been a considerable increase in juvenile offences during the past year, and it is generally believed that one of the causes is to be found in the character of some of the films shown at the cinematograph theatres.'[37] Consequently, he fully endorsed an independent enquiry into the 'physical, social, moral and educational influence of the cinema, with special reference to young people' to be undertaken by the National Council of Public Morals (NCPM) in November 1916.[38]

At the heart of the Home Office's discussions over the cinema and juvenile crime during 1916–17 was the issue of whether state censorship of films should be introduced.[39] The existing censorship system relied on local authorities to prohibit the screening of controversial films since under the regulations of the

Cinematograph Act, 1909 they were empowered to issue (or refuse) licences to local cinema owners.[40] No clear rules were laid down in that Act, however, on the types of films to be prohibited. The Act was primarily concerned with safety in cinemas.[41] Few local authorities, it seems, took their film censorship duties seriously. When the Home Office canvassed opinion on the issue of state censorship in May 1916 the vast majority of local licensing bodies raised no objections.[42]

There were, nevertheless, examples of film censorship in action in the interests of local youth. Following a court case against a cinema owner in St. Helens, the judge decreed that no film was henceforth to be screened in the town which was 'objectionable or indecent or likely to educate the young in the wrong direction'.[43] Early in 1916, London's licensing committee, London County Council, prohibited films 'representing criminal and repulsive scenes'.[44] These, however, were isolated cases.[45] The Home Office was thus seriously considering state censorship of films when informed of the NCPM investigation, on the grounds that the cinema was linked to the juvenile crime statistics and was to some degree responsible for the wartime increase in juvenile crime but local authorities were apparently indifferent to this situatation. In the meantime, the Home Office waited patiently for the NCPM's report, which was finally sent to the Home Office in October 1917.[46]

Among the committee of 25 that undertook the NCPM inquiry were youth leaders and clergymen. The most distinguished youth leader of the day, Sir Robert Baden-Powell (the Chief Scout) sat on the committee, along with representatives of other youth organisations including the YMCA, the Sunday School Union, and the Ragged School Union.[47] The clergymen and churchleaders involved included the Bishop of Birmingham (the chairman of the inquiry); a representative from the Salvation Army, and one from the Jewish community.[48] The committee sat between January and July 1917 and heard evidence from 40 witnesses who included chief constables, probation officers, educationists, churchmen, industrialists, magistrates, social workers, and school children.[49]

Much of the evidence heard on the cinema's role in juvenile crime was contradictory, even that presented by single witnesses.[50] Members of the legal profession, for example, were divided over this issue. On the one hand, there were alarmist statements from Cecil Leeson, a highly respected probation officer in Birmingham, and Secretary of the Howard Association, who claimed that many films made 'children, whose thoughts should be happy and wholesome, familiar with ideas of death by exhibiting shootings, stabbings, and the like'.[51] The probation officer at Old Street Court in London, by contrast, was not at all perturbed by the films shown to the young, pointing out: 'The films chiefly complained of, crime and crook films, have, in my opinion, little if anything to do with the increase in juvenile crime. Let any keen observer attend a cinema when a "crook" film and detective story is shown and listen to the children's cheers when the crook has been run to earth and punished.'[52] In the end, the committee reinforced this view and gave short shrift to the cinema's critics. In their summary of the evidence, they described cases where juveniles had apparently committed copycat crimes as 'exceptional' and pointed out that boys who allegedly stole money in order to gain admission to a cinema might simply have done so in order to buy sweets, 'penny dreadfuls' or 'any objects on which their hearts are set'.[53] Boys convicted for theft always told the court they stole in order to obtain money to visit the cinema because they knew they would be treated leniently for saying this.[54]

Though the NCPM inquiry became preoccupied with the issue of juvenile crime, some witnesses addressed other issues and the committee made recommendations on these. A subject that worried the chief constable of Guildford (more than juvenile crime) was immorality in the cinema. One of the many abuses that the darkness in cinemas made possible, he claimed, was 'one... where young men and...women attend together, not for the purpose of following the pictures, but...to become spoony...'.[55] He even hinted that sexual offences against women were committed in the cinema. A girls' club official from the East End of London was not convinced by such claims. She admitted that 'spooning' went on, but saw nothing sinister in the act, remarking lightheartedly to the committee: 'the elder children do not go [to the cinema] with their parents: they go with their "bird". The expression down there is that you take your "bird" to the pictures'.[56] The act of 'spooning' was, in other words, merely part of the courtship process. The committee recommended that there should be more lighting in cinemas; but this proposal was a response to the complaints of eye strain among school children, not an attempt to eradicate a supposed juvenile immorality. [57] The NCPM's report convinced the Home Office that there was no cause for alarm over juvenile behaviour, but it was by no means a severe blow to the critics. A key witness before the committee was Roderick Ross, the Chief Constable of Edinburgh, whose statement impressed so much it was circulated to all the chief constables in the United Kingdom.[58] His testimony was, however, ambivalent. He was certain that boys did not emulate burglars or other criminals, but felt that crime films were potentially dangerous matter. 'I consider that there is grave danger', he told the committee, 'in such representations. Boys are generally of an adventurous disposition, and ever ready to emulate anything in the way of an example....For this reason I am decidedly opposed to representations of such a nature being shown to the young.'[59]

After receiving the NCPM's report the Home Office withdrew from the cinema debate, not re-entering it until the early 1930s. Since so much of the evidence adduced for and against the cinema was inconclusive, however, there was scope for further campaigns by the cinema's critics. Concern continued to be voiced after 1917 and campaigns against the cinema were instituted.[60] In Manchester, a local branch of the National Council for Women set up a committee, in May 1927, which campaigned vigorously (albeit unsuccessfully) to have all 'A' films shown in the city to the under-16s removed from public circulation.[61] As we shall see, other action was taken in a number of cities.

Prominent among the critics of the cinema during the 1920s and 1930s were youth leaders. In *Rovering to Success*, 98,000 copies of which had been sold by 1930, Baden-Powell subtly denigrated the cinema:

> One little form of 'fun' in which I sometimes indulge myself when I have had too long a day in office or at committee work, is to go to – for goodness' sake don't tell anyone – a music hall or a cinema.
>
> I know that I shall be told by respectable folk that this is most degrading. Well, I can't help it. No man expects to be perfect.
>
> I have been urging ACTIVE change of occupation as your best form of recreation. I have no defence for this occasional lapsing into being passively amused by others.[62]

It emerges that, in fact, Baden-Powell was not amused by cinema stars since once inside the cinema he invariably fell asleep.[63] He confessed that he disliked the new 'super cinemas', where the 'talkies' were shown, because he was not able to fall asleep so easily in them.[64] More forthright than Baden-Powell in attacking the cinema was Lilian Russell, the widow of Charles Russell and president of a lads' club in Manchester. She deplored the 'cinema habit' among working boys of 14 to 18, remarking in 1932:

> The cinema-play, though not exactly vicious, is often very low in tone, giving young people who frequent it an altogether false and vulgar, foolishly sentimental, and in the worst sense, Americanised view of life. It is not the single 'talkie' drama that does the harm, but the cumulative effect of many which affect the impressionable mind as a stone is worn by the dropping of water.[65]

She believed, as her husband had done, that boys who fell into the habit of visiting cinemas regularly frequently turned to crime in order to pay for their outings. 'We have seen not a few weak-willed young fellows in prison,' she noted, 'who have been convicted for thefts committed, as they confessed, to get money "to buy some tabs and go to the pictures".'[66]

Among youth leaders, Baden-Powell and the Russells were not exceptional in believing that cinemas were potentially harmful to young people. In December 1915, the officials at a lads' club in Manchester joined forces with a local clergyman and lodged a complaint with the chief constable of the city over 'the notorious character' of the film *Five Nights* (showing at a cinema close to the club). They feared that many of their members, known to frequent the cinema, would see the film.[67] Though labelled a 'Romance' by the film historian Denis Gifford, it was banned by many local authorities.[68] In Manchester, the youth leaders and the clergyman won their appeal. The chief constable and his Watch Committee, the censorship committee for the city, removed the offending film from public circulation. Furthermore, the cinema manager who showed the film was subsequently taken to court by the youth leaders. They won the case and were awarded £3--4 costs which they spent on books for their club library.[69] This conflict of interests between, on the one hand, clergymen and youth leaders who believed passionately that working boys should 'use' their leisure time pursuing 'rational recreation' under the guidance of a youth organisation and, on the other, cinema managers who believed that all working boys wanted in their leisure time was entertainment and escapism, was to resurface during the 1930s over the issue of Sunday opening.[70]

The Campaign for Rational Recreation

During the 1920s, youth leaders and other advocates of 'rational recreation' seem not to have entered into a public conflict with cinema managers. Nevertheless, the former continued to criticise cinemas and, implicitly, their managers. At a national conference on the theme 'The Leisure of the People', held in Manchester during November 1919, the advocates of rational recreation were given an opportunity to outline their criticisms of the cinema and to propose alternatives. On the former subject, their criticisms tended to be savage and colourful, but extremely vague attacks. For instance, C. G. Ammon, the Organising Secretary of the Union of Post Office Workers, referred to 'the sloppiness and sensationalism of the kinema, the extravagances and inanities of...jazz, and the bestiality of the public house'.[71] Another speaker, Dr Arthur H. Norris, a member of the Home Office Juvenile Organisations Committee and a former youth leader with Charles Russell in Manchester,[72] felt that the free time of an adolescent presented 'immense possibilities for good or evil'.[73] One of the few to propose a viable alternative to the cinema was Alderman J.H. Lloyd of Birmingham. He suggested that to draw young people away from cinemas local authorities should build winter gardens:

> The Winter Garden I have in mind is a place where there will be cafés, reading rooms, and libraries, concert rooms, lecture halls, and billiard rooms, and a Repertory Theatre....There should be provision for recreation in the open air, such as bowls, cricket, etc., al fresco concerts, and pleasant shady walks where young couples can lose themselves – if you don't provide the means they will find them themselves, probably under worse conditions.[74]

Although this speaker was a little vague about the potential dangers young people faced if such ambitious schemes did not materialise, Dr Norris spelt out the probable consequences in his speech. The 'growing boy', he argued, would spend his free time 'with other restless spirits in places...which are harmful to himself...in mischief, in petty or even serious crime'.[75]

The golden opportunity for critics of the cinema to confront cinema managers came, however, during the Sunday opening debates of the 1930s.[76] It might be assumed that the cinema's influence over young people would be peripheral to this debate. The important issues, surely, would be that Sunday cinemas would draw people – adults as well as young people – away from the church; that cinema employees should not be forced to work on Sundays, and that cinema managers should not be allowed to make money out of people on the one day of the week most people did not work. The issue that dominated the debate, however, was whether cinemas were a good or a bad influence in the lives of the young.[77]

In Manchester, the issue was debated by the local council in January 1933. Among those opposed to Sunday cinemas was Alderman West, who told the city council: 'our younger generation is not sufficiently serious-minded... I consider it would be disastrous to pander still further to this unhappy craze for excitement and amusement by sanctioning Sunday cinemas'.[78] His view was shared by Councillor Richardson, a church warden, who felt that if local cinemas were allowed to open on Sunday evenings 'promenading', that 'excellent custom' which gave young people 'an opportunity to converse with each other after church', would die out.[79] Councillor Ackroyd opposed Sunday opening because 'the large number of organisations whose work amongst our young children is one of Manchester's greatest assets' would suffer; 'never', he argued, 'was there a time when they needed more encouragement and protection.'[80] He also suggested, without providing any evidence, that many of the films that would be screened on Sundays would be 'harmful and unsavoury' and expose young people to 'calamitous views of the institutions of marriage, the home and the family'.[81]

Such arguments proved sufficient to convince a substantial majority of Manchester's local councillors that cinemas should not be allowed to open on Sundays: 73 voted against Sunday opening and only 17 for it.[82] In nearby Salford the debate was not so one-sided, but a motion to introduce Sunday opening to the city was still defeated by six votes.[83] Elsewhere, cinema managers who requested permission to open on Sundays invariably lost the argument to sabbatarians and advocates of 'rational recreation'. In Stoke-on-Trent, for instance, 3,000 angry protesters sang hymns outside the city council chamber, contributing to the defeat of a motion to open cinemas on Sundays there.[84] In Croydon, a large yellow flag emblazoned with the words 'Hold on to your Sunday' was pinned to one of the local churches when the issue was being debated by the local council, along with posters calling upon the mothers of Croydon to 'Guard Your Children's Heritage' and 'Vote Against Sunday Cinemas'.[85]

In Manchester, the Lord's Day Observance Society played a key role in rallying sabbatarian opposition to Sunday cinemas. A few days before a further city council meeting on the subject in March 1939 this pressure group sent a letter outlining why they were opposed to Sunday cinemas to every member of the city council. In addition, many local clergymen who belonged to the Society explained why they were opposed to Sunday cinemas in their sermons on the Sunday preceding the city council debate.[86] They also urged their congregations to write to their local councillors expressing their opposition to Sunday cinemas.[87] This propaganda campaign proved highly effective. When the issue was again debated by the Manchester council on 1 March 1939 a motion to open local cinemas on Sundays was resoundingly defeated by 79 votes to 14.[88]

Sunday cinemas only became a reality in Manchester in 1941 and even then only for the duration of the war. They were introduced to meet the needs of young soldiers stationed in the city rather than the needs of local youth. Consequently, cinema managers were required to obey certain rules with regard to local youth. First, they were not to admit boys or girls under 16 to Sunday matinée performances because local civic leaders feared this would sabotage the work of churches and Sunday schools locally.[89] Second, they were not to show films on Sunday evenings which were suitable for adults only because the council were worried that the under-16s were sneaking into 'A' films unaccompanied by a parent or guardian.[90]

This temporary arrangement prevailed throughout the war, but, soon after it, the Sunday opening issue was raised again at an open meeting held in Manchester's town hall. The two main opponents of Sunday cinemas at this meeting were a local clergyman, the Reverend Desmond Dean, and a local youth leader, a Miss

Kennett.[91] The Rev. Dean told the 500 local citizens who attended the meeting that Sunday was a 'spiritual oasis in a desert of weekday materialism – a gift we shall lose at our own peril'.[92] He was especially worried that Sunday cinemas would be a threat to the 'welfare' and 'morals' of the young, declaring: 'What hypocrisy it is to talk about the young people having nowhere to go on Sunday nights! How long have the cinemas been showing any regard for the welfare or morals of our...boys and girls?'[93] He continued: 'Sunday stands as almost the last national bulwark against complete materialism. If this strongpoint is swept away, is there anything can save our nation from headlong disaster?'[94] The villains in the Sunday cinema debate, according to the Reverend, were cinema managers. He described them as 'uncharitable, money-grabbing businessmen'.[95]

Another local minister, a Mr Boumphey from a Methodist church in Wythenshawe, also spoke out against cinemas and, by implication, their managers. He declared: 'During the last few years the cinemas have been open, Manchester has been going into the depths of sin and poverty. We have the churches today. We have had them for hundreds of years. Do you want the churches or cinemas?' (Roars of 'cinemas' from the audience).[96] Despite this hostile reception, he continued to press his point: 'We open the doors of our church... for our children and we take pride in the fact that we are able to do something towards teaching children the proper ways of life....What do they get at cinemas – hooliganism and destruction...'[97] The real fears of the local clergy were revealed in the speech by Miss Kennett. She noted that, in her own district, parents were sending their children to the cinemas on Sundays instead of to Sunday school and that the children were growing up ignorant of Christianity.[98]

It thus becomes apparent why churchmen and youth leaders were opposed to cinemas in general and to Sunday cinemas in particular. Both groups were profoundly worried that cinemas were undermining their own work with young people, luring them away from the church and away from youth movements. These fears were certainly justified. Youth movements began to lose members at a dramatic rate after 1929, when Hollywood gangster films such as *The Perfect Alibi* were attracting huge audiences.[99] In fact, as we saw earlier, those in their teens (the main recipients of youth movements) were the staple audiences not just at gangster films but at most films by the 1930s.[100] A number of social investigators remarked upon the poor performance of youth movements during the 1930s, and linked this to the corresponding rise of the cinemagoing 'habit'. A. D. K. Owen obtained information on the leisure interests of 1,000 14-18s in Sheffield. He found that 72 per cent of all the boys in the sample and 73 per cent of all the girls visited the cinema at least once a week; but only 19 per cent of the boys and only 11 per cent of the girls belonged to a youth movement and less than a fifth of the sample attended church or chapel on Sundays.[101] Rowntree discovered an identical pattern among the teenage population of York in the mid-1930s. Young wage-earners of both sexes flocked to cinemas, dance halls and music halls on most nights of the week; but youth movements appealed to a mere handful.[102] As an advocate of 'rational recreation', Rowntree was as concerned about this state of affairs as youth leaders and clergymen. He fretted that: 'there is every temptation for them to spend their evenings in ways which...are often not helpful. Two or three nights in the week they will go to cinemas...which involves no effort or initiative on their part. Such use of leisure does not make for strength of character...'[103] Two points arise from this; first, whether during the 1930s those young wage-earners who watched gangster films and the like were resorting to crime as a consequence and, second, whether cinemagoing was simply a passive pursuit.

Cinemas and the Juvenile Crime-Rate

Those who still believed that the cinema was, to some extent, responsible for a certain amount of juvenile crime were in a distinct minority by the 1930s and, whenever they tried to argue their case, they either ended up simply criticising certain films for portraying crime or resorting to extremely questionable logic when trying to link the influence of the cinema with particular crimes. The chief constable of Wallasey adopted the former approach. In his annual report for 1936, he declared: 'Any film that prompts a child to commit crime, teaches him to conceal stolen goods, or to evade the Police or the truth, should never be allowed to circulate. An incalculable amount of damage may be caused to the impressionable mind of a child.'[104] Few chief constables were so extreme by the 1930s, but some still believed that crime films gave boys bad ideas. 'Some of the methods adopted by children for breaking into premises show extraordinary cunning and audacity,'

128

the chief constable of Lancaster recorded in his annual report for 1936. 'In other instances', he noted, 'their acts savour of the films – stolen property having been secreted in the hollow trunks of trees.'[105] The chief constable of Leicester believed boys learnt the rudiments of breaking and entering from the gangster films they went to see, and the chief constable of Birkenhead was also of this opinion, remarking in his annual report for 1936: 'I am convinced that the great majority of juveniles embark on... offences as 'a great adventure'; and I also believe half the trouble is caused by a desire to imitate what is seen in films, or read of in trashy literature'.[106]

Chief constables who argued along these lines produced little or no concrete evidence to support their case. Their arguments were based simply on unproven assumptions about the monocausal relationship between crimes portrayed in films and crimes committed by juveniles. The pressure groups that campaigned against the cinema during the 1930s relied on even more doubtful evidence when discussing how the cinema influenced young people. The Birmingham Cinema Enquiry Committee produced, in Jeffrey Richards's words, 'a highly impressionistic case for the prosecution'. In their report on the effects of the cinema on 1,439 children and adolescents, they drew attention to the testimony of three individuals:

> 'One child said she would show me how to strangle people', remarks one commissioner. There is a boy who revels in burglar films and says 'Only potty children are frightened'. 'The picture taught me how to shoot' says another boy.[107]

Such dubious use of the evidence contained in questionnaires completed by children and adolescents undoubtedly weakened the cinema critics' case against the cinema. Debates in Parliament during the 1930s on the issue of the so-called juvenile 'crime wave' certainly suggest this conclusion. In the House of Commons debates the cinema's critics, arguing without concrete evidence at their disposal, were invariably given short shrift and the Home Office was never seriously concerned about the cinema's role in juvenile delinquency. When the House of Commons debated juvenile crime in April 1932 the Home Secretary, Herbert Samuel, who spoke with some authority on the subject in the light of his earlier experience of dealing with it as Home Secretary, pointed out:

There are some who think that the cinema is another factor contributing [to the increase in crime], especially among the young....My very expert and experienced advisers at the Home Office are of the opinion that on the whole the cinema conduces more to the prevention of crime than to its commission. It keeps the boys out of mischief....In general, the Home Office's opinion is that if the cinemas had never existed there would probably be more crime than there is rather than less.[108]

During a Commons debate in 1938 the new Home Secretary, Sir Samuel Hoare, reported:

Our inquiries...show that...today the young are not more wicked than they were, but that they are less controlled by their parents. They... show that it is not so much films and shilling shockers that make juvenile crime, but broken homes, indulgent mothers, unkind stepmothers or unemployment.[109]

The criminologist Dr Cyril Burt had, as early as 1927, dismissed the cinema as an influence on the juvenile crime-rate. In his influential book *The Young Delinquent*, he ridiculed the arguments of the cinema's critics:

It is alleged...that what is called his 'faculty of imitativeness' renders the child peculiarly prone to copy whatever he witnesses upon the screen. On sifting the evidence adduced by those who express these fears, it is plain that both their inferences and their psychological assumptions are by no means free from fallacy. Nor are their facts better founded.. The direct reproduction of serious film crimes is, in my experience, exceedingly uncommon....It is clear that, in comparison with the incalculable number of films, the offences resulting are infinitesimally few.[110]

He even suggested that the cinema prevented juvenile crime, remarking:

I could, I think, cite more than one credible instance where the opening of a picture-palace had reduced hooliganism among boys, withdrawn young men from the public-house, and supplied the girls with a safer substitute for lounging with their friends in the alleys or the parks.[111]

Finally, it is even doubtful whether there was in fact a juvenile crime wave during the 1930s. The juvenile crime statistics certainly do not indicate the existence of one. The statistics on indictable or serious crimes committed by young (16–21) adults show no consistent pattern over the decade: 400,000 were found guilty of such offences in 1932; 360,000 in 1935; 440,000 in 1938, and 390,000 in 1939.[112] Over the decade, then, the number of young adults found guilty of serious offences fluctuated between a narrow band of 350,000 and 450,000 annually. It was only after 1939 that something indicative of a juvenile 'crime wave' occurred. From an annual figure of 390,000 young adults found guilty of serious offences, the numbers multiplied, reaching 650,000 by 1941 and 700,000 by 1945.[113]

Cinema and Youth Culture

It should not be assumed that because cinemagoing was habitual in the teens it required little thought or 'initiative', as Rowntree argued. On the contrary, it appears that this age-group used cinemas for a number of purposes. Cinemas were meeting places for rival male gangs who visited them specifically to 'taunt one another';[114] and places where young males could take their girlfriends in order to impress them (the 'posh' city centre cinemas were used for this purpose).[115] They were also patronised by courting couples who wished to indulge in heavy petting in a warm, dark, and relatively congenial environment.[116] Even social investigators seem to have been aware of the multifarious functions cinemas performed for young wage-earners. Two psychologists who studied the leisure behaviour of young workers in Manchester during the summer of 1939 discovered that the young workers of Hulme, a working-class district of the city, visited cinemas to indulge in 'love-making', by which they presumably meant kissing and heavy petting.[117] An investigator working for Mass Observation in Bolton noted the same pattern of behaviour. He was dismayed by the 'continual petting' and 'chatting' that went on even during the film.[118] Joan Harley assumed that girls who attended Manchester cinemas frequently did so to meet the boys of their neighbourhood. 'There is proof of this', she argued, 'in the fact that quite a number of girls will see the same film twice.'[119]

For the young worker, a visit to a 'posh' city centre cinema had little to do with the films showing, most of which could eventually be seen at cinemas in the suburbs at a reduced rate, but much to do with flaunting his or her status as an independent wage-earner. As Gilbert Fisher, a teenage worker during the 1930s, remarked: 'If we got money and we could just go to pictures, ooh it was thrilling that, it was great to go t'pictures. Ooh, you were well off, you were like a king; more so if you went upstairs...you was somebody – "I've been upstairs in New Vic", you were proud of that. Other people couldn't afford it.'[120] Such evidence is invariably overlooked by those historians who have written about the interwar cinema and its 'function'. Jeffrey Richards, for instance, argues that cinemas were institutions which allowed those with power in society the opportunity to make the powerless cinemagoing public accept the established ordering of society.[121] John MacKenzie argues along similar lines.[122] Both subscribe to the view that the cinema was a potent social control mechanism which, during the 1920s and 1930s, contributed to the growth of a deferential and patriotic working class.[123]

The argument developed in this chapter and the evidence cited suggests that cinemas were by no means simply institutions where a passive working-class audience would sit in silence and receive, unquestioningly, all the images and messages peddled in the films shown to them. Young wage-earners certainly did not believe all they were told in films. When A. E. H. Fielder asked Manchester adolescents what they had learnt about nature, life in other lands, life in the higher ranks of society, life in the underworld, and the 'ways of living of ordinary men and women' in the films they had seen, he was told: 'We don't go to the pictures to learn.'[124] Those who did go specifically to see the film – by no means the overwhelming majority – preferred crime films. These were as popular with teenage girls as they were with boys. Adventure films and comedies were also popular with this age-group, but educational films and war films were despised. Only five (out of 142) boy apprentices in Fielder's study, for instance, said they liked war films; and only three (out of 120 secondary school boys) did so.[125] Fielder, like his contemporaries, was worried that crime films gave boys ideas about how to commit certain crimes. He, in fact, asked a loaded question about what his sample had 'gained from films about life in the underworld'. The answers he received surprised him. Very few boys (or girls) were at all attracted by the underworld – 'the majority look upon it as horrible and dangerous', he commented.[126] He was forced to conclude that films:

> do not consciously have a bad moral effect on adolescents...often the adolescents recognise films as poor stuff; they are distinctly critical of what they see. They claim to be unaffected because they feel that the life depicted on films is unreal...[127]

This judgement seems far closer to the truth than the judgements of most other investigators who wrote about the cinema's influence on young people during the 1920s and 1930s.

NOTES

1. Pearson, *Hooligan, passim*;. Springhall, *Coming of Age*, Ch. 4. For a different view see Frith, *Sound Effects*, Ch. 8; idem, 'Time To Grow Up'; Hoggart, *The Uses of Literacy*, chapter 8(A).
2. For some discussion of these issues see J. Richards, *The Age of the Dream Palace: Cinema and Society in Britain, 1930–1939* (London, 1984), Chs. 3 and 4; A. Field, *Picture Palace: A Social History of the Cinema* (London, 1974), pp.61–3, 65, 89–90, 111, 114, 150.
3. See below, pp.118–20, 122–7. See also Richards, *Dream Palace*, pp. 50–4, 70, 74.
4. Richards, *Dream Palace*, Ch. 4; Field, *Picture Palace*, Chs. 2 and 3. For the best discussion of juvenile crime during the interwar years (though it makes no reference to the cine ma debate) see Bailey, *Delinquency and Citizenship*, especially Chs. 1,5, and 6.
5. On the impact of the cinema and other mass media on the population as a whole see Le Mahieu, *A Culture for Democracy, passim*.
6. National Council of Public Morals (NCPM), *The Cinema: Its Present Position and Future Possibilities* (London, 1917), p.xxiv; Caradog Jones, *Social Survey of Merseyside*, Vol. 3, p.281; H. Llewellyn Smith, *The New Survey of London Life and Labour*, Vol. IX (London, 1935), p.46; Rowntree, *Poverty and Progress*, p.413; Cameron, Lush and Meara, *Disinherited Youth*, pp. 104–5.
7. See A. E. H. Fielder, 'Adolescents and the Cinema, Report of an Enquiry', Diploma in Social Studies, Department of Economics, University of Manchester, 1932, p.5.
8. Harley, 'Report', pp.107–9, 157.
9. Ibid., p.107.
10. James and Moore, 'Adolescent Leisure in a Working–Class District', pp.139–40.
11. On the significance of the Saturday visit see above, p.104, and Walter Greenwood, *Love on the Dole*, (1933, repr.Middlesex, 1981), p.66.
12. Cameron *et al.*, *Disinherited Youth*, pp.104–5.
13. Ibid., p.104.
14. Ibid., pp.iv, 2–5.
15. Harley, 'Report', pp.151–7.

16. See below, pp.131–2.
17. Harley, 'Report', p. 111; L. Sutton, *Mainly About Ardwick*, Vol.1 (Manchester, 1975), pp.2–3; S. Rowson, 'A Statistical Survey of the Cinema Industry in Great Britain in 1934', *Journal of the Royal Statistical Society*, Vol.XCIX (1936), p.71.
18. Harley, 'Report', p.111.
19. Rowson, 'Cinema Industry', pp.70–1.
20. Ibid., p.71; R. Stone and D.A. Rowe, *The Measurement of Consumers' Expenditure and Behaviour in the United Kingdom, 1920–1938*, Vol II (Cambridge, 1966), p.78.
21. See below, pp.131–2.
22. Manchester Studies Oral History Archive, tapes J14, 996, 1001. See also the testimony of York residents in York Oral History Project, *York Memories Of Stage and Screen: Personal accounts of York's theatres and cinemas, 1900–1960* (York, 1988), especially pp.9–12.
23. York Oral History Project, *York's cinemas*, p.9.
24. In Bolton, double seats were popularly known as 'lovers' couches'. See L. Halliwell, *Seats In All Parts: Half a Lifetime at the Movies* (London, 1985), p.65.
25. Richards, *Dream Palace*, pp.12–14; C. Chisholm (ed.), *Marketing Survey of the United Kingdom, 1937* (London, 1938), p.203; Llewellyn Smith, *London Life and Labour*, Vol.IX, pp.44–6; James and Moore, 'Adolescent Leisure in a Working–Class District', pp.139–40; Halliwell, *Seats In All Parts*. ('For a film fanatic, Bolton was almost like Mecca... there lay within my easy reach no fewer than forty– seven cinemas of varying size ...', p.12.)
26. R. Low, *The History of the British Film, 1906–14* (London, 1949), p.50; Chisholm, *Marketing Survey, 1937*, p.203.
27. Chisholm, *Marketing Survey, 1937*, p.203; Census of England and Wales, 1931, *County of Lancaster* (London, 1932), p.2.
28. Rowson, 'Cinema Industry', p.84.
29. Ibid.
30. For biographical details see Bailey, *Delinquency and Citizenship*, pp 10–11, 329.
31. C. E. B. Russell, *The Problem of Juvenile Crime* (Oxford, 1917), pp.5–6.
32. Ibid.
33. Ibid.
34. Ibid.
35. PRO, HO 179/312, 491/20.
36. PRO, HO 179/Entry Books relating to Entertainments and Theatres in the years 25 July 1910–31 December 1921, *passim*.
37. *Hansard (Parl.Debs.)*, Fifth Series, Vol. LXXXII, 1916 (London, 1916), col.132.
38. PRO, HO 179/312, 397/124 ; Richards, *Dream Palace*, p.70. On the NCPM's interest in eugenics and involvement in 'social purity' campaigns see A. Kuhn, *Cinema, Censorship and Sexuality, 1909–1925* (London, 1988), pp.38–42.
39. PRO, HO 179/264, 149/52; HO 179/284, 149/86; HO 179/312, 397/14; HO 179/312, 491/20.
40. Kuhn, *Cinema, Censorship and Sexuality*, pp.17–18; Richards, *Dream Palace*, p.90.
41. Kuhn, *Cinema, Censorship and Sexuality*, p.16; Richards, *Dream Palace*, p.90.
42. Kuhn, *Cinema,Censorship and Sexuality*, p.23.
43. PRO, HO 179/312, 397/14.
44. PRO, MEPO 2/1696. Letter to the Commissioner of the Metropolitan Police London, from Sgt. F. Hennequin of Paris, dated 2 May 1916.
45. PRO, HO 179/Entry Books. These cite no further cases relating to young people during 1916. No cases are cited either by Kuhn, *Cinema, Censorship and Sexuality*.
46. Kuhn, *Cinema, Censorship and Sexuality*, p.43; R. Low, *The History of the British Film, 1914–1918* (London, 1950), p.135.
47. See NCPM, *The Cinema*, pp. viii–ix.
48. Ibid.
49. NCPM, *The Cinema, passim*; Low, *History of British Film, 1914–1918*, p.135.
50. NCPM, *The Cinema*. See, for example, the evidence given by Spurley Hey, Manchester's Director of Education (pp. 161, 166–7).
51. Ibid., p.187. Leeson was also the author of a wartime survey of juvenile crime; see C.

Leeson, *The Child and the War* (London, 1917).

52. NCPM, *The Cinema*, p.219.

53. Ibid., pp. xxxiv–xxxviii.

54. Ibid., pp. xxxiv–xxxv. See also C. Burt, *The Young Delinquent* (1925, repr. London, 1938). Burt recalled overhearing the following dialogue in a remand home he visited. 'Newcomer (due at court on the following day): "Oo's the 'beak' tomorrer?" Veteran: "Old W.....". N: "What d'yer s'y to him?" V: "S'y it's the pitchers: 'e always makes a speech about it and nods at yer for provin' 'is p'int". So shrewdly do these young rascals plume themselves upon an insight into their elders and their judges' (p.143, note 1).

55. Cited in Field, *Picture Palace*, p.63.

56. Ibid., pp.63, 65.

57. NCPM, *The Cinema*, p.1xxix.

58. Richards, *Dream Palace*, pp.60–1, 73.

59. NCPM, *The Cinema*, pp.176–7.

60. During 1925–26, for example, there were deputations to the British Board of Film Censors (BBFC) from the National Council of Women; the National Association of Head Teachers; London Public Morality Council, and London County Council. See R. Low, *The History of the British Film, 1918–1929* (London, 1971), p. 187.

61. Minutes of the Child and the Cinema Meetings held at the local branch of the National Council of Women during 1927. Manchester Central Library, Archives Department (M271/Box 5).

62. Lord Baden–Powell of Gilwell, *Rovering to Success: A Book of Life-Sport for Young Men* (London, 1930), p.82.

63. Ibid., pp.82–3.

64. Ibid., p.83. On the strategies youth leaders adopted to try to compete with the cinema see below, Ch. 6.

65. C. E. B. Russell and L.M. Russell, *Lads' Clubs: Their History, Organisation and Management* (London, 1932), p.215. Lilian Russell was, of course, reiterating the fears her husband had voiced in 1917; but she embellished his original comments and was, if anything, more concerned than he had been about the cinema's corrupting influence on young people.

66. Ibid.

67. Hugh Oldham Lads' Club, Minute Book, 1 March 1915–7 November 1921, Manchester Central Library, Archives Department (M7/1/5). See the minutes of the meeting held on 1 December 1915.

68. D. Gifford, *The British Film Catalogue 1895–1970: A Guide to Entertainment Films* (Devon, 1973), 05606; PRO, HO 179/312, 397/14.

69. Hugh Oldham Lads' Club, Minute Book, 1 December 1915.

70. See below, pp.125–7.

71. *The Leisure of the People, A Handbook* (Manchester, 1920), p.15. The conference was organised by the Manchester and Salford Temperance Council and was spread over six days.

72. Norris also held the post of Chief Inspector of Reformatory and Industrial Schools at the Home Office, replacing Charles Russell in November 1917. See Bailey, *Delinquency and Citizenship*, p.12.

73. *Leisure of the People*, pp.45–6.

74. Ibid., pp.18–19.

75. Ibid., pp 45–6

76. On the debate in Birmingham see J. Richards, 'The cinema and cinema–going in Birmingham in the 1930s' in J.K. Walton and J. Walvin (eds), *Leisure in Britain, 1780–1939* (Manchester, 1983), Ch. 3. See also Richards, *Dream Palace*, pp.50–4.

77. The issue arose following the passage of the Sunday Entertainments Bill in 1932 which made it legal for cinemas to open on Sundays if their owners were granted permission to do so by local councils. They, in turn, needed the permission of the Home Office. See Richards, 'Cinema–going in Birmingham', p.41; idem, *Dream Palace*, p.51. On the anxieties over young people's attendance see *Manchester Evening Chronicle*, 6 Dec. 1932 and 3 Jan. 1933; *Manchester Evening News*, 4 Jan. 1933; *Manchester City News*, 7 Jan. 1933;

Daily Dispatch, 5 Jan. 1933; *Daily Herald*, 25 Nov. 1932; *Manchester Guardian*, 19 Jan. 1933.

78. *Manchester City News*, 7 Jan. 1933.
79. *Manchester Evening News*, 4 Jan. 1933.
80. *Manchester City News*, 7 Jan. 1933.
81. Ibid.
82. *Manchester Evening News*, 4 Jan. 1933.
83. Ibid.
84. *Daily Dispatch*, 23 Nov. 1932.
85. *News Chronicle*, 26 Nov. 1932. In Croydon, local ratepayers voted in favour of Sunday cinemas; but they were rejected either by local ratepayers or the town council in Oldham, Northampton, Rochdale, and Sidcup (Kent). See, for instance, *Manchester Guardian*, 6 and 22 Dec. 1932; *Daily Dispatch*, 14 Jan. 1933; *Manchester Evening Chronicle*, 6 Dec. 1932.
86. *Manchester Evening Chronicle*, 27 Feb. 1939.
87. Ibid.
88. *Manchester Evening News*, 1 March 1939.
89. *Manchester Guardian*, 18 April 1947; *Manchester Evening News*, 1 March 1944; *Daily Herald*, 20 March 1944.
90. *Manchester Guardian*, 18 April 1947.
91. The Reverend Dean was Rector of St. Clement's Church in Higher Openshaw and also Chairman of the Manchester Sunday Defence Committee; Miss Kennett was Superintendent of Manchester Girls' Institute. See *Manchester Evening Chronicle*, 21 April 1947; *Manchester City News*, 25 April 1947.
92. *Manchester Evening Chronicle*, 21 April 1947.
93. *Manchester Evening Chronicle*, 6 May 1947.
94. Ibid.
95. Ibid.
96. *Manchester City News*, 25 April 1947.
97. Ibid.
98. Ibid.
99. During a two-week period in August 1929, 65,000 people saw *The Perfect Alibi*, starring Roland West, in Manchester. See *The Manchester Programme: Entertainments and Pleasures*, 19 and 26 Aug. 1929; 2 and 9 Sept. 1929. For further consideration of the decline in youth movement membership see below, Ch. 6.
100. See above, pp.99–101, 116–17.
101. A. D. K. Owen, *A Survey of Juvenile Employment and Welfare in Sheffield* (Sheffield, 1933), pp.39, 41, 43.
102. Rowntree, *Poverty and Progress*, p.447.
103. Ibid., p.349.
104. *The Police Review and Parade Gossip: Organ of the British Constabulary* (hereafter *Police Review*), 21 Feb. 1936.
105. *Police Review*, 13 March 1936.
106. *Police Review*, 28 Feb. 1936.
107. Cited in Richards, *Dream Palace*, p.76.
108. *Hansard (Parl.Debs.)*, Fifth Series, Vol.264, 1931–32 (London, 1932), col.1141.
109. *Hansard (Parl.Debs.)*, Fifth Series, Vol.342, 1938–39 (London, 1939), col.272.
110. Burt, *Young Delinquent*, pp.144–50.
111. Ibid., p.150.
112. See Bailey, *Delinquency and Citizenship*, Appendix, Fig.2.
113. Ibid.
114. Manchester Studies Oral History Archive, tape 214.
115. Manchester Studies Oral History Archive, tape 996.
116. Manchester Studies Oral History Archive, tape 1001.
117. James and Moore, 'Adolescent Leisure in a Working–Class District', p.137.
118. Mass Observation Archive, University of Sussex Library (Box W21).
119. Harley, 'Report', p.112.
120. Manchester Studies Oral History Archive, tape 996.

121. Richards, *Dream Palace*, pp.323–4. 'There can be little doubt that...the cinema in the 1930s played an important part in the maintenance of the hegemony of the ruling class. The film industry was run by men who desired to be seen as part of the Establishment. The actual films were used either to distract or to direct the audience's views into approved channels, by validating key institutions of hegemony, such as monarchy and Empire, the police and the law, and the armed forces, and promoting those qualities useful to society as presently constituted: hard work, monogamy, cheerfulness, deference, patriotism' (p.323).
122. See J.M. MacKenzie, *Propaganda and Empire: The Manipulation of British Public Opinion, 1880–1960* (Manchester, 1984), Ch. 3. During the 1920s and 1930s, Mackenzie argues, an ideology of imperialism, militarism and monarchism was presented to the pub–lic through the medium of film and internalised by the audience.
123. Ibid., p.91; Richards, *Dream Palace*, pp.323–4.
124. Fielder, 'Adolescents and the Cinema', p.2.
125. Ibid., p.13.
126. Ibid., pp.29–30.
127. Ibid., pp.35–6.

6

'Lads Can Get Recreation Elsewhere Nowadays': Youth Movements and the Young Wage-Earner

The interwar years were difficult ones for the numerous youth organisations active in Britain's towns and cities offering rational recreation under responsible adult supervision as an antidote to commercialised entertainments. Historians have not dwelt on this theme. They have focused instead on the ideological origins of movements such as the Boy Scouts and the related issue of whether youth movements were a form of social control inflicted on working-class boys by middle-class adults.[1] Nevertheless, it is clear from the records of some of the principal youth organisations active during this period that they experienced protracted recruitment and other problems. In some cases, this led to a reorientation of youth work and the emergence of clubs not dissimilar to youth clubs of the 1960s.[2] Other organisations, as we shall see, proved unwilling to innovate and, as a consequence, a progressive decline in membership set in. This chapter surveys developments in four organisations: lads' clubs, the Boy Scouts (including the Rover section), the Jewish Lads' Brigade, and selected girls' organisations.

Lads' Clubs

The principal centres of lads' club work in interwar Britain were Manchester and London. In 1932, provision was greatest in London, but not by much. There were 14,000 lads' club members in that city; only slightly fewer (12,000) in Manchester.[3] These statistics seem impressive, but they disguise problems that arose relating to the composition of the membership. The lads' club movement was originally pitched at working lads of 14 to 18. Indeed, the first historian of the movement Charles Russell gave his book on the subject, published in 1908, the title *Working Lads' Clubs*.[4] By 1932, however, the movement was no longer exclusively for working boys; it admitted boys from 10 to 18. In Manchester, schoolboys predominated by 1917, though in London the 14–18s still dominated the movement in 1931.[5] A question that needs to be answered, therefore, is why Manchester's lads' clubs fared so badly, and London's so well, in appealing to working boys.

The poor recruitment record of Manchester's lads' clubs among 14–18-year-olds began during the First World War and, initially, resulted from wartime circumstances: many 14–18s in the city were working long hours in munitions factories and simply could not find the time to attend a youth organisation of any sort.[6] Given these circumstances, the fact that almost 3,000 lads' club members in the city were between 14 and 18 (one in seven boys in the age group) seems impressive.[7] The lads' clubs' 14–18 recruitment was certainly far superior to that of any other youth organisation active locally. They attracted twice as many boys as the Boy Scouts and almost three times as many as the Church Lads' Brigade, Cadets, and Catholic Boys' Brigade.[8] By the interwar period, however, problems had emerged.

Though the difficulties encountered were common to all lads' clubs, the officials responded in different ways. The principal problem facing the leaders was the emergence of the casual club member. At the Hugh Oldham Lads' Club in the city centre, one of the city's largest before the First World War with almost 1,000 members in 1913,[9] the changing nature of the membership was reflected in the numbers attending the club event of the year, the annual Whit Week camp. Before the war, the number of boys in camp averaged 250 each year and 500 did so in 1914.[10] Statistics for the interwar period are patchy, but in 1938 fewer than 100 club members went to camp; the lowest figure in the club's fifty-year history.[11] It is clear that the decline was progressive, not episodic, since it was reported in the club's annual report for 1922 that:

> A number of circumstances – the cost (nowadays considerable), unemployment, and, we fear, disinclination to make any effort to save their money – resulted in a much smaller number of lads being able to go to camp at Whit.[12]

At other lads' clubs, the emergence of the casual member proved an intractable problem. An official at Heyrod Street Men's and Lads' Club, where Charles Russell had worked before the War, wrote in the club's annual report for 1927: 'In common with all similar institutions, we find ourselves face to face with such problems as unemployment, increased facilities for sensational amusement, and the deplorable strengthening of the money interest in sport'.[13] The officials at the club and those at other Manchester clubs were obviously not prepared to say by how much their membership had declined since the war. Their annual reports clearly indicate, however, that there was a general malaise in lads' club work during the 1920s.[14] The officials at Heyrod Street openly admitted, for instance, in 1929 that their club had less of an appeal to working boys than in former years: 'the great increase in amusements of all kinds tends to make the appeal of a club such as this less attractive than of old – lads can get recreation elsewhere nowadays'.[15] The officials at Ancoats Lads' Club shared this view. One wrote in their club's annual report for 1930: 'Lads' Clubs nowadays must be up-to-date if they are in any way to be a counter attraction to the growing and not too elevating influence of the cinema'.[16] As we shall see, the officials at this club proved more willing to adapt to the changing leisure interests of young wage-earners than those at other Manchester clubs. Nevertheless, they were forced to acknowledge, in 1938, that most of their members were only casually attached to the club. As one official put it in the club's annual report that year:

> A lad who can afford to go to the pictures twice a week; go to the seaside for his holidays, and get out on his bicycle at weekends has a very much wider outlook on life than was previously possible, and there is no doubt that self-reliance and initiative have been greatly fostered...[17]

This official was in no doubt that, owing to 'the greater independence of the modern Lads' Club member', the lads' club movement was experiencing unprecedented difficulties by the late 1930s.[18] For one thing, 'their [his members'] bi-weekly sojourn at the local cinema house means two nights less at the Club, and their hiking and biking activities are liable to lead to a disinclination to attend our Annual Camp and Sunday Services'.[19]

Faced with the changing lifestyles of young wage-earners, lads' club officials in Manchester began, during the 1920s and 1930s, to alter the nature of club life. This was clearly in order to avoid the prospect of wage-earning members deserting the clubs altogether. At the Hugh Oldham Lads' Club, the change was signalled by the installation of a film projector in 1936;[20] and the lifting of a ban on smoking in March 1939.[21] At Heyrod Street and Ancoats clubs, the changes introduced were far more dramatic. At the Heyrod Street club, the Boys' Brigade company set up by Charles Russell in 1893 to instil discipline and 'esprit de corps' into the working boys of the district – which, in 1927, still formed 'the backbone' of the club's work – was disbanded in 1928. 'We have become convinced', a club official wrote in the club's annual report for 1928, 'that its methods had ceased to appeal to the lads of this district for which....our Club primarily exists'.[22] Russell, who died in 1917, would have been deeply shocked by this decision. He saw the Brigade as indispensable to the functioning of the club and ruled that membership of the Boys' Brigade company was a prerequisite for membership of the club.[23] Furthermore, each Brigade member had to demonstrate commitment to it. In practice, this meant he had to attend drill once a week and Bible class every Sunday.[24] The decision to abolish the Brigade company was, therefore, a radical departure from previous club policy. After 1928, the club's officials effectively abandoned their attempts to 'build up the characters' of working boys and decided instead to make the activities which interested their members – billiards, table tennis and draughts – the centre of club life. From 1929, they also began showing films at the club.[25]

Ancoats Lads' Club was far more successful than other Manchester clubs at retaining the interest of working boys. Hugh Oldham and Heyrod Street clubs began to attract fewer working boys and more schoolboys.[26] The Ancoats Lads' Club, by contrast, continued to appeal to large numbers of working boys. In 1928, for instance, the club had over 1,700 members (1,710), 50 per cent of whom were 'working lads' of 14 or older.[27] This partial success was achieved because the officials were far more responsive to the demands of their older members than was the case at the other two clubs. From 1925, they allowed senior members (boys over 14) to hold dances regularly which the officials were aware was an extremely progressive move: 'The Officers are well aware that... the Club may gain an exaggerated reputation of frivolity but, after all, dancing is...more or less...a necessity with modern youth...'[28] The senior boys were put in charge at these dances and, interestingly, the club's officials were hardly every present.[29] In fact, from the 1920s they remained very much in the background of club

141

life, but this was part of a deliberate policy rather than a sign of their lack of control. By delegating responsibility to senior boys and enabling them to organise their own activities, the club's officials were being pragmatic. A more informal approach would, they felt, attract to the club boys who 'will not face the more regular discipline of organisations such as the Boy Scouts and the Boys' Brigades'.[30] During the 1920s, it proved a remarkably successful policy.

By the 1930s, however, senior members had begun to drift away from the club. Few attended the annual camp in 1930, many preferring instead trips to 'the much-advertised pleasure resorts'.[31] The club's officials, realising that a novel approach to club organisation was not solving the problem of the casual member, introduced new activities in an attempt to lure older members away from the cinemas. In 1930, a wireless set was installed at the club;[32] a dance class was started in 1936 and roller-skating introduced in 1938.[33] These experiments did not halt the drift of senior boys from the club, both to see 'talkies' and to pursue other activities such as cycling and hiking.[34] Ironically, the senior boys' interest in club life was retained not by the introduction of novel pursuits such as roller-skating, but traditional ones such as football and cricket, both of which had featured prominently at the club before the First World War.[35] In the mid-1930s, Ancoats Lads' Club had seven football teams and, whenever these performed well, other areas of club life flourished. 'It may seem a strange thing', a club official reported in 1934, 'but our Sunday Evening Services are better attended when our football teams are doing well...A greater loyalty pervades the Club and teams come along en masse throughout the season.'[36] The club was still in a precarious position by the late 1930s, however, because its football teams were not successful during these years and the rank-and-file member, it was acknowledged, was only very casually attached to the club.[37]

Three conclusions emerge from this analysis of lads' clubs in Manchester. First, the experiences of officials at three of the largest clubs active in the city were strikingly similar; all experienced severe difficulties in trying to keep working boys interested in club life. Second, in order to avoid the prospect of working boys drifting away from the clubs, lads' club officials were forced to introduce quite drastic changes to club life. Third, it is evident from the annual reports and manuscript records of the lads' club movement in Manchester that during the interwar years club leaders had no clearly defined aims. The original aims of the movement, character building and the provision of 'wholesome' or rational leisure, were forgotten in the struggle to think up new innovations to try to prevent boys drifting away from the clubs.

Superficially, the 1920s and 1930s seem to have been far more successful years for the lads' club movement in London. The membership figures during the 1920s were a dramatic improvement on the previous fortunes of the movement in the capital. There were, for example, 8,000 lads' club members in London in 1920 compared with only 2,800 in 1910.[38] Moreover, the membership held up during the 1920s and had even increased (to 14,000) by the early 1930s.[39] Furthermore, a detailed analysis of the age composition of London lads' clubs undertaken in 1931 for the *New Survey of London Life and Labour* revealed that the typical member was 15-17 and employed in unskilled and skilled manual work.[40] On closer inspection however, these statistics are misleading because the sample of clubs analysed in the survey was biased in favour of those that catered exclusively for working boys. Of eight clubs whose membership was scrutinised, only three admitted boys younger than 14; namely, schoolboys.[41] That lads' clubs in London, in common with those in Manchester, encountered difficulties maintaining their 14-18 membership is apparent from the fortunes of the Federation of London Working Boys' Clubs, the co-ordinating body for lads' club work in the capital.[42]

The Federation was established in 1887 and, until the 1920s, catered exclusively for working boys.[43] From an early date, the Federation's work was far more orientated towards promoting sporting activities such as football, cricket, boxing, athletics and swimming rather than discipline.[44] Its principal responsibility, in fact, was to promote inter-club competitions, mainly comprising sporting and billiard competitions.[45] There was no emphasis on religion and moral training; a clear contrast with early lads' club work in Manchester. This approach, moreover, proved highly successful: the membership grew from 1,600 in 1887 to 3,000 in 1911; 7,000 in 1919; 7,200 in 1926, and had reached 17,000 by 1936.[46]

Problems regarding the working boy began to surface, however, immediately after the First World War. Many affiliated clubs began reporting 'the sudden disappearance' of 16- and 17-year-olds.[47]

Club leaders attributed this to girls ('a chance meeting at a street corner', as they put it)[48] and undertook measures to try to lure older boys back into the clubs. From 1919, many club leaders introduced 'mixed evenings' and dances to enable members 'to enjoy petticoat society under decent conditions'.[49] As the membership statistics cited indicate, this change of focus proved a success. Never, after 1919, was concern expressed over leakage of 16- and 17-year-olds in the Federation's annual reports. It is conceivable that the sharp increase in membership after 1926 was due to an influx of schoolboys into the clubs. In 1927, for example, this was made possible when the Federation dropped 'Working Boys' from its title and re-named itself the London Federation of Boys' Clubs.[50] This appears unlikely, however, given the absence of comment on working boys in subsequent annual reports. The limited evidence available suggests that the London lads' clubs' success in retaining the allegiance of working boys seems to have been due to a much greater sensitivity to their interests, and from a much earlier date, than was the case in Manchester.

The Boy Scouts

The principal problem for Boy Scout leaders during the 1920s and 1930s was not the casual member that afflicted lads' club work but what was termed 'leakage'.[51] This denoted the permanent drift of boys away from the movement at 14 or 15.[52] The problem is far easier to illustrate statistically than that of the casual member. It is apparent, for instance, in the membership statistics of the Rover Scouts; an organisation for boys above Scout age (17 and older) established in 1919 and active until 1967 when it was disbanded.[53] As Table 6.1 demonstrates, the Rover Scout movement was never able to reach anything like the strength of the Boy Scouts despite the fact that there was no upper age limit governing eligibility.[54] During the interwar years, the Rover membership never reached even a fifth of the strength of the Boy Scouts.[55] Why was this so?

During the 1930s, the movement's official paper *The Rover World*, launched in 1934, attributed the problems over recruitment to difficult circumstances beyond the ability of the movement to rectify. First of all, there was the unfavourable demographic situation in the mid-1930s: a shortage of boys of Rover age owing to the sharp decline in the birth rate during the First World War.[56] Second, the persistence of the Depression in certain parts of the country apparently reduced recruitment (London, the West Riding of Yorkshire, south-east Lancashire, south-west Lancashire and, curiously, Kent were singled out as experiencing severe recruitment difficulties as a consequence).[57] Third, the lack of Scout and Rover troops on the new housing estates was seen as another problem.[58] None of these theories, all elaborated upon in *The Rover World*, seems very plausible.

First, the demographic theory seems highly spurious. The decline in the birth rate, a long-term trend under way from the late nineteenth century, would in theory have affected recruitment over the course of the late nineteenth and early twentieth centuries.[59] As to the impact of the Depression on boys in their late teens, this was minimal in south-east Lancashire and London where youth unemployment was extremely short-term.[60] Finally, the problem on the new housing estates was not so much the supply of Scout and Rover troops as the lack of demand for them.[61] It is also clear from the Rover movement's own literature that its problems began in the early 1920s.

Baden-Powell, it appears, was part of the problem. Despite receiving numerous letters from Rover leaders anxious for the Chief Scout to devise a more imaginative programme for Rover Scouts he remained wedded to the idea that the sole function of the Rover movement was to promote the concept of service.[62] In 1932, in a letter to Rover leaders, he outlined the type of organisation he wished to see develop.[63] It should promote, first, the concept of 'service to self' by which he meant a boy of 18 and older should be encouraged by his leader to settle in a career 'so that he is not a burden to his relations'; to safeguard his health through taking up outdoor activities such as hiking, and to work hard 'as his contribution to the national welfare'. Second, the Rovers should develop the concept of service to the Scout movement by which he meant Rover leaders should try to train Rovers to be Scout leaders. Third, Rover leaders should promote the idea of service to the community with the aim of turning a Rover into a 'good citizen'. The orientation of Rover work during the 1920s had been precisely as Baden-Powell intended. The London Rovers' theme was 'social service' which involved visits to hospitals, hospices, and work with young offenders.[64] The 39th Croydon Rover Crew, meanwhile, competed for a horseshoe trophy signifying service to the community, and inscribed with the message 'as this horse shoe had devoted its life to the service of a humble servant of Mankind, let it now act as a constant reminder and to inspire the Spirit of Service in others'.[65]

By the early 1930s, the Headquarters Rover leadership were becoming sensitive to grassroots feeling that the ethos of the movement was growing stale and a greater range of activities was required if substantially more boys of Rover age were to be drawn into the movement.[66] In the absence of initiatives from Baden-Powell on this matter the Headquarters leadership began to shift the orientation of the movement, though very gradually. Baden-Powell's absence from the second national Rover conference in 1933 ('owing to a chill') helped matters. A statement from the Chief Scout reiterating his desire to see the movement 'develop in our young men a balanced *Character* and a sense of *Service*' was read out, but the Headquarters Commissioner for Rover Scouts, Colonel Walton, then issued instructions on how the movement was to be made more attractive (more emphasis was to be placed on sport).[67]

By 1934, more radical proposals were being outlined at grassroots level. At a conference of Surrey Rover leaders in October one speaker urged Rover leaders to encourage political discussions among their crews, expressing a wish to see 'every Rover Crew at the beginning of every meeting going at it hammer and tongs with their political arguments'.[68] Another addressed the theme 'The Failure of Rovering'. This speaker found fault with virtually every aspect of the movement. Its personnel was 'too exclusive'. It had no coherent aim. In Surrey, the professed aim was to produce men; but, in practice, the emphasis was on producing Scout leaders. This speaker also felt there was a need to promote political awareness as an aspect of citizenship and severely to curtail theoretical discussion of the concept.[69] The programme was also in need of modification. More time ought to be spent outdoors. Finally, he suggested that Rover leaders needed to alter their approach. They ought to reduce the emphasis on discipline and become more sensitive to older boys' chief preoccupation: namely, girls.[70]

The issue of 'The Rover and the girl' was raised in *The Rover World* during 1934. It was suggested that the movement's refusal to address the issue was the main reason 75 per cent of Scouts left the movement before the age of 18.[71] An article on this subject suggested as a solution to the problem the introduction of a weekly 'ladies' night'.[72] Baden-Powell provided no guidance on this matter. In a message to Rovers, drafted towards the end of his life, he disclosed his age ('over 82') and instructed them to 'make sure that you are not frittering away the few short years you have before you, but are trying to do something worthwhile – maybe for yourself, and your family, but especially for others'.[73] He did not, however, even mention girls. Nor did he allude to them in any of his correspondence with Rover leaders. His only publicly expressed views on this subject, meanwhile, were that girls who belonged to youth movements were not to be encouraged to mix with Rovers. In fact, they were to be discouraged from doing so. Scout policy laid down during the 1920s was clear on this matter: 'It is most undesirable that Guides and Scouts should be trained together, and Commissioners are requested to see that this rule is strictly enforced.'[74] By the 1930s, the Rover movement's unwillingness to accommodate girls was seen as the main barrier to its expansion.[75]

To what extent were some of the problems of the Rover Scouts nationally addressed at a local level? Manchester, which staged the Rovers' annual conference during 1935[76] and had a Scout movement almost 4,000 strong in 1930[77] and thus the potential for a flourishing Rover movement, forms a useful case study for analysis.[78]

It is as well to begin with a consideration of the interwar record of the Boy Scouts in Manchester. Even the official membership statistics of Manchester and District Boy Scouts' Association (MDBSA) reveal that the membership was contracting at this period. In 1921, the membership stood at 4,310. By 1924, it had fallen below 4,000 (to 3,796) and never recovered its 1921 level. In 1938, the membership stood at 3,164. In effect, between 1921 (the year of the first Scout census) and 1938 the MDBSA's membership had contracted by 25 per cent.[79] Furthermore, few MDBSA Boy Scouts entered the ranks of the Rovers. That movement never reached even a quarter of the strength of the Boy Scouts, although its relative strength did increase over these two decades.[80]

Rover statistics are, however, misleading. Other evidence reveals that the Rovers of Manchester, like the Boy Scouts, experienced leakage. By the 1930s, Rover troops in every district of the city were losing members. At a meeting of local Rover leaders in March 1936, the following statement was recorded in the minutes of the meeting:

Openshaw. Numbers down.
North Central. Things slow.
Gorton. Down on Census. 2 Crews closed.
South East. A few good Crews, several bad. Poor Divisional
meetings...
Bury. 3 Crews, going forward slowly...
Middleton. 1 Crew, Nightschool a hindrance.[81]

By September 1936, the predicament of local troops had still not
improved. The following comments were recorded in the minutes
of a meeting held on 1 September 1936:

Openshaw. Numbers not up.
North Central. Quiet summer. No Scouts coming up...
Farnworth. Slack in summer, but hiking and camping.
Bolton. Regular few at monthly meetings.
East Central. No Scouts coming up...
Chorlton. As usual...[82]

Rover membership in Manchester declined markedly after 1936.
There were 707 Rovers locally in that year, but under 600 (587) the
following year, and only slightly over 600 (611) in 1938.[83]
    The contraction of the Boy Scout movement in Manchester was
not an isolated case. In Liverpool, the movement was also losing
boys at a serious rate by the late 1920s. Two youth workers in that
city remarked in 1928:

The leakage from the clubs and Scouts is serious, the more so
as the figures greatly understate the membership turnover.
Boys drift aimlessly from club to club. Most leave altogether
during the summer. When one of the large Liverpool clubs
claims a permanent membership of only 100 on an annual
turnover of 800, the gravity of the problem can be realised.[84]

The authors of this statement, Ernest S. Griffith and R.A. Joseph,
ran a boys' club at Liverpool University Settlement in the city
centre.[85] They tackled leakage from their club in two ways: first, by
means of a jobs scheme for boys of 14-16 and, second, for the same
group, a 'gang club' consisting of boys who socialised together
outside the club. Neither of these experiments solved the problem

of boys drifting away from the club; they merely reduced the turnover.[86]

Though boys' clubs in cities such as Liverpool and Manchester had some success retaining the interest of working boys, the Boy Scout movement had a far worse record in this respect. Griffith and Joseph believed there were two reasons for this. First, the typical Boy Scout troop was dominated by schoolboys, which gave rise to the belief among working boys that the movement was 'for kids'. Second, working boys were unlikely to remain in a movement which required them to wear a uniform that included short trousers; not least because they would be ridiculed by their workmates.[87] Unfortunately, Griffith and Joseph produced no concrete evidence to support their thesis that the most serious leakage from the Boy Scout movement occurred when boys reached the age of 14 and began wage-earning. Their argument seems plausible, but it was based simply on their own 'experience' of boys in a slum district of Liverpool.

The absence of statistical data on the age composition of the Boy Scouts, either nationally or locally, is a severe handicap to the testing of their hypothesis. It is borne out, however, by a sample survey of youth organisations active in London, undertaken in 1931.[88] Also, social investigators in Manchester argued along similar lines to Griffith and Joseph. In a 1939 survey of adolescent leisure in Hulme, Manchester, two psychologists from Manchester University, H. E. O. James and F. T. Moore, noted the poor record of Scouts, Guides, and clubs with young wage-earners of both sexes.[89] They attributed this to the fact that the organisations available in Hulme were all single-sex ones catering, primarily, for schoolboys and schoolgirls.[90] They concluded that the youth organisations of Hulme would only begin to attract large numbers of young workers if mixed-sex clubs were introduced.[91]

As we saw earlier, lads' club leaders in other parts of Manchester and in London had made definite steps in this direction by 1939. The Boy Scout and Rover leadership in Manchester were, however, insensitive to such matters. The tone of their annual reports during the 1920s and 1930s was smug and self-congratulatory. Much was said about the qualities required to join the local Boy Scouts; a boy must, for instance, 'satisfy his Scoutmaster that he knows the Scout-law, signs and salute; the composition of the Union Jack and the right way to fly it; uses of the Scout Staff...; and the following knots: Reef, sheet bend, clove hitch, bowline, fisherman's, sheepshank, and understand their special uses'.[92] Similarly, much was said about the qualities required to join the Rovers: a boy had to be 17 or over and 'he must satisfy his Scoutmaster that he knows:- The Scout Law; Signs and Salutes; Six Knots...; First Aid; How to lay and light a fire and cook a simple meal; the use of the compass and how to read a map'.[93] In addition, he must know 'the right way to fly the Union Jack and what it stands for, and the underlying principles of the constitution of the British Commonwealth'.[94] Next to nothing was said about either the falling membership or the need to devise new activities to broaden the appeal of the movements.

In fact, far from wanting to achieve this objective, local Scout and Rover leaders seemed quite prepared to accept that their movements appealed to only a tiny minority of boy wage-earners. During the 1930s, the Rover leadership even introduced stricter rules governing entry. By 1938, boys who wished to join the Manchester Rovers were no longer automatically admitted at 17, as had been the case during the 1920s. Those who were 'not sufficiently well developed physically and mentally' had to wait until they reached 18.[95] In addition, they had to satisfy a Rover Scout leader that they had read and studied both *Scouting for Boys* and *Rovering to Success* (both, of course, written by the Chief Scout Lord Baden-Powell); they had to be familiar with the Scout Promise and the Scout Law, and also had to be 'sufficiently knowledgeable to train a boy of Scout age in the tenderfoot tests'.[96] Furthermore, any boy wishing to become a Scout or a Rover in 1938 was forbidden from joining a political organisation and from attending political meetings. It is unlikely, therefore, that any of the 13,000 engineering apprentices who participated in the Manchester apprentices' strikes during 1937 were members of either organisation.[97]

The Boy Scouts and the Rovers required boys to possess schoolboyish knowledge about the Monarchy, the Commonwealth, the British Constitution and to be susceptible to strict discipline. Given this ethos, it is worth considering whether the movements ever appealed to the working-class boy. Despite the fact that membership of the Scouts was more costly than membership of a lads' club (the uniform alone, for instance, cost 15s in the early 1920s),[98] the Manchester Boy Scouts did attract working-class boys.

One indication of this is that Boy Scout troops were set up in the poorest districts of the city. Hulme, a densely populated district, consisted almost entirely of working-class families whose wage-earners worked in unskilled and semi-skilled manual employment.[99] Though only one square mile in surface area, it was home in 1917 to seven Boy Scout troops; six Boys' Brigade companies; a Boys' Life Brigade branch; four Church Lads' Brigade branches; two lads' clubs; a girls' club; four Girls' Friendly Society branches; six Girl Guide companies; a Girls' Life Brigade branch, and a Wesleyan girls' club.[100] Interestingly, few of these organisations survived the interwar period. When a survey of all the youth organisations operating in the city was undertaken in 1940 there were only two Boy Scout troops in Hulme; two Church Lads' Brigade branches; one lads' club; and one Girl Guide company.[101] Both sets of statistics are illuminating. They clearly reveal that the Boy Scout movement appealed to working-class boys. Furthermore, Hulme was not atypical. The Boy Scouts thrived in other working-class districts of the city and local engineering firms even set up troops.[102] Manchester's Boy Scout movement also attracted middle-class boys. Manchester Grammar School, for instance, had five Scout troops in 1924 and Manchester Central High School for Boys also had its own troop.[103] Scout Troops were also set up in middle-class suburbs such as Chorlton-cum-Hardy, Didsbury, Fallowfield and Withington.[104] It appears, however, that working-class boys deserted the movement at an earlier age than middle-class boys.[105]

The contraction of Manchester's Boy Scout movement is difficult to fathom, not least because the local leadership did not dwell on this issue in their annual reports. The worst years for the local movement were from 1930 onwards.[106] These were also, coincidentally, years when talking pictures were beginning to be shown regularly at cinemas in the city. Boys of Scout age were among the most habitual cinemagoers and this struck a nerve with youth leaders from Baden-Powell down. As revealed in Chapter 5, they were among the most vociferous critics of the cinema.[107] They also believed that the emergence of the 'super cinema' contributed to the contraction of Boy Scout membership.[108] Another theory, developed by John Springhall, suggests that the decline in the membership nationally was linked to the emergence of hiking as a popular leisure pursuit.[109] The membership of the Youth Hostel

Association (YHA), for example, grew at a dramatic rate during the 1930s; from 16,000 in 1931 the membership soared to 83,417 in 1939.[110] In Manchester, however, the YHA did not prove to be an appealing counter-attraction to the Boy Scouts. Of the 4,607 members in 1936–37, only 154 were boys and of the 5,458 a year later only 141 were boys.[111] The local YHA was dominated by young professionals, particularly teachers.[112]

Neither did political youth movements such as the Clarion Cyclists and the Young Communist League (YCL) lure significant numbers of boys away from the Boy Scouts. The Manchester branch of the Clarion Cyclists had only 25 members in 1936. A year later, the total membership (adults and youths) was still 'less than a hundred' and the youth membership began to fall off, largely because that 'some members have started courting'.[113] As to the Young Communist League, its main problem in Manchester was not how to keep working boys interested in the organisation, but how to persuade them to join it. The local branch only had around 70 members in the mid-1920s, and not all of these were local residents. Some were from as far afield as Wigan and Preston. Ten young miners from Wigan, for example, cycled 20 miles to attend a local branch meeting in July 1926. Only 70 'comrades' were present at this meeting; yet it was the best attended ever according to the chairman of the local YCL.[114] Recruiting young workers into the local YCL was a painfully slow process. During 1926–27, local activists canvassed the whole of Salford and Pendleton. The sum total of their 'house-to-house' canvassing was eight new recruits from Salford and the possibility of three more from Pendleton.[115]

It is apparent, therefore, that the Boy Scout movement of Manchester does not appear to have lost members to other youth movements at this period. No doubt it lost most of its older members to the 'super cinemas'. But another reason the membership began to fall off was that the Boy Scouts required too much effort. Scout leaders who tried to set up a troop on a new housing estate in Wythenshawe encountered insuperable difficulties trying to interest the boys of the estate in the movement: 'Our attempt to run an old farmhouse at Wythenshawe, as a kind of communal club-room for groups on the Wythenshawe estate has been defeated...by the physical difficulties of getting boys to come to a club-room which is not on their own doorstep.'[116] This reveals that the problem for youth workers on the new housing estates was not simply a lack of facilities and personnel, but insufficient demand for youth organisations.

It would be wrong, however, to conclude on this pessimistic note. Despite the numerous problems the Boy Scout and Rover movements failed to address at this period, either at local or national level, in certain circumstances – even during the lean years of the 1930s – individual troops did flourish. Those organised around Manchester Grammar School apparently enjoyed a halcyon period during the 1930s. One master at the school, who was also a Scout official, gave a glowing account of the school's scouting activities during the 1930s in the official history of scouting at the school:

> Saturday by Saturday Scouts came faithfully to the clubroom for six or seven hours of busy scouting activity. The parade was at 2.30. After the inspection and 'flag-up' there would be a scouting game...which might take the form of a convoy run, a prince game which was a form of escorting royalty through hostile country, a flag raid, a treasure hunt. As long as there was rivalry, a certain amount of friendly 'scrapping', and a fair measure of success it was considered a good game...Tea would follow in the clubroom. The evening would then be devoted to patrol work, badge work and tests, indoor games, mostly of the wilder sort – tilting, obstacle races, boxing – and a sing-song would generally bring the evening to a close.[117]

The Jewish Lads' Brigade

The fortunes of the Jewish Lads' Brigade (JLB) at this period mirrored those of the Boy Scouts and lads' clubs. 'It is difficult in all Lads' Clubs today to secure a stability of membership,' it was pointed out in the movement's annual report for 1935. 'Outside attractions, many of a doubtful character, are numerous, and it is becoming increasingly difficult to interest large numbers in an organisation of this kind.'[118] This statement is slightly misleading, since the JLB had never attracted large numbers at any time before 1935. When the first Manchester branch was set up in February 1899 it initially attracted only 80 boys.[119] This figure had increased to 278 by May 1899, but the membership did not increase significantly thereafter. By 1917, the Manchester JLB had only 300 members and 180 of these were under 14.[120] As with the Boy Scouts, schoolboys continued to dominate the movement after 1917. By the late 1920s, the Manchester JLB was heavily dependent on the support of schoolboys. In 1927, for example, one of the local JLB's officers complained that few of the members were planning to go on the annual camping trip that year, 'many having stated that they were going to the school camps in preference'.[121] One reason the Manchester JLB was far less popular with boys over 14 was the fact that all the local companies were organised around schools.[122] It is worth pausing to consider whether the movement's organisers deliberately sought to exclude all but schoolboys from joining the movement.

It appears from the JLB's records that the national policy was to pitch the movement at working-class Jewish boys who were about to leave elementary school, in the hope that they would be so hooked on Brigade life by the time they left school they would not want to leave the movement until they were obliged to at 18. The real goal of the organisers, clearly stated in the JLB's annual report for 1919, was: 'to extend the working of the Jewish Lads' Brigade so that there may eventually be no Jewish lad of between 14 and 17 years of age who (if he is not already a member of some similar organisation) does not belong to [our] body'.[123] This ambitious policy did not even come close to being achieved during the 1920s and 1930s, for a number of reasons. First, as has already been pointed out, the JLB was dominated by schoolboys, which was bound to make the movement seem inappropriate to the wage-earning boy who had 'money to spend' on cinemas and dance halls; unless, of course, he had become extremely attached to club life. Even the dedicated member, however, tended to leave the movement at about the age of 16. Martin B. is a case in point. He joined the Manchester JLB during the 1920s while still a pupil at Salford Grammar School. He joined the Brigade because it had a 'proper gym' in which he could practise his favourite hobby, boxing. He attended the JLB most evenings during the 1920s, mainly to box, but also to play table tennis and draughts. As he was a member of a successful boxing team (which won the Prince of Wales Boxing Shield when he was aged 15), he remained in the movement longer than most boys. Nevertheless, although a keen and successful JLB member, he left the movement at 16 when he began attending dance halls regularly.[124]

A second reason the movement was never able to attract large numbers of working-class boys was its ethos. Jewish parents apparently objected to the JLB's militaristic tone. Working-class resistance to the JLB, in Manchester and around the country, was frequently commented upon in the *Jewish Chronicle*.[125] During the First World War, the Manchester JLB was seen by some working-class Jewish parents as a recruiting ground for the British Army. One ex-member during the First World War recalled, for instance, how 'a lot of people objected to the wearing of khaki and rifle drill and wouldn't send their boys to the club. They thought it was a recruiting place for the army.'[126] Such feelings must also have been rife after the First World War because boys who joined the Manchester JLB were still required to wear khaki uniforms on certain occasions (in camp and on special ceremonial occasions) as late as 1932.[127] The officers also preferred it if members wore khaki uniform when parading on Sundays, although this was not obligatory by the 1930s.[128]

The other source of much working-class opposition to the JLB was rifle drill. This continued to be practised at Manchester JLB into the 1920s and, in addition, local JLB members were taught rifle shooting: 'a very large number of lads have been...trained to shoot well', it was reported in the movement's annual report for 1921.[129] During the 1920s, provincial JLB companies were advised by the Headquarters Staff in London to tone down the militaristic flavour of the movement.[130] The Manchester JLB, however, simply ignored these instructions and even proceeded to consolidate the military spirit.[131] In London, the khaki uniform was abolished altogether in 1921 and replaced by a less symbolically laden uniform of 'leather belt, white haversack and blue service cap with blue band and Brigade badge'.[132] JLB officers in Manchester, by contrast, not only insisted on retaining the khaki uniform after 1921; they also remained convinced that 'a system of military training' was still the best way to inculcate 'orderly and cleanly habits in boys'.[133] This system comprised military parades, indoor and outdoor rifle shooting, drill (infantry, physical and rifle), and, during the summer months, military camps.[134] These remained the core activities in Manchester up to the Second World War.[135]

The militaristic tone of the Manchester JLB did nothing to improve its image, either with working-class Jewish families or the citizens of Manchester as a whole. Consequently, the interwar years were ones of acute financial difficulty for the movement in Manchester. In 1921, the local movement was described in the annual report as 'in a critical position, depleted of officers, low in numbers of members, and nearly at the end of its financial resources'.[136] It survived the 1920s, largely thanks to the help it received from rich Jewish businessmen locally;[137] but the debt began to mount during the 1930s and, with fewer people prepared to donate money, its very existence was clearly threatened.

The reality was that by April 1932 the Manchester JLB was over £4,000 in debt.[138] Various schemes were initiated to try to raise revenue. In May 1934, the local JLB's Treasurer and Medical Officer, Dr P. I. Wigoder, wrote to ex-members inviting them to become annual subscribers; in effect, donors.[139] Following a 'disappointing' response, more ambitious fund-raising schemes were launched. Among these were boxing competitions, a wrestling match, dances and book competitions.[140] None of these initiatives significantly alleviated the local JLB's financial problems. In November 1937, the movement's debt still stood at over £3,000.[141] Moreover, the unresolved debt problem of Manchester JLB was compounded by other problems. The leadership spent much time considering how the movement could retain the support of older boys; but, despite their efforts, they were never able to overcome a high turnover: 'it is still found that large numbers are constantly passing through after a membership of only a few weeks or months', they reported gloomily in 1932.[142] A further problem for the leadership was that they had to provide activities members demanded rather than ones they thought would be beneficial. Educational classes were considered desirable by the leadership; but they were rejected by the membership and had to be withdrawn. English and Hebrew classes were introduced at the Manchester JLB in 1932; because of low attendances they had to be dropped after only a few months.[143] Educational classes met with a similar fate in other lads' clubs.[144] The activity that proved most popular at the Manchester JLB was boxing. Its boxing team won the Prince of Wales Boxing Shield, inaugurated in 1925, five times in the first six years of the competition.[145] Billiards was another popular activity; billiard tables being an important source of revenue at the JLB and at lads' clubs.[146]

Girls' Organisations

Girls' organisations, it appears, were not immune from the developments that so clearly afflicted youth work among boys. Joan Harley's interviews with 169 girl wage-earners in 1935–36 revealed that only one-third of her sample belonged to youth organisations.[147] Moreover, the majority admitted to being only casual members. Two-thirds of the girls Harley spoke to who were members of organisations attended them only once a week, though meetings were held usually two or three times a week.[148] This casual attitude was engendered partly by an aversion to wearing a uniform. One 16-year-old told her: 'I think Girl Guides are daft. I don't like wearing a uniform and parading through the streets.'[149] Other girls who had belonged to the Girl Guide movement as schoolgirls shared this view. Many thought they had outgrown the movement and would have felt 'silly and self-conscious in uniforms'.[150] Another criticism among the girls interviewed was that the Girl Guides especially was dominated by schoolgirls.[151] A further reason for the Girl Guides' and Rangers' limited impact with girl wage-earners was the limited opportunities provided for meeting boys.[152] Moreover, the activities on offer in most girls' organisations were not conducive to a large 14–18 membership. These were either associated with day school and Sunday school (gymnastics and bible classes); or with marriage (mothers' meetings, clothing clubs, laundry classes, and sick nursing).[153] There were, however, organisations that catered exclusively for single, working girls. In Manchester one such, the Pioneer Club for Girl Clerks and Typists, opened in May 1916. It survived into the interwar period and the records of the organisation survive, enabling a judgement to be made on its fortunes at this period.[154]

The Pioneer Club was set up to provide a meeting place for girl clerks and typists who worked at business firms in Manchester's city centre. An early report outlined the purpose of the club thus:

> the girl [clerk or typist], placed suddenly in the whirl of city life, alone perhaps and unable to secure for herself a sufficient amount of rest, recreation and nourishing food, tends to lose both health and spirits. She needs above all companionship; some place where she can go if she is tired and lonely or depressed, where she will be sure of meeting with comfort and sympathy...[155]

The officials who ran the club, a group of philanthropic middle-class women, clearly hoped it would be more than simply a meeting place for such girls. Their intention was to make it the centre of a Manchester girl clerk or typist's social life.[156]

By the end of 1917, the organisers had gone a long way towards achieving this aim. A wide range of activities had become established at the club: art classes, Bible study, drama, gymnastics, music, and physical efficiency classes. In addition, there was a 'Rambling Circle' which organised regular rambles and picnics during the summer months; a hockey team; a 'Riding Circle', and a swimming club.[157] In March 1918, the club even launched its own magazine, *The Pioneer News*.[158] By the early 1920s, a vibrant social and cultural life centred on the club had emerged. In a typical week, the evening activity included dancing classes, embroidery classes, gymnastics, millinery, painting, singing classes, orchestral practice, bridge, and a 'Reading Circle'.[159] The membership had reached 600 by 1923.[160]

The club's existence was, however, shortlived. A turnround in its fortunes began in 1926 when members started to 'find their evening recreation nearer home', attending the club only at lunchtimes.[161] In 1927, the club's country residence, Candlin House in West Kirby, closed because members were not visiting it.[162] Furthermore, when city centre cafés and restaurants serving 'astonishingly cheap meals' began to appear in the early 1930s this not only seriously eroded the lunchtime membership but also threatened the financial solvency of the club.[163] Owing partly to the depletion of its finances, and partly to the decline in the membership, the club was forced to close in March 1933 and it never reopened.[164] The club's officials accepted its demise as an act of fate. They were, however, in no sense responsible for it, but the victims of commercial forces. They did not dwell on this issue in their reports, but it appears that the erosion of the lunchtime membership had a knock-on effect on the rest of club life.[165]

Conclusion

The four case-studies discussed in this chapter suggest that the fortunes of both major youth movements (lads' clubs, the Boy Scouts and Rovers, the Jewish Lads' Brigade, and Girl Guides) and minor ones such as the Pioneer Club for Girl Clerks and Typists, were similar. During the 1920s and 1930s, they all experienced recruitment and other problems. These have not, as yet, been investigated by other historians; but that has been the principal purpose of this chapter. As revealed, there was no uniform response among youth leaders to the principal problem with which they had to deal; namely, leakage. Lads' club officials, in an effort to retain the patronage of working boys, introduced radical changes to club life; some even transformed their clubs into embryonic youth clubs. Boy Scout and Rover leaders, however, eschewed modernisation. The Rover Movement's ethos was social service, embracing work for the community such as giving blood, helping out at hospitals, and at civic events. Though obviously worthwhile, this work must have seemed astonishingly staid to former Boy Scouts, few of whom made the transition from the Scouts into the Rovers. The JLB's major problem was a lack of finance, which threatened to obliterate the organisation in its strongest provincial recruiting ground, Manchester.[166] The movement's failure to attract money and a mass following was undoubtedly the result of its overtly militaristic methods and ethos.

As regards the aims of youth organisations, in the case of the lads' clubs these were either modified or simply abandoned. Certainly, by the 1930s 'building up character' was no longer central to club life, although club leaders still claimed that it was. As late as 1935, for instance, the JLB claimed that it existed 'to train its members in loyalty, honour, discipline and self-respect, that they shall become worthy and useful citizens, and a credit to their Country and their Community'.[167] But such training was bound to be a protracted process. Moreover, as we have seen, boys did not remain members of youth organisations long enough for such noble ideals to have been realised. There was also an obvious discrepancy between the ideals of youth leaders and the activities that were popular at their clubs. It is difficult to see, for instance, how the character of working boys was built up through activities such as billiards and table tennis which, along with football, dominated club life during the 1920s and 1930s.[168]

It is apparent, therefore, that the interwar years were significant ones in the history of British youth movements. A reorientation of youth work was instituted during these years which was less a matter of design than a hurried response to the increasing affluence of young wage-earners and the new leisure opportunities becoming available to them. These changes affected all youth organisations and even within those that failed to introduce changes, such as the Boy Scouts and Rovers, pressure for reform was mounting.

NOTES

1. See especially M. Rosenthal, *The Character Factory: Baden-Powell and the Origins of the Boy Scout Movement* (London, 1986); J. Springhall, *Youth, Empire and Society: British Youth Movements, 1883–1940* (London, 1977); idem, 'Lord Meath, Youth and Empire', *Journal of Contemporary History*, Vol.5, No.4 (1970), pp.97–111; idem, 'The Boy Scouts, Class and Militarism in Relation to British Youth Movements 1908–1930', *International Review of Social History*, Vol.XVI (1971), pp.125–58; idem, 'Baden-Powell and the Scout Movement before 1920: Citizen Training or Soldiers of the Future?', *English Historical Review*, Vol.CII, No.405 (October 1987), pp.934–42; A Warren, 'Sir Robert Baden-Powell, the Scout Movement and Citizen Training in Great Britain, 1900–1920', *English Historical Review*, Vol.CI, No.399 (April 1986), pp.376–98; idem, 'Baden-Powell: a final comment', *English Historical Review*, Vol.CII, No. 405 (October 1987), pp. 948–50; idem, 'Citizens of the Empire: Baden-Powell, Scouts and Guides, and an imperial ideal' in J.M. MacKenzie (ed.), *Imperialism and Popular Culture* (Manchester, 1986), Ch. 10; Hendrick, *Images of Youth*, Ch. 6. For studies of movements which have stimulated rather less debate see B. Harrison, 'For Church, Queen and Family: The Girls' Friendly Society, 1874–1920', *Past and Present*, Vol.61, No. 61 (Nov. 1973), pp.107–38; D. Prynn, 'The Woodcraft Folk and the Labour Movement, 1925–1970', *Journal of Contemporary History*, Vol.18, No.1 (Jan. 1983), pp.79–95; P. Wilkinson, 'English Youth Movements, 1908–1930', *Journal of Contemporary History*, Vol.4, No.2, (1969), pp.1–23; V. Bailey, 'Bibles and Dummy Rifles: The Boys' Brigade', *History Today*, Vol.33 (Oct. 1983), pp.5–10; Z. Layton-Henry, 'Labour's Lost Youth', *Journal of Contemporary History*, Vol.11 (July 1976), pp.275–308; R.A. Voeltz, '"A Good Jew and a Good Englishman": The Jewish Lads' Brigade, 1894–1922', *Journal of Contemporary History*, Vol.23, No.1 (Jan. 1988), pp.119–27.
2. See below, pp.140–2. On youth clubs during the 1960s see T.R. Fyvel, *The Insecure Offenders: Rebellious Youth in the Welfare State* (Middlesex, 1964), especially pp.80, 250–6; J.B. Mays, *Growing up in the City: A Study of Juvenile Delinquency in an Urban Neighbourhood* (Liverpool, 1964), *passim*.
3. Statistics on lads' club membership, either nationally or at a regional level, are extremely rare. For the London and Manchester figures see C. E. B. Russell and L. M. Russell, *Lads' Clubs: Their History, Organisation and Management* (London, 1932), p.24. For London, reasonably comprehensive statistics are available for the years 1910–32 (see Appendix, Table 6.3), but no similar index is for Manchester. For lads' club membership in Manchester in 1917 see Appendix, Table 6.4.
4. See C. E. B. Russell and L.M. Rigby, *Working Lads' Clubs* (London, 1908).
5. On the Manchester membership see Appendix, Table 6.4; on London, H. Llewellyn Smith (ed.), *The New Survey of London Life and Labour*, Vol.IX, Ch. VII, Tables III (A) and III (B), pp.193–4.
6. Manchester Juvenile Organisations Committee, *Handbook* (Manchester, 1918), p.7.
7. Appendix, Table 6.4.
8. Ibid.
9. Hugh Oldham Lads' Club, *Annual Report*, 1914, p.3. The annual reports of this and other Manchester lads' clubs referred to below are held in the Local History Library of Manchester Central Library. The manuscript records of the club are in the Archives Department of the same library (M7).
10. Hugh Oldham Lads' Club, *Annual Report*, 1913, p.3.
11. W.A. Richardson, 'The Hugh Oldham Lads' Club, 1888–1958', *Manchester Review* (Autumn 1959), p.342.
12. Hugh Oldham Lads' Club, *Annual Report*, 1922, p.4.
13. Heyrod Street Men's and Lads' Club, Ancoats, *Annual Report*, 1927, p.4. On Charles Russell's period at the club see below, p.141.

14. See, besides the clubs discussed here, the recruitment difficulties experienced by club officials at Ardwick Lads' Club discussed in Ardwick Lads' and Men's Club, *Annual Report*, 1924–25, p.8. In an effort to stir casual members into taking a more active interest in the club, the club's officials abolished the entrance fee of 1d for boys aged 14 and older and ½d for those under 14. Moreover, members were henceforth entitled to admit guests (on payment of 1d per guest).

15. Heyrod Street Men's and Lads' Club, *Annual Report*, 1929, p.4.

16. Ancoats Lads' Club, *Annual Report*, 1930, p.16.

17. Ancoats Lads' Club, *Annual Report*, 1938, p.6.

18. Ibid., p.7.

19. Ibid.

20. Hugh Oldham Lads' Club, Minute Book, 5 March 1928–5 October 1942, Manchester Central Library, Archives Department, M7/1/7. See the entry for 31 Aug.1936.

21. Hugh Oldham Lads' Club, Minute Book, 6 March 1939.

22. Heyrod Street Men's and Lads' Club, *Annual Report*, 1927, pp.5–6; *Annual Report*, 1928, p.6.

23. Russell and Rigby, *Working Lads' Clubs*, p.407. On Russell's period at the club see also F.P. Gibbon, *A History of the Heyrod Street Lads' Club And of the Fifth Manchester Company of The Boys' Brigade, 1889–1910* (Manchester, 1911), pp.11, 14.

24. Gibbon, *History of Heyrod Street Lads' Club*, pp.11, 14. In 1927, club members were still obliged to attend the Bible class every Sunday and drill once a week; see, for instance, Heyrod Street Men's and Lads' Club, *Annual Report*, 1927, p.5.

25. Heyrod Street Men's and Lads' Club, *Annual Report*, 1928, p.9; *Annual Report*, 1929, pp.4–5, 10. In the 1929 *Report* it was admitted that members' attendance at church and chapel services was also falling away: 'unfortunately, the general decline in the habit of church-going has spread to our lads, and the attendance on Sunday evenings [at the Russell Chapel attached to the club] is not nearly so large as we should desire' (p.5).

26. On the prominence of schoolboys at Heyrod Street Lads' Club see Heyrod Street Men's and Lads' Club, *Annual Report*, 1928, p.5; on the same phenomenon at the Hugh Oldham club see Richardson, 'Hugh Oldham Lads' Club', p.345.

27. Ancoats Lads' Club, *Annual Report*, 1924–25, p.14; *Annual Report*, 1926, pp.6–7; *Annual Report*, 1927, p.9; *Annual Report*, 1928, p.5.

28. Ancoats Lads' Club, *Annual Report*, 1927, p.8.

29. Ibid.; idem, *Annual Report*, 1926, pp.6–7; *Annual Report*, 1929, p.9.

30. Idem, *Annual Report*, 1929, p.4.

31. Idem, *Annual Report*, 1930, p.14.

32. Ibid., p.16.

33. Idem, *Annual Report*, 1936, p.11; *Annual Report*, 1938, pp.6–7, 9–10, 12.

34. Idem, *Annual Report*, 1938, pp.6–7.

35. Idem, *Annual Report*, 1935 ('...the success of a season in a Lads' Club...can be gauged pretty accurately by the success of its football and cricket teams', p.4). On the members' obsession with football (playing and discussing) before the First World War see *Annual Report*, 1902–3, pp.6–7.

36. Idem, *Annual Report*, 1934, p.6; *Annual Report*, 1935, p.8; *Annual Report*, 1936, p.10.

37. Idem, *Annual Report*, 1938, pp.6–7.

38. See, for instance, Hugh Oldham Lads' Club, *Annual Report*, 1891. ('The object of this Club is to secure, so far as possible, an upright mind in an upright body for the lads who are members', p.5.). Fifteen years later, character-building was still seen as the most important task of the officials at the club: 'A feature of Lads' Clubs, maybe the most important feature...is the formation of character through their agency' (*Annual Report*, 1906, p.3). The most effective way of 'building up the characters' of working boys, the officials found, was through encouraging them to participate in 'fresh air' and 'manly sports'. See, for instance, *Annual Report*, 1898, p.6. On the importance of character-building at the Heyrod Street Lads' Club before the War see Gibbon, *History of Heyrod Street Lads' Club*, pp.5, 11. Interestingly, the officials at Ancoats Lads' Club were never interested in character-building. See, for instance, Idem, *Annual Report*, 1902–3, *passim*, and *Annual Report*, 1904–5, *passim*.

39. For these and the following statistics see Appendix, Table 6.3.
40. Llewellyn Smith, *New Survey of London*, Vol. IX, Ch. 7, Tables III (A) and III (B), pp.193–4.
41. Ibid., p.193, note 3.
42. The records of the London Federation of Boys' Clubs are held at Bridge House, Bridge House Quay, Prestons Road, London E14. Access to the records was kindly granted by Nichola Willoughby of the Federation. For details of the scope of the Federation's work during the interwar period see Llewellyn Smith, *New Survey of London*, Vol. IX, pp.22 64, 136, 142, 155–6, 172.
43. See Federation of London Working Boys' Clubs, *Annual Reports* 1910–1923, *passim*.
44. See, for example, the Federation's *Annual Report* for 1910–11 (not paginated).
45. Federation of London Working Boys' Clubs, *Annual Report*, 1919–20, p.2; *Annual Report*, 1921–2, pp.7–8.
46. E.W. Pead, 'Eighty-Nine Years On: London Federation of Boys' Clubs' (typescript), p.28; Federation of London Working Boys' Clubs, *Annual Reports*, 1910–1938, *passim*.
47. Idem, *Annual Report* 1918–19, p.3.
48. Ibid.
49. Ibid.
50. See idem, *Annual Report*, 1927–28, p.1.
51. See, for example, the correspondence between Baden–Powell and Rover leaders in the Scout Association Archives, London (TC/34) and, for a case-study of leakage from the Boy Scouts, see E.S. Griffith and R.A. Joseph, 'The Unknown Years', *Social Service Bulletin*, Vol.IX, No.7 (July 1928), pp. 112–19.
52. Scout Association Archives (TC/34). Letter to Baden–Powell from Mr A.J. Wakeford of London, dated 7 August 1929, who was worried that 'at about 14 years of age, and after, the Scouts fall away...'. On the same subject see also an earlier letter by Mr Sam Darrington of Finchley, dated 18 August 1921. Baden–Powell was himself clearly worried about leakage. In a letter to Rover leaders (n.d. 1932?) he called for a conference on the question of 'the leakage between Scouts and Rover Scouts'.
53. For the membership statistics of the Rovers see Appendix, Tables 6.1 and 6.2. For the ideology of the Rovers and the movement's impact in Cambridge and Bromley see A. Warren, 'Popular Manliness: Baden-Powell, Scouting, and the Development of Manly Character' in J.A. Mangan and J. Walvin (eds), *Manliness and Morality: Middle-class Masculinity in Britain and America, 1800–1940* (Manchester, 1987), Ch. 10.
54. Appendix, Table 6.1; The Boy Scouts Association, *Policy, Organisation And Rules*, Jan. 1925, British Library (WP 8501), p.26.
55. Appendix, Tables 6.1 and 6.2.
56. See the editorial in *The Rover World*, March 1935, p.401.
57. Ibid.
58. Ibid.
59. N. L. Tranter, *Population and Society, 1750–1940: Contrasts in Population Growth* (London, 1985), p.92.
60. See above, pp.16, 80–1; Appendix, Table 3.1.
61. See below pp.152–3.
62. For the correspondence between the Chief Scout and Rover leaders see Scout Association Archives (TC/34), *passim*.
63. Letter from Baden-Powell on leakage from the Boy Scouts (n.d. 1932?), Scout Association Archives, London.
64. Letter to the Chief Scout from the London Rover Commissioner dated 26 April 1924, Scout Association Archives, TC/34. See also 'Look Wide!', a publicity leaflet published by the London Rover Committee (n.d.1924?), Scout Association Archives, TC/34.
65. Details of the scheme are contained in a letter to the Chief Scout, dated 15 Dec. 1931, from Edward G. Wood of the 39th Croydon Rover Crew, Scout Association Archives, TC/34.
66. On grassroots feeling see, for example, the proceedings of a conference of Rover leaders in Surrey during October 1934 entitled 'Surrey Rover Leaders and Mates Conference, October 1934', Scout Association Archives, TC/34, *passim*.
67. See the 'Typed report of a meeting of Assistant County Commissioners For Rover Scouts

at Gilwell Park, January 28–29, 1933', Scout Association Archives, TC/34.

68. See 'Surrey Rover Leaders and Mates Conference', Scout Association Archives, TC/34, pp.1–3.
69. Ibid., pp. 8–11.
70. Ibid., pp.10–11.
71. *The Rover World*, August 1934, p.157.
72. Ibid.
73. Letter from the Chief Scout headed 'To Rovers', dated 1939, Scout Association Archives, TC/34.
74. The Boy Scouts Association, *Policy, Organisation and Rules*, p.42.
75. *The Rover World*, Aug. 1934, p.157.
76. *The Rover World*, March 1935. At the conference one of the speakers, a Rover leader in Northumberland, described the Scout movement as in a state of 'crisis' (p.429).
77. Appendix, Table 6.2.
78. The records of Manchester Boy Scouts and Rovers are held at the Greater Manchester Record Office in Manchester. For a more detailed analysis of this material and the fortunes of other youth movements in Manchester c.1919–39 see D.M. Fowler, 'The Lifestyle of the Young Wage–Earner in Interwar Manchester, 1919–1939', unpublished PhD thesis, University of Manchester, 1988, Ch. 6.
79. Appendix, Table 6.2.
80. Ibid.
81. Greater Manchester Rover Scouts, Minute Book, 1935–1958. See the meeting on 3 March 1936.
82. Ibid. See the minutes of the meeting held on 1 Sept. 1936.
83. Appendix, Table 6.2.
84. Griffith and Joseph, 'Unknown Years', pp.118–19.
85. Griffith was the Warden of Liverpool University Settlement from 1922 to 1928. For a brief account of his youth work for the Settlement see C.M. King and H. King, *'The Two Nations': The Life and Work of Liverpool University Settlement And Its Associated Institutions, 1906–1937* (Liverpool, 1938), pp. 87–9.
86. Griffith and Joseph, 'Unknown Years', p.119.
87. Ibid. They argued that the Scout uniform 'to the average slum boy makes him an object of ridicule at his most self-conscious age' and suggested that '[a] Scout troop which is exclusively over the age of 14 and does not require a uniform might be worth trying'.
88. Llewellyn Smith, *New Survey of London*, Vol. IX, Ch. VII, Table III (A) p.193.
89. H. E. O. James and F. T. Moore, 'Adolescent Leisure in a Working-Class District', *Occupational Psychology*, Vol.XIV, No.3 (July 1940), pp. 144–5. On the same pattern in York see Rowntree, *Poverty and Progress*, pp.393–4, 447.
90. James and Moore, 'Adolescent Leisure in a Working-Class District', pp.144–5.
91. Ibid., p.145.
92. Manchester and District Boy Scouts Association, *Yearbook* 1924 (incorporating the 15th Annual Report), p.17.
93. Idem, *Yearbook* 1926, p.23.
94. Ibid.
95. Manchester and District Boy Scouts Association, *Yearbook* 1938, p.4.
96. Ibid.
97. Ibid. See also Ch. 2.
98. R. Roberts, *The Classic Slum*, p.161, note 4.
99. James and Moore, 'Adolescent Leisure in a Working-Class District', pp.133–4.
100. Manchester Juvenile Organisations Committee, *Handbook*, pp.68–9.
101. Manchester Education Committee, *Youth Committee Report 1940–41* (Manchester, 1941), pp. 33–4.
102. Manchester and District Boy Scouts Association, *Yearbook* 1924, pp. 38–9, 40–1, 51–2.
103. Ibid., pp. 49–50. On school troops see also Manchester Grammar School, *Scouting at the Manchester Grammar School, 1912–1955* (Manchester, 1955); J. A. G. Dymond, *Scouting and the Adolescent* (Manchester, 1920), Chs. III–V.
104. Manchester and District Boy Scouts Association *Yearbook*, 1924, pp. 36–7, 53–4.

105. Whereas working–class boys deserted the Scouts at 14 or 15, according to Dymond (a teacher at Manchester Grammar School and a Scout leader there) boys of 16 were actively involved in the school's troops. See Dymond, *Scouting and the Adolescent*, Ch. V.

106. Appendix, Table 6.2.

107. See Ch. 5.

108. See, for example, the comments of 'a Holborn Rover' published in *The Scouter* in June 1935: 'Something is attracting our boys, and it is something on what we class as the "out side" of Scouting...skating rinks, prize fights, dirt track races, talkies...'.

109. Springhall, *Youth, Empire and Society*, pp. 63–4.

110. Ibid., p.70, note 82.

111. Youth Hostel Association (England and Wales), Manchester and District Regional Group, *Annual Report 1936–37*, p.8; *Annual Report 1937–38*, p.8.

112. See, for instance, Youth Hostel Association, Manchester and District, *Annual Report*, 1932–33, p.2; *Annual Report*, 1933–34, p.2. For the same pattern in York see Rowntree, *Poverty and Progress* ('The local leaders of the [YHA] state that the membership tends to be confined to teachers, clerks and students', p.396).

113. *The Clarion Cyclist*, Dec. 1936 and April 1937, Manchester Central Library, Archives, Department (016/Box 5).

114. *Young Worker*, 7 Aug. 1926. Held at British Library Newspaper Section, Colindale.

115. *Weekly Young Worker*, 12 Feb. 1927, British Library Newspaper Section, Colindale.

116. Manchester and District Boy Scouts Association, *Handbook for 1939*, p.12.

117. Manchester Grammar School, *Scouting At The Manchester Grammar School*, p.16.

118. Jewish Lads' Brigade (JLB), *Annual Report*, 1935, p.67. The movement's annual reports were published in London. News from the regions was included at the end of each report. Copies of the annual reports from 1907 to 1935 are held with the manuscript records of Manchester Jewish Lads' Brigade in Manchester Central Library, Archives Department (M130).

119. Manchester Jewish Lads' Brigade, 1st *Annual Report*, 1899–1903, p.25.

120. Appendix, Table 6.4.

121. Manchester Jewish Lads' Brigade, Officers' Minutes, 4 Sept. 1923–5 March 1934. See the minutes of the meeting held on 5 April 1927.

122. See, for instance, Manchester Juvenile Organisations Committee, *Handbook*, p.58.

123. Jewish Lads' Brigade, *Annual Report*, 1919, p.4.

124. Manchester Studies Oral History Archive, tape J43.

125. H. Solomon, 'The Aims, Methods and Achievements of the Manchester Jewish Lads' Brigade against the Background of British Youth Movements 1883–1914', Diploma in Local History, Manchester Polytechnic, 1984, Ch. 5.

126. Manchester Studies Oral History Archive, tape S1.

127. Manchester Jewish Lads' Brigade, Officers' Minutes, 4 Sept. 1923–5 March 1934. See the comments made at a meeting on 4 April 1932.

128. Ibid. See the minutes of a meeting held on 7 Dec. 1931. See also Manchester Jewish Lads' Brigade, Officers' and Managers', Executive and Subscribers', Minutes, March 1934 – June 1939. At a meeting held on 29 April 1935 it was suggested that the khaki uniform should be abolished altogether, but this proposal was rejected by those present.

129. Jewish Lads' Brigade, *Annual Report* 1921, pp. 16, 60.

130. Ibid., p.12.

131. See note 128.

132. Jewish Lads' Brigade, *Annual Report* 1921, p.12.

133. See note 128; Jewish Lads' Brigade, *Annual Report* 1921, p.6.

134. Ibid., p.60; idem, *Annual Report*, 1923, pp. 35–6; *Annual Report*, 1932, p.55; *Annual Report*, 1933, pp. 61–2; *Annual Report*, 1934, p.51; *Annual Report*, 1935, pp. 68–9. See also Manchester Jewish Lads' Brigade, Officers' Minutes, *passim*; Officers' and Managers', Executive and Subscribers', Minutes, *passim*.

135. See, for example, Jewish Lads' Brigade, *Annual Report*, 1923. Manchester Jewish Lads' Brigade companies 'drill nightly' and battalion parades were held once a month (p.35). See also Manchester Jewish Lads' Brigade, Officers' and Managers', Executive and Subscribers', Minutes, March 1934–June 1939. In July 1934, the 'shooting section' were

attending a barracks every week. See the Minutes of the meeting held on 2 July 1934.

136. Jewish Lads' Brigade, *Annual Report*, 1921, p.5.
137. See Manchester Jewish Lads' Brigade, Officers' Minutes, 4 Sept. 1923–5 March 1934. See, in particular, minutes of a meeting held on 18 Oct. 1926. See also R.D. Livshin, 'Aspects of the Acculturation of the Children of Immigrant Jews in Manchester 1890–1930', unpublished MEd thesis, University of Manchester, 1982, pp. 130–48.
138. Scrapbook of newspaper cuttings re Manchester Jewish Lads' Brigade, Manchester Central Library, Archives Department (M130/).
139. Manchester Jewish Lads' Brigade, Officers' and Managers' Minutes. See minutes of meeting held on 4 June 1934.
140. Ibid. Minutes of meetings held on 7 Jan. 1935; 11 Feb. 1935; 3 June 1935; 1 July 1935; 3 Feb. 1936; 15 July 1936.
141. Ibid. Minutes of meeting held on 29 Nov. 1937.
142. Cited in Manchester Jewish Lads' Brigade, 'Scrapbook'.
143. *Manchester Guardian*, 27 May 1932.
144. Educational classes (reading, writing, arithmetic, elementary book–keeping and shorthand) were introduced at the Ancoats Lads' Club in September 1926; but, owing to low atten– dances, these were stopped in 1933. See idem, *Annual Report*, 1926, p.7; *Annual Report*, 1933, p.4. On the lack of appeal of educational classes at other local lads' clubs see Ardwick Lads' and Men's Club, *Annual Report*, 1924–25, p.5; *Annual Report*, 1935–36, p.4; Heyrod Street Men's and Lads' Club, *Annual Report*, 1927, p.6; *Annual Report*, 1928, p.9; *Annual Report*, 1929, p.8.
145. Manchester Jewish Lads' Brigade, 'Scrapbook'; *Jewish Gazette*, 1 Oct. 1931; *Daily Express*, 11 Sept. 1931.
146. Manchester Jewish Lads' Brigade, Officers' and Managers' Minutes. See the meetings held on 9 April 1934; 11 March 1935; 2 Dec. 1935; 28 March 1938. On billiard tables as an important source of revenue in lads' clubs see Russell and Russell, *Lads' Clubs*: 'If the club is fortunate enough to possess one, there will...be receipts from a billiard-table, and assuming that this is used for three hours each evening for six days a week, at a charge of 1d a half hour for every lad playing...there will be a revenue from this source of 2s a night – 12s a week, and, let us say, £20 during the season' (p.44).
147. Harley, 'Report', p.85.
148. Ibid., p.89.
149. Ibid., p.84.
150. Ibid.
151. Ibid. 'The Girl Guide movement seems to appeal much more to girls of school age than to older girls. At 16, when the time comes for them to join a Ranger company, many leave the movement altogether'.
152. Ibid., pp. 92, 95.
153. Two clubs mentioned by Harley, Manchester Girls' Institute and Heyrod Street Girls' Club, provided Madeleine Rooff with details of their age–structure. The former had 600 members (in 1934), 300 of whom were under 14 and 225 over 18. The latter club was dominated by schoolgirls. Of the 400 members (in 1934), 312 were under 14. A further 56 were over 18. Most of the latter, it appears, were married women. See M. Rooff, *Youth and Leisure: A Survey of Girls' Organisations in England and Wales* (Edinburgh, 1935), pp. 191–2. On the activities at girls' clubs see Manchester and Salford Girls' Institutes, *Annual Reports*, 1918–1923, *passim*.
154. The records of The Pioneer Club for Girl Clerks and Typists are held in Manchester Central Library, Archives Department, MS F 369.48 M40.
155. Handwritten report on 'The Opening of the Pioneer Club for Girl Clerks and Typists'.
156. See, for example, *The Pioneer News*, March 1918. In this issue of the club's paper, the first one, its editor Margaret Pilkington (the club's secretary) wrote: 'I think we all want this club to be a training ground for good citizens as well as a pleasant centre of social life'.
157. The Pioneer Club, Winter Programme, 1917; idem, *Annual Report*, 1917–18.
158. *The Pioneer News*, a monthly, sold for 6d a copy. Only one issue survives. This may have been the only one printed.
159. Pioneer Club, *Annual Report*, 1919–20, p.2; *Annual Report*, 1920–21.

160. Idem, Annual Report, 1922–23, p.3.
161. Pioneer Club for Girl Clerks and Typists, 'Reports, 1916–1933'.
162. Pioneer Club, *Annual Report*, 1926–27 (not paginated).
163. Idem., *Annual Report*, 1932–33, p.1.
164. Ibid.
165. Ibid., pp.1–2.
166. In 1926, the Manchester JLB had 450 members; significantly more than other provincial battalions. The other provincial centres were: Glasgow (121 members), Birmingham (112) and Liverpool (108). See Jewish Lads' Brigade, *Annual Report*, 1927, p.12.
167. Jewish Lads' Brigade, *Annual Report*, 1935, p.70.
168. On London see above p.143. On Manchester see, for example, Ancoats Lads' Club, *Annual Reports*, *passim*; Ardwick Lads' and Men's Club, *Annual Reports*, *passim*; Jewish Lads' Brigade, *Annual Report*, 1923, p.35; idem, *Annual Report*, 1925, pp.51–2; Manchester Jewish Lads' Brigade, Officers' and Managers'..., Minutes, March 1934–June 1939. At a meeting held on 11 March 1935 it was disclosed that the local JLB had four table tennis teams, billiard teams (number not specified) and only one football team.

Conclusions

What broad conclusions emerge from this study? A principal theme in the existing accounts of young wage-earners at this period is their lack of autonomy either in the labour market, at the workplace, or in the leisure sphere. This interpretation needs to be heavily qualified. In a number of Britain's towns and cities young wage-earners of both sexes, because of the shortage of juvenile labour at this period and its relative cheapness compared with unemployed adult labour, possessed bargaining power in the labour market and utilised this to their advantage. The best examples of this are the nationwide apprentices' strikes during 1937. But it is clear from the above account that other young workers, girls as well as boys, sought to improve their living standards by leaving low-paid for higher-wage occupations when it suited them to do so. Given the short spells many young wage-earners, in a number of locations, invariably spent in a single occupation and the fact that even apprentices usually began their careers in high-wage 'blind-alley' jobs, it appears that the search for pecuniary rewards was a preoccupation of the young wage-earners of interwar Britain. As revealed, there were good reasons for this; namely, the significant wage differentials between 'blind-alley' and 'progressive' juvenile occupations and even within the blind-alley sector; also, the greater relative affluence of young wage-earners in relation to adults in terms of their disposable income, and the emergence of leisure goods and services aimed specifically at the teenage group.

That young wage-earners possessed, and exercised, autonomy is apparent in each of the spheres central to their lives: the labour market, the workplace, and the leisure sphere. In the labour market, they frequently rejected the advice supplied by parents or Juvenile Employment Bureau officials on suitable and unsuitable occupations and decided themselves which work was suitable. The advice they received was, in any case, flawed, and presumably their experience of the labour market (or that of their peers) revealed this to them. To contemporaries (academics, school teachers, social investigators all agreed) there were 'progressive' and 'blind-alley' juvenile occupations; namely, white collar work, apprenticeships, and other jobs involving some degree of skill and, on the other hand, messenger and van boy work. Contemporaries believed there were no long-term prospects in so-called blind-alley work and not even medium-term ones. On reaching 16 or 18 juvenile employees, it was thought, would be sacked and a fresh supply of school- leavers recruited. This, however, was a simplistic and alarmist view. As revealed in Chapter 1, it certainly underplayed the fluidity of the juvenile labour market. Many juveniles at about the age of 16 moved out of so-called blind-alley jobs into apprenticeships. There was even movement from apprenticeships into blind-alley jobs. Moreover, the critics of blind-alley employment overlooked the statistical evidence produced for census reports which clearly showed that many juveniles remained in such employment well beyond the dangerous ages of 16 and 18. They were concerned about such employment partly because of the lack of prospects, but also the working environment. Those in blind-alley jobs worked long hours which restricted their opportunities to seek further education. To young workers, however, such work was attractive because in comparison with apprenticeships it offered far greater remuneration.

Young wage-earners also possessed and exercised a degree of autonomy at the workplace. The teenage group were not deferential workers. Their relationship with employers, even paternalistic employers, was a fragile one. On occasions, as during 1937, they came into conflict with employers and were involved in strike action. This was nothing new, but the scale and duration of the disputes was unprecedented. The 1937 strike action was overwhelmingly by boys; but girls were not absent. In the north-west of England girls participated in the disputes and were involved in acts of industrial sabotage in certain parts of the country.[1] Girl wage-earners with a grievance against an employer were no more deferential than boys.

Outside the workplace, young wage-earners were relatively free from constraints of any kind. Elizabeth Roberts found that 'while young people [in central and north Lancashire] remained at home, they had to live according to their parents' rules'.[2] One such rule, she argues, was that they handed over their unopened wage-packets to their mothers and received only a few coppers back for spending money. Such a system meant that saving up for marriage was a protracted process and lack of savings explains why young people from working-class families married late.[3] In Chapter 4, a different argument was developed. In big cities such as Manchester young wage-earners, of both sexes, spent much of their free time indulging in pursuits which cost money. Cinema visits and dancing were habitual pursuits for boys and girls in their teens and even for those in their early twenties. Some spent most evenings at cinemas or dances. Those in their teens certainly possessed the disposable income to pursue such activities habitually. All the social investigators who studied the income and expenditure of working-class households acknowledged this. They either implied, or stated explicitly, that young wage-earners in such families enjoyed a higher standard of living than other members of the family and especially mothers and young children.

Moreover, this superior lifestyle only became possible during the interwar years. It resulted, in part, from the dramatic improvement in young wage-earners' earnings since the pre-First World War period; and, in part, from the emergence of a welfare system covering most manual families which shielded young workers from having to support families in which the chief wage-earner was unemployed.[4] Other economic and demographic developments contributed to the improvement in young wage-earners' living standard; among these, the improvement of real wages among manual as well as white-collar workers and the decline in family size.[5] The increasing affluence of young wage-earners can be demonstrated another way; in terms of the shift in the leisure supply. During the 1920s and 1930s, as revealed in Chapter 4, entertainment entrepreneurs, manufacturers of consumer products, and magazine proprietors began to tap the teenage market. Dance halls began to cater exclusively for young wage-earners and young people's dances, music and fashions emerged. Cinema managers began showing films with the teenage group in mind. Magazines aimed at young wage-earners appeared and proliferated. Moreover, manufacturers of consumer products began advertising their products in them, as did the proprietors of other magazines. A hard-sell youth market was emerging.

It appears from this study that the principal beneficiaries of commercialised leisure provision during the interwar years were young wage-earners from working-class families. Their spending patterns and lifestyles were not unlike those of 1950s teenagers. They frequented the same establishments (cinemas, dance halls and milk bars); were as preoccupied with clothes and fashion, and spent their disposable income on similar products (clothes, cosmetics, magazines, motor cycles and soft drinks). It is clear, in fact, that the phenomenon market researchers claimed they discovered in the late 1950s was already visible in Britain's towns and cities by the 1930s. Moreover, the changing lifestyles of young wage-earners had some impact on the age of marriage. As a Preston weaver interviewed about his youth during the interwar years put it: 'I can't weigh these young 'uns up; they want to end their lives befoor they've started 'em. They're savin' up fer an 'ouse afore they've left schoo'. Why don't they 'ave their fun first like we did?'[6] Given the developments documented here, the trend of late marriages among 15-24 year olds of both sexes, and especially in relation to the same age group during the 1950s and 1960s, cannot be explained purely in terms of poverty. Lack of savings in what was at this period an extremely protracted (10-year) phase of the life-cycle was presumably the result, in part, of spending on gregarious and other pursuits in an environment in which there were pressures to do so.

The changing lifestyles of young wage-earners at this period posed problems for youth movements. Youth leaders either had to adapt their movements to the changing interests of young wage-earners, or accept the tendency towards a casual and uncommitted membership; or even, as in the case of the Boy Scout movement, the permanent drift of young wage-earners from the ranks. Lads' club officials chose a reorientation of lads' club work, involving the abandonment of activities central to the ethos of lads' clubs before the First World War such as drill and the installation of billiard tables, film projectors, wirelesses, and even roller-skating rinks. As part of the same process, rules were relaxed. Girls began to be admitted to the clubs for regular (usually weekly) dances; the members were given greater autonomy; entrance fees were lowered and, in some clubs, abolished. In effect, lads' clubs were transformed from sedate institutions where working boys could seek solace and play chess or read into embryonic youth clubs. The Boy Scout movement, on the other hand, eschewed modernisation and, consequently, lost the support of working boys. Its membership was drawn, increasingly, from schoolboys.

In many respects, therefore, the young wage-earners of the 1920s and 1930s were as much the beneficiaries of increasing economic, social, and cultural opportunities as those of the 1950s. Their lifestyles, in fact, show a remarkable resemblance to those of 1950s' teenagers, as Chapter 4 sought to demonstrate; and, as revealed in Chapter 5, moral guardians were as shocked by their behaviour as a later generation were about affluent postwar teenagers. But adults had little influence over the lives of young wage-earners in interwar Britain, who created their own lifestyles despite (and perhaps because of) attempts by adults to shape their behaviour.[7]

NOTES

1. On the first point see above Ch.2. On the acts of industrial sabotage orchestrated by girl wage-earners see *Daily Herald*, 11 Sept. 1937. This contains a report on 50 factory girls at the Massa Sparking Plug company in Wimbledon who, on hearing they were to be sacked, 'began to wreck the building. They dismantled machinery, pulled down benches, overturned desks and destroyed material.'
2. E. Roberts, *Woman's Place*, p.44.
3. Ibid., pp. 42—3.
4. See Ch. 4.
5. On the first point see S. G. Jones, *Workers At Play: A Social and Economic History of Leisure, 1918-1939* (London, 1986), Ch. 2; on the latter, Tranter, *Population and Society*, pp. 181—2.
6. Cited in D. Thompson, 'Courtship and Marriage in Preston between the Wars', p.43.
7. For a similar interpretation of a different subject see E.P. Thompson, *The Making of the English Working Class* (1963 repr. Middlesex, 1979).

Appendix

TABLE 1.1

THE TEENAGE WORKFORCE OF ENGLAND AND WALES, 1921

	Number in employment or seeking it	*Number in the age group*	*Those in employment or seeking it as a percentage of the age group*
Boys (14—19)	1,758,089	2,092,545	83.7
Girls (14—19)	1,365,131	2,138,384	63.8

Source: Census of England and Wales 1921, *Occupational Tables* (London, 1924), Tables 2 and 4.

TABLE 1.2

THE TEENAGE WORKFORCE OF ENGLAND AND WALES, 1931

	Number in employment or seeking it	*Number in the age group*	*Those in employment or seeking it as a percentage of the age group*
Boys (14-20)	2,003,106	2,355,355	85.1
Girls (14-20)	1,680,283	2,378,508	70.8

Source: Census of England and Wales 1931, *Occupation Tables* (London, 1934), Tables 2 and 3.

TABLE 1.3
OCCUPATIONS OF BOYS IN ENGLAND AND WALES, 1921 AND 1931

Occupation	Number		Percentage of Boy Labour Force	
	1921	1931	1921[a]	1931[b]
Agriculture	197,063	171,542	11.2	8.5
Mining and quarrying	190,862	145,913	10.8	7.2
Brickmakers, pottery and glass	20,194	12,035	1.1	0.6
Chemicals	5,317	2,241	0.2	0.1
Metal workers (includes precious metals)	276,810	226,428	15.6	11.3
Electricals	30,595	37,582	1.7	1.8
Watch and clock makers (includes scientific instruments)	3,488	2,823	0.1	0.1
Textiles (includes textile goods workers and textile workers)	132,523	78,840	7.5	3.9
Foods, drinks and tobacco	25,922	24,376	1.4	1.2
Wood and furniture workers	71,470	92,278	4.0	4.6
Transport and communication	252,660	267,406	14.3	13.3
Commerce, finance and insurance	119,673	222,253	6.7	11.1
Professionals	20,098	22,462	1.1	1.1
Entertainments and sport	8,085	10,592	0.4	0.5
Personal service	37,583	57,582	2.1	2.8
Clerks	113,523	161,382	6.4	8.0
General labourers	43,549	58,327	2.4	2.9
Others[c]			13.0	21.0

Notes:

a Boys aged 12–19
b Boys aged 14–20
c Includes fishermen; makers of leather goods; makers of paper and cardboard boxes; printers; builders; painters and decorators; utility workers; workers in public administration, and workers in defence

Source: Census of England and Wales 1921, *Occupation Tables*, Table 2; Census of England and Wales 1931, *Occupation Tables* Table 2.

TABLE 1.4
OCCUPATIONS OF GIRLS IN ENGLAND AND WALES, 1921 AND 1931

Occupation	Number		Percentage of Girl Labour Force	
	1921	*1931*	*1921*[a]	*1931*[b]
Agriculture	17,358	12,025	1.2	0.7
Mining and quarrying	1,058	897	0.0	0.0
Brickmakers, pottery and glass	17,876	7,784	1.2	0.4
Chemicals	7,091	1,307	0.5	0.0
Metal workers (includes precious metals)	48,777	44,560	3.5	2.6
Electricals	8,390	12,469	0.5	0.7
Watch and clock makers (includes scientific instruments)	874	616	0.0	0.0
Textiles (includes textile goods workers and textile workers)	353,435	326,349	25.9	19.4
Foods, drinks and tobacco	38,596	27,889	2.7	1.6
Wood and furniture workers	9,302	7,750	0.6	0.4
Transport and communication	29,564	27,740	2.1	1.6
Commerce, finance and insurance	129,417	182,946	9.4	10.8
Professions	25,568	31,266	1.8	1.8
Entertainments and sport	5,481	3,774	0.3	0.1
Personal service	376,337	523,208	32.4	31.1
Clerks and typists	157,132	202,713	11.5	12.0
Warehouses, storekeepers and packers	59,398	78,146	4.3	4.6
Others[c]			2.1	12.2

Notes:

a Girls aged 12–19
b Girls aged 14–20
c Includes fishing; makers of leather goods; makers of paper and cardboard boxes; printers; builders; painters and decorators; utility workers; workers in public administration, and workers in defence

Source: Census of England and Wales 1921, *Occupation Tables*, Table 4; Census of England and Wales 1931, *Occupation Tables* Table 3.

APPENDIX

TABLE 2.1
AVERAGE WEEKLY EARNINGS OF YOUNG WORKERS IN SELECTED
OCCUPATIONS, OCTOBER 1935[a]

Occupation	Boys[b]	Girls[c]
Aircraft manufacture	22s 6d	21s 6d
Boot and shoe repairing	26s 6d	16s 9d
General engineering	21s 0d	18s 4d
Hosiery	26s 1d	17s 6d
Locomotive engineering	17s 3d	–
Textiles (bleaching, printing etc)	24s 2d	16s 0d
Textile machinery (making)	17s 10d	15s 1d
Transport (trams)	31s 9d	24s 5d

Notes:

a The following statistics were obtained by the Ministry of Labour for a national survey of the earnings of industrial workers throughout Britain undertaken in 1935. Employers from 76,000 industrial establishments supplied wages information for the survey.

b Denotes boys under 21.

c Denotes girls under 18.

Source: Ministry of Labour Gazette, 1937, various issues.

TABLE 3.1

YOUTH UNEMPLOYMENT IN SELECTED BRITISH CITIES, 1927–36 (%)a

Dateb	Bristol	Glasgow	Liverpool	Londonc	Manchester	Newcastle	Salford	Sheffield
1927	–	–	17.5	2.6	3.4	–	10.8	11.2
1928	–	–	16.4	2.3	4.4	–	14.8	11.8
1929	–	–	15.8	1.7	5.2	–	10.1	9.0
1930	10.7	14.3	16.9	2.8	9.3	15.2	18.4	14.8
1931	9.9	18.0	17.2	4.2	6.5	18.5	13.3	17.4
1932	13.6	20.2	16.7	4.1	9.1	19.2	12.0	17.3
1933	15.1	17.1	13.1	1.9	5.4	14.8	9.8	7.2
1934	20.7	22.8	20.2	2.3	5.6	21.6	12.1	6.1
1935	16.0	23.4	21.8	2.1	3.6	22.0	9.6	4.2
1936	7.0	16.4	22.3	1.7	2.1	15.5	5.0	1.7

Notes:

a The figures relate to those 14–18-year-olds registered as unemployed as a percentage of the insured juvenile population.

b The statistics were collected monthly. Because the source is incomplete the figures for 1927–29 are for November; those for 1930–36, November (Salford and Sheffield) and December (Bristol, Glasgow, Liverpool, London, Manchester and Newcastle).

c Denotes Greater London.

Source: Ministry of Labour, *Local Unemployment Index, January 1927–December 1937* (London, 1938).

APPENDIX

TABLE 3.2
YOUTH UNEMPLOYMENT IN MANCHESTER, 1931[a] (BOYS)

Occupation	In Work		Out of Work	
	N	%	N	%
Metal workers	4,296	81.5	978	18.5
Commerce, finance and insurance	4,503	93.1	332	6.9
Transport and communication workers	4,315	92.2	368	7.8
Messengers and porters[b]	4,094	92.5	332	7.5
Clerks, draughtsmen and typists	3,955	93.5	274	6.5
Labourers and unskilled factory workers	2,885	75.7	927	24.3
Warehousemen and storekeepers	2,236	90.5	234	9.5
Road transport workers	957	91.1	191	8.9
Workers in wood and furniture	1,623	90.4	172	9.6
Textile goods workers	1,333	88.6	171	11.4
Workers in precious metals	953	90.4	101	9.6
Van boys[c]	903	93.0	68	7.0
Personal service	863	88.0	118	12.0
Textile workers	746	83.0	153	17.0
Others[d]	4,759	81.5	1,082	18.5
TOTAL	34,424	87.6	4,851	12.4

Notes:

a   Those covered comprise 14-21 year olds who, regardless of whether they were registered as such, were unemployed on 27 April 1931.

b   Excludes railway porters.

c   Includes bus and tram conductors.

d   Includes printers, photographers, builders, painters and decorators, professionals, agricultural workers, miners, defence and public administration.

Source: Census of England and Wales 1931, *Occupation Tables*, London 1934, Table 18.

TABLE 3.3
YOUTH UNEMPLOYMENT IN MANCHESTER, 1931[a] (GIRLS)

Occupation	In Work		Out of Work	
	N	%	N	%
Textile goods workers	11,823	96.1	484	3.9
Clerks and typists	5,357	96.2	211	3.8
Personal service	4,570	94.2	281	5.8
Commerce, finance and insurance	2,913	92.8	226	7.2
Textile workers	2,525	89.7	289	10.3
Labourers and unskilled factory workers	2,396	90.2	260	9.8
Textile workers	2,525	88.6	289	11.4
Storekeepers and packers	2,273	92.4	187	7.6
Paper and cardboard makers and workers	1,224	93.5	85	6.5
Transport and communication workers	1,050	96.9	34	3.1
Messengers	772	96.6	27	3.4
Others[b]	9,977	95.1	522	4.9
TOTAL	37,828	93.6	2,579	6.4

Notes:

a See Table 3.2, note a.

b Includes professionals, metal workers, wood and furniture makers, agricultural workers, entertainment and sport, public administration, and defence.

Source: Census of England and Wales 1931, Occupation Tables, Table 18.

TABLE 3.4
MANCHESTER JUVENILE EMPLOYMENT SERVICE, 1921–38

	1921			1926		
	B	G	T	B	G	T
Registrations	6,355	5,049	11,404	5,828	4,359	10,187
Placements:						
Manchester juveniles in Manchester	1,211	901	2,112	3,144	2,355	5,499
Manchester juveniles outside Manchester	58	16	74	80	30	110
Outsiders	166	144	310	124	154	278
Total	1,435	1,061	2,496	3,348	2,539	5,887
Vacancies notified	1,642	1,321	2,963	3,615	2,946	6,561

	1931			1935			1938		
	B	G	T	B	G	T	B	G	T
Registrations	9,229	6,794	16,023	9,690	6,864	16,554	8,870	7,381	16,251
Placements:									
Manchester juveniles in Manchester	3,725	4,302	8,027	5,435	5,330	10,765	5,933	5,102	11,035
Manchester juveniles outside Manchester	48	29	77	115	60	175	95	29	124
Outsiders	87	230	317	140	326	466	281	322	603
Total	3,860	4,561	8,421	5,690	5,716	11,406	6,309	5,453	11,762
Vacancies notified	4,196	5,143	9,339	6,665	7,588	13,853	8,392	7,594	15,986

Sources: Manchester Education Committee, Juvenile Employment Bureaux, *Annual Reports*, various issues; H. E. Canner, 'The Juvenile Employment Service in Manchester, 1910–1939', unpublished MEd thesis, University of Manchester, 1958.

179

TABLE 3.5
AGE PROFILE OF BOYS IN 'BLIND-ALLEY' EMPLOYMENT IN MANCHESTER, 1931

Age	N	%
Van Boys[a]		
14	112	12
15	150	15
16–17	346	36
18–20	363	37
Total	971	100
Messengers and Porters[b]		
14	1,375	31
15	1,451	33
16–17	1,257	28
18–20	343	8
Total	4,426	100
Warehouses		
14	102	4
15	221	9
16–17	883	34
18–20	1,314	53
Total	2,470	100

Notes:

a Includes bus and tram conductors.

b Excludes railway employees.

Source: Census of England and Wales 1931, *Occupation Tables*, Table 18.

APPENDIX

TABLE 4.1
AGE PROFILE OF THE POPULATION OF ENGLAND AND WALES, 1921–61

Age-Group	1921 %	1931 %	1951 %	1961 %
0–4	8.7	7.4	8.4	7.7
5–9	9.2	8.3	7.2	7.0
10–14	9.6	8.0	6.4	8.0
15–24	17.5	17.3	12.8	13.1
25–34	15.2	16.0	14.4	12.6
35–44	14.0	13.6	15.2	13.6
45–54	11.6	12.3	13.6	13.9
55–64	7.6	9.2	10.4	11.6
65–74	4.3	5.3	7.4	7.6
75+	1.7	2.0	3.5	4.2

Source: Census of England and Wales, *General Tables*, 1921–1961.

TABLE 4.2
MARITAL STATUS OF YOUNG PEOPLE IN
ENGLAND AND WALES, 1921–61[a] (%)

Boys

		15–19		20–24	
Date	Single	Married	Single	Married
1921	99.5	0.4	82.1	17.6
1931	99.7	0.2	86.1	13.8
1951	99.4	0.5	76.2	23.7
1961	98.9	1.0	68.9	30.9

Girls

		15–19		20–24	
Date	Single	Married	Single	Married
1921	98.1	1.7	72.6	26.9
1931	98.2	1.8	74.2	25.6
1951	95.5	4.4	51.7	47.9
1961	93.4	6.5	42.0	57.7

Note:

a Excludes widowed and divorced.

Source: Census of England and Wales, *General Tables*, 1921–1961.

TABLE 4.3
AVERAGE WEEKLY EARNINGS OF YOUNG WORKERS IN SELECTED
OCCUPATIONS, 1906 AND 1935

Boys (Under 21)

	Weekly Earnings			
Occupation	*1906*		*1935*	
	s.	d.	s.	d.
Engineering	9	7	21	0
Shipbuilding	11	10	16	1
Cotton textiles	12	8	19	1
Tailoring	6	10	21	2
Laundries	8	9	20	4
Confectionery	–	–	22	10
Tobacco	10	0	37	1
Building	9	7	21	9
Transport (trams)	11	3	31	9
Transport (goods)	11	10	26	4
Warehouses	–	–	21	0

Girls (18 and Over)

	Weekly Earnings			
Occupation	*1906*		*1935*	
	s.	d.	s.	d.
Engineering	13	1	32	9
Cotton textiles	18	8	28	8
Tailoring	14	2	31	11
Dressmaking	13	10	35	9
Laundries	12	10	28	1
Confectionery	–	–	32	6
Tobacco	11	5	39	7
Transport (trams)	–	–	48	6
Transport (goods)	–	–	27	2
Warehouses	–	–	29	9

Girls (Under 18)

	Weekly Earnings			
Occupation	*1906*		*1935*	
	s.	d.	s.	d.
Engineering	8	2	18	4
Cotton textiles	11	0	16	6
Tailoring	5	5	14	4
Dressmaking	3	9	15	2
Laundries	6	6	15	7
Confectionery	–	–	16	8
Tobacco	6	6	20	7
Transport (trams)	–	–	24	5
Transport (goods)	–	–	16	11
Warehouses	–	–	16	2

Sources: Board of Trade Labour Gazzette, 1909–13, various issues; *Ministry of Labour Gazette*, 1937, various issues.

APPENDIX

TABLE 6.1
BOY SCOUT AND ROVER MEMBERSHIP IN UK, 1919–38

Year	Scouts^a	Rovers^b	Rovers as % of Scouts
1919	150,446	5,580	4
1920	152,141	7,263	5
1921	149,817	7,638	5
1922	154,566	8,938	6
1923	158,413	11,603	7
1924	163,767	14,361	9
1925	169,917	17,300	10
1926	175,691	19,257	11
1927	183,350	20,790	11
1928	186,949	23,944	13
1929	189,459	25,565	13
1930	196,773	31,111	16
1931	202,010	34,751	17
1932	213,473	38,735	18
1933	216,857	38,927	18
1934	205,610	35,809	17
1935	198,665	33,464	17
1936	195,058	35,268	18
1937	194,592	31,194	16
1938	200,082	31,276	16

Notes:

a Boys of 11–17. Excludes Scout leaders.
b Boys of 17 and older. Excludes Rover leaders.

Source: The Scout Association, *Annual Census Figures*.

TABLE 6.2
BOY SCOUT AND ROVER MEMBERSHIP IN MANCHESTER, 1921–38

Year	Scouts[a]	Rovers[b]	Rovers as % of Scouts
1921	4,310	209	5
1922	4,165	199	5
1923	4,111	218	5
1924	3,796	287	8
1925	3,789	365	10
1926	3,657	367	10
1927	3,697	501	16
1928	3,808	599	16
1929	3,833	621	16
1930	3,989	716	18
1931	–	–	–
1932	–	–	–
1933	–	–	–
1934	–	–	–
1935	–	–	–
1936	3,151	707	22
1937	3,200	587	18
1938	3,164	611	19

Notes:

a, b As Table 6.1

Source: Manchester and District Boy Scouts Association, *Year Books*, 1924–40.

APPENDIX

TABLE 6.3
YOUTH MOVEMENT MEMBERSHIP IN LONDON, 1910–32

Year	Boys' Brigade[a]	Church Lads' Brigade[b]	Scouts[c]	Rovers[d]	Boys' Clubs[e]
1910	7,424	7,283	13,062	–	2,841
1915	6,661	11,970	21,558	–	2,335
1920	6,063	8,138	25,904	1,502	8,017
1925	8,035	8,352	26,746	3,698	6,428
1930	13,062	6,857	27,116	5,185	8,638
1932	12,947	4,961	26,272	5,488	7,538

Notes:

a Boys aged 12 to 18. Includes warrant officers and staff sergeants, but excludes officers.
b Boys aged 10–21. Excludes officers.
c Boys aged 11 to 18. Excludes officers and cubs.
d Boys of 17 and older. Excludes officers.
e 14–18 membership only. Excludes officers.

Source: H. Llewellyn Smith (ed.), *The New Survey of London Life and Labour*, Vol. IX, *Life and Leisure* (London, 1935), Table 1, p. 189.

TABLE 6.4
YOUTH MOVEMENT MEMBERSHIP IN MANCHESTER, 1917 (BOYS)

Organisation	14–18s	Total (10–18)
Boys' Brigade	814	2,378
Boys' Life Brigade	200	600
Boy Scouts	1,600	6,600
Cadets	172	234
Catholic Boys' Brigade and Scouts	1,100	2,000
Church Lads' Brigade	1,166	2,241
Jewish Lads' Brigade	120	300
Lads' Clubs	2,880	6,450
Street Children's Mission	75	195
YMCA	750	1,050
Total	8,877	26,048 [a]
Total boy population	21,000	47,000

Note:

a Includes 4,000 14–18-year-olds attending evening play centres organised by Manchester Education Committee.

Source: Manchester Juvenile Organisations Committee, Handbook (Manchester, 1918), p. 8.

TABLE 6.5
YOUTH MOVEMENT MEMBERSHIP IN MANCHESTER, 1917 (GIRLS)

Organisation	14–18s	Total (10–18)
Ancoats Settlement	50	130
Catholic Girls' Club	140	160
Girls' Friendly Society	2,200	2,700
Girl Guides	1,875	2,411
Girls' Institute	300	600
Girls' Life Brigade	180	460
Jewish Girls' Club	250	250
Street Children's Mission	50	290
Wesleyan Girls' Clubs	472	752
Total	6,017	12,853 [a]
Total girl population	21,000	47,000

Note:

a Includes 4,000 14–18-year-olds attending evening play centres organised by Manchester Education Committee.

Source: Manchester Juvenile Organisations Committee, Handbook (Manchester, 1918), p. 8.

Bibliography

1. Manuscript Sources

Greater Manchester Record Office, Manchester
Greater Manchester Rover Scouts: Minute Books, 1935–1958; Daybook, 1927–1948.

Manchester Central Library, Archives Department
Church Lads' Brigade – St. James branch, Gorton: miscellaneous papers 1922–1957 (M432).

Clarion Cycling Club: pamphlets, handbooks, *The Clarion Cyclist* and other records (016).

Grey Mare Lane Day Continuation School, Openshaw, Log Book, 1923–1937 (M66/32 additional/Box 1).

Grove House Lads' Club: Managers' and Subscribers' Meetings, Minutes, November 1916–March 1934 (M130).

Hugh Oldham Lads' Club: Minute Books, 1 March 1915–5 October 1942 (M7/1/5–7).

Israel Wolf Slotki Papers: Hebrew Educationalist, Scholar and Minister (M191): various boxes.

Jewish Lads' Brigade (M130): Officers' Minutes, May 1908–August 1912; September 1923–March 1934.

Officers' and Managers', Executive and Subscribers', Minutes, March 1934–June 1939.

Scrapbook of Newspaper Cuttings re Manchester JLB.

Letters from Packing Case Firms About Apprentices, 1913–1939 (M308/4/3–8).

Minutes of the Child and the Cinema Meetings held at the local branch of the National Council of Women during 1927 (M271/Box 5).

Papers of Lucien Harris of Crumpsall, President of the Manchester Zionist Youth Council (M350): including a copy of *The Young Zionist: Organ of the Federation of Zionist Youth*, dated June 1939; South Manchester and District Women's Zionist Society, *Annual Report* 1939–40; Manchester Junior Zionist Society, correspondence *c.*1938 and correspondence from the Zionist Central Council of Manchester and Salford to Lucien Harris as Chairman and President of the Zionist Youth Council, February 1935–December 1939.

Pioneer Club for Girl Clerks and Typists: Reports etc. 1916–1933 (MS F369. 48 M40).

Minute Books (MS F369.48 M10).

Seymour Road Municipal Girls' School, Clayton, Log Book 1907–1935 (M66/134/Box 1).

Wright Robinson Papers (M284): including newpaper cuttings which record his criticism of the cinema's influence over young people in the 1940s (M284/Box 15).

Manchester Central Library, Local History Library.

Newspaper cuttings: Amusements: General (Box 462). Cinema in general (Th.791.43 MA1).

Mass Observation Archive, University of Sussex Library.

Youth: Boxes 1–3 – including material on youth peace movements; a Mass Observation youth survey in Paddington and Bermondsey, 1940–1, and an interview with a London Boys' Brigade leader.

Worktown: Bolton, Boxes 21 and 22 including material on special occasions.

Public Record Office, Kew

CAB 24/160/281 – Juvenile Unemployment Centres. Memorandum by the Minister of Labour, Sir Montague Barlow 13/6/1923.

CAB 27/202 – Report, Proceedings and Memorandum of a Cabinet Committee on Juvenile Unemployment, March 1924.

CAB 27/228 – Report and Proceedings of a Cabinet Committee on Juvenile Unemployment, December 1923.

CAB 27/267 – Report, Proceedings and Memorandum of a Cabinet Committee on Juvenile Unemployment, 1925.

HO 179/ Entry Books relating to Entertainments and Theatres in the years 25 July 1910–31 December 1921.

LAB 2/1078. Juvenile Unemployment Centres – Manchester Education Authority Centres at Byrom Street Course 1929–30, (typescript).

LAB 2/1311/EDJ 525/4/1928. National Advisory Committee on Juvenile Employment – Inquiry into the Usefulness of Juvenile Unemployment Centres, 1927 (typescript).

MEPO 2/1696/ON 993640 – Cinema films: effect on juveniles and proposed censorship.

Scout Association Archives, Baden-Powell House, London
Founder's Files re. Rover Scouts (TC/34).

Working-Class Movement Archive and Library, Salford

E. Frow, 'The Apprentice Strike And Our New Tasks: How the Strike Started And Developed', handwritten notes dated 1937. This library also has other material relating to the engineering apprentices' strikes of 1937, including strike bulletins produced by the apprentices.

2. Printed Reports

Ancoats Lads' Club, *Annual Reports* 1895–1938, MCL, Local History Library.

Ardwick Lads' and Men's Club, *Annual Reports* 1924–1946, MCL, Local History Library.

Census of England and Wales, 1911, Vol. X, *Occupations and Industries*, Part II (London, 1913), MCL, Social Sciences Library. (Censuses cited below are also at this location.)

Census of England and Wales 1921, *County of Lancaster* (London, 1923).

Census of England and Wales 1921, *Occupation Tables* (London, 1924).

Census, 1931 *Classification of Occupations* (London, 1934).

Census of England and Wales 1931, *County of Lancaster* (London, 1932).

Census of England and Wales 1931, *Occupation Tables* (London, 1934).

City of Manchester Education Committee, Juvenile Employment Bureaux, *Annual Reports*, 1914–1939, MCL, Local History Library.

City of Manchester Education Committee, *Youth Committee Report 1940–41* (Manchester, 1941), MCL, Social Sciences Library.

Federation of London Working Boys' Clubs, *Annual Reports* 1910–1926, LFBC Archive.

Heyrod Street Men's and Lads' Club, Ancoats, *Annual Reports* 1927–1929, MCL, Local History Library.

Hugh Oldham Lads' Club, *Annual Reports* 1890–1957, MCL, Local History Library.

Jewish Lads' Brigade, *Annual Reports* 1907–1935, MCL, Archives Department (M130).

London Federation of Boys' Clubs, *Annual Reports* 1927–1938, LFBC Archive.

Manchester and District Boy Scouts Association, *Year Books* 1924–1940, MCL, Local History Library.

Manchester and Salford Girls' Institutes, *Annual Reports* 1918–1923, MCL, Local History Library.

Manchester and Salford Trades Council, *Annual Reports* 1918–1938, MCL, Local History Library.

Manchester University Settlement, *Annual Reports* 1920–1938, MCL, Social Sciences Library.

Pioneer Club for Girl Clerks and Typists, *Annual Reports* 1917–1933, MCL, Archives Department (MS F369.48 M40).

Procter Club Gymnasium and Hulme Lads' Club, *Annual Reports* 1917–1940, MCL, Local History Library.

The Boy Scouts Association, *Policy, Organisation and Rules*, January 1925, B.L. (W.P. 8501).

The Boys' Brigade, Manchester Battalion, *Annual Report* 1937–38, MCL, Local History Library.

Youth Hostel Association (England and Wales), Manchester and District Regional Group, *Annual Reports* 1932–1939, MCL, Social Sciences Library.

3. Parliamentary Papers

Final Report of the Departmental Committee on *Juvenile Education in relation to employment after the War*, Vol.I, Report, Cd 8512 (London, 1917).

Final Report of the Departmental Committee on *Juvenile Education in relation to employment after the War*, Vol.II, Summaries of Evidence and Appendices, Cd 8577 (London, 1917).

Hansard, 1915–1939.

Ministry of Education, *The Youth Service in England and Wales*, Report of the Committee Appointed by the Minister of Education in November, 1958, Cmnd 929 (London, 1960).

Ministry of Labour, *Local Unemployment Index, January 1927–December 1937* (London, 1938).

Ministry of Labour, *Memorandum on the Shortage, Surplus and Redistribution of Juvenile Labour during the Years 1928–1933* based on the views of Local Juvenile Employment Committees, Cmd 3327 (London, May 1929).

Ministry of Labour, *Report for the Year 1932*, March 1933, Cmd 4281 (London, 1933).

Ministry of Labour, *Report of an Enquiry into Apprenticeship and Training for the Skilled Occupations in Great Britain and Northern Ireland, 1925–6*, Vol. VII, General Report (London, 1928).

Ministry of Labour, *Report of the Committee on Education and Industry England and Wales*, First Part (London, 1926).

Ministry of Reconstruction, *Juvenile Employment During the War – and After. The Report of an Enquiry* (London, 1919?).

Report of the Departmental Committee on the *Hours of Employment of Young Persons in Certain Unregulated Occupations*, March 1937, Cmd 5394 (London, 1937).

Royal Commission On the Poor Laws and Relief of Distress, Appendix Vol. XX, Report by Mr Cyril Jackson on Boy Labour (London, 1909).

The Public General Acts 8 and 9, Geo.V (London, 1918).

The Public General Acts 24 and 25, Geo.V (London, 1934).

4. Newspapers, Journals, and Magazines

Boys' Cinema
Bulletin of the Society for the Study of Labour History
Challenge
Change: Bulletin of the Advertising Service Guild
Daily Dispatch
Daily Express
Daily Herald
Daily Worker
Economic History Review
Economic Journal
English Historical Review
Feminist Studies

Girls' Cinema
Historical Journal
History of Education
History Today
History Workshop
Hobbies
International Review of Social History
Jewish Chronicle
Jewish Gazette
Journal of Contemporary History
Journal of Educational Administration and History
Journal of Further and Higher Education
Journal of the National Institute of Industrial Psychology
Journal of the Royal Statistical Society
Manchester City News
Manchester Evening Chronicle
Manchester Evening News
Manchester Faces and Places
Manchester Guardian
Manchester Region History Review
Manchester Review
Ministry of Labour Gazette
Motor Cycle
New Society
New Writing
News Chronicle
Occupational Psychology
Odds and Ends: A Manuscript Magazine
Oral History
Our Journal: The Magazine of the Employees of Mather and Platt Ltd.
Peg's Paper
Social History
Social Service Bulletin
Social Service Review
Social Welfare
The Advertiser's Annual and Convention Year Book
The Blackshirt
The Clarion Cyclist
*The Fifth: Monthly Chronicle of the Heyrod Street Lads' Club, and
    of the 5th Manchester Company of the Boys' Brigade*
The Manchester Programme: Entertainments and Pleasures
The Militant
The Milk Trade Gazette

The Motor Cycle Book for Boys
The Police Review and Parade Gossip: Organ of the British Constabulary
The Rover World
The Scouter: The Headquarters Gazette of the Boy Scouts Association
The Sunday Times
The Times
The Weekly Young Worker
The Worker Sportsman
The Young Worker
Transactions of the Manchester Statistical Society
Young Engineer
Young Worker

5. Contemporary Publications

Articles

'A Day in a Juvenile Employment Officer's Life', *Human Factor*, Vol. XI, No.3 (March 1937), pp.106–10.

Bottomley, C., 'The Recruitment of Juvenile Labour in Warrington', *Transactions of the Manchester Statistical Society* (Session 1930–31), pp.129–44.

Bray, R. A., 'The Apprenticeship Question', *Economic Journal*, Vol. XIX (September, 1909), pp.404–15.

Carter, C. F., 'Youth Work in Manchester, The Report of the Youth Survey', *Social Welfare*, Vol. IV, No.6 (October 1940), pp.108–11.

Cross, T. K., 'Social Service or Bureacracy – A Problem for the Juvenile Employment Departments and Bureaux', *Human Factor*, Vol. X, No.10 (October 1936), pp.347–50.

Godwin, G., *Town Swamps and Social Bridges* (1859, repr. Leicester, 1972).

George, R. F., 'A New Calculation of the Poverty Line', *Journal of the Royal Statistical Society*, Vol. C, Pt.I (1937), pp.74–95.

Greenwood, A., 'Blind-Alley Labour', *Economic Journal*, Vol. XXII (June 1912), pp.309–14.

Greenwood, W., 'The Apprentice' in idem, *How the Other Man Lives* (London, 1939?), Chapter XVII.

Griffith, E. S. and Joseph, R. A., 'The Unknown Years', *Social Service Bulletin*, Vol. IX, No.7 (July 1928), pp.112–19.

Hadden, E. A., 'Women's Recreations in Ancoats', *Odds and Ends: A Manuscript Magazine*, L (1904), pp.305–22.

Harrisson, T., 'Whistle While you Work' in J. Lehmann (ed.), *New Writing*, 1 (Autumn, 1938), pp.47–67.

Hindshaw, W., 'Works Schools For Engineers' in J.J. Findlay (ed.), *The Young Wage-Earner and the Problem of his Education* (London, 1918), pp.162–74.

Hobbins, J. H., 'From the Threepenny Gallery: Some Impressions of the Cheap Theatre', *Odds and Ends: A Manuscript Magazine*, XLIX (1903), pp.365–82.

'Impressions and Animadversions By a Juvenile Bureaucrat', *Human Factor*, Vol. X, No.5 (May 1936), pp.190–4.

James, H. E. O. and Moore, F. T., 'Adolescent Leisure in a Working-Class District', *Occupational Psychology*, Vol. XIV, No.3 (July 1940), pp.132–45.

McG. Eagar, W., 'The Next Step in Education', *Social Service Bulletin*, Vol. IX, No.8 (August 1928), pp.135–42.

Morley, F., 'The Incidence of Unemployment by Age and Sex', *Economic Journal*, Vol. XXXII (1922), pp.477–88.

Paton, J. L., 'The Adolescence of the Working Lad in Industrial Towns', *Transactions of the Manchester Statistical Society* (Session 1911–12), pp.85–101.

Rowson, S., 'A Statistical Survey of the Cinema Industry in Great Britain in 1934', *Journal of the Royal Statistical Society*, Vol. XCIX, Pt.I (1936), pp.67–119.

Tawney, R. H., 'The Economics of Boy Labour', *Economic Journal*, Vol. XIX (1909), pp.517–37.

Taylor, W. E., 'Educational Opportunities', *Odds and Ends: A Manuscript Magazine*, Vol. LXXXVI (1946), pp.179–94.

'The Problems of Adolescents as Seen by a Juvenile Employment Officer, A Birmingham Survey', *Social Service Review*, Vol. X, No. 9 (September 1929), pp.175–8.

Warrington, S., 'Unemployment Statistics – Some Observations upon North Western Figures', *Manchester Statistical Society Group Meetings* (1935–36), pp.28–43.

Watson, W. F., 'Is There a Shortage of Skilled Craftsmen?', *Human Factor*, Vol. X, No.1 (January 1936), pp.29–33.

Welldon, Right Reverend Bishop James, 'Education After the War', *Transactions of the Manchester Statistical Society* (Session 1916–17), pp.57–8.

Books and Pamphlets

Baden-Powell of Gilwell, Lord, *Rovering to Success: A Book of Life-Sport for Young Men* (London, 1930).

Baden-Powell, Sir Robert, *Scouting and Youth Movements* (London, 1929).

Bell, V. A., *Junior Instruction Centres and their Future: A Report to the Carnegie U.K. Trust* (Edinburgh, 1934).

Bowley, A. L., *Wages and Income In the United Kingdom Since 1860* (Cambridge, 1937).

Bowley, A. L., and Hogg, M. H., *Has Poverty Diminished?* (London, 1925).

Burt, C., *The Young Delinquent* (1915, repr. London, 1938).

Butler, C. V., *Social Conditions in Oxford* (Oxford, 1912).

Cadbury, E., Matheson, C. and Shann, G., *Women's Work and Wages* (London, 1906).

Cameron, C., Lush, A. and Meara, G., *Disinherited Youth: A Report on the 18+ Age Group Enquiry Prepared for the Trustees of the United Kingdom Trust* (Edinburgh, 1943).

Caradog Jones, D. (ed.), *The Social Survey of Merseyside*, Vol. 1 (London, 1934).

The Social Survey of Merseyside, Vol.3 (London, 1934).

Chisholm, C. (ed.), *Marketing Survey of the United Kingdom, 1937* (London, 1938).

Marketing Survey of the United Kingdom, 1938 (London, 1939).

City of Manchester, *The Signpost: A Guide for Young People and Their Elders* (Manchester, 1928).

Collier, D. J., *The Girl in Industry* (London, 1918).

Dobbs, S. P., *The Clothing Workers of Great Britain* (London, 1928).

Durrant, H., *The Problem of Leisure* (London, 1938).

Dymond, J. A. G., *Scouting and the Adolescent* (Manchester, 1920).

Ferguson, R. W. and Abbott, A., *Day Continuation Schools* (London, 1935).

Findlay, J. J. (ed.), *The Young Wage-Earner and the Problem of his Education* (London, 1918).

Fleming, A. P. M. and Pearce, J. G., *The Principles of Apprentice Training* (London, 1916).

Ford, P., *Work and Wealth In A Modern Port: An Economic Survey of Southampton* (London, 1934)

Ford, R., *Children in the Cinema* (London, 1939).

Freeman, A., *Boy Life and Labour: The Manufacture of Inefficiency* (London, 1914).

Gibb, S. J., *The Problem of Boy Work* (London, 1906).

Gibbon, F. P., *A History of Heyrod Street Lads' Club and of the Fifth Manchester Company of The Boys' Brigade, 1889–1910* (Manchester, 1911).

Gollan, J., *Why Youth Strikes* (London, 1937).

Youth in British Industry: A survey of labour conditions today (London, 1937).

Greenwood, W., *Love On The Dole* (1933, repr. Middlesex, 1981).

How The Other Man Lives (London, n. d. 1939?).

Hallsworth, J., *Protective Legislation for Shop and Office Employees* (3rd edn. London, 1939).

Hallsworth, J. and Davies, R. J., *The Working Life of Shop Assistants: A Study of Conditions of Labour in the Distributive Trades* (Manchester, 1910).

Hannington, W., *The Problem of the Distressed Areas* (1937, repr. Wakefield, 1976).

Harrison, G. and Mitchell, F. C., *The Home Market* (London, 1936).

Jewkes, J. and Jewkes, S., *The Juvenile Labour Market* (London, 1938).

Jewkes, J. and Winterbottom, A., *Juvenile Unemployment* (London, 1933).

Keynes, M. N., *The Problem of Boy Labour in Cambridge* (Cambridge, 1911).

King, C. M. and King, H., *'The Two Nations': The Life and Work of Liverpool University Settlement and its Associated Institutions, 1906–1937* (Liverpool, 1938).

Leeson, C., *The Child and the War* (London, 1917).

Lewis, E. L., *The Children of the Unskilled: An Economic and Social Study* (London, 1924).

Llewellyn Smith, H., *et al.* (eds), *The New Survey of London Life and Labour*, Vol. IX, (London, 1935).

Manchester and District Boy Scouts Association, *Handbook for 1939* (Manchester, 1939).

Manchester and Salford Council of Social Service, *Report of the Second Youth Survey* (Manchester, 1942).

Manchester Education Committee, *General Survey, 1914–1924* (Manchester, 1926).

Young People's Week June 17–23 1928, Handbook (n.d., 1928?).
Education in Manchester: A Survey of Progress, 1924–1934 (Manchester, 1935).

Juvenile Employment Bureaux, *A Summary of Occupations Open to Boys and Girls in the City* (Manchester, 1936).

Manchester Juvenile Organisations Committee, *Handbook* (Manchester, 1918).

Manchester University Settlement, *Ancoats: A Study of a Clearance Area, Report of a Survey Made in 1937–38* (Manchester, 1945).
Day Clubs for Men and Boys, An Experiment And An Appeal For Volunteers (Manchester, 1932).

Mather, L. E. (ed.), *The Right Honourable Sir William Mather, 1838–1920* (London, 1926).

Mather, Sir William, *The Co-operation of Employers and Educational Authorities* (Nottingham, 1913).

McG. Eagar, W., and Secretan, H. A., *Unemployment Among Boys* (London, 1925).

Meara, G., *Juvenile Unemployment In South Wales* (Cardiff, 1936).

Mendl, R. W. S., *The Appeal of Jazz* (London, 1927).

National Council of Public Morals, *The Cinema: Its Present Position and Future Possibilities* (London, 1917).

Owen, A. D. K., *A Survey of Juvenile Employment and Welfare in Sheffield* (Sheffield, 1933).

Phillips, M., *The Young Industrial Worker: A Study of his Educational Needs* (Oxford, 1922).
The Adolescence of the Young Wage Earner (Birmingham, 1930).

Pilgrim Trust, *Men Without Work* (Cambridge, 1938).

Pollock, M. A. (ed.), *Working Days* (London, 1926).

Rooff, M., *Youth and Leisure: A Survey of Girls' Organisations in England and Wales* (Edinburgh, 1935).

Rowntree, B. S., *Poverty and Progress: A Second Social Survey of York* (London, 1941).

Russell, C. E. B., *Manchester Boys: Sketches of Manchester Lads at Work and Play* (1905, repr. Manchester, 1984).

Social Problems of the North (1913, repr. London, 1980).

The Problem of Juvenile Crime (Oxford, 1917).

For Remembrance 1866–1917: A Memoir written specially for the Members and Old Members of the Heyrod Street Lads' Club (Manchester, 1917).

Russell, C. E. B. and Rigby, L. M., *Working Lads' Clubs* (London, 1908).

Russell, C. E. B. and Russell, L. M., *Lads' Clubs: Their History, Organisation and Management* (London, 1932).

Sadler, M. E. (ed.), *Continuation Schools in England and Elsewhere* (Manchester, 1907).

Save The Children Fund, *Unemployment and the Child: The Report on an Enquiry into the effects of Unemployment on the Children of the Unemployed and on Unemployed Young Workers in Great Britain* (London, 1933).

Simon, S. D., *A Century of City Government: Manchester 1838–1938* (London, 1938).

Slotki, I. W., *Jewish Education In Manchester and Salford* (Manchester, 1928).

The Film In National Life, An Enquiry conducted by the Commission on Educational and Cultural Films into the service which the cinematograph may render to education and social progress (London, 1932).

The Leisure of the People, A Handbook (Manchester, 1920).

Toole, J., *Fighting Through Life* (London, 1935).

Tout, H., *The Standard of Living in Bristol* (Bristol, 1938).

Urwick, E. J. (ed.), *Studies of Boy Life In Our Cities* (London, 1904).

Waterfall, E. A., *The Day Continuation School In England: Its Function and Future* (London, 1923).

Winterbottom, A., *An Enquiry into the Employment of Juveniles in Lancashire* (Manchester, 1932).

Wyatt, S., *Incentives in Repetitive Work: A Practical Experiment in A Factory* (London, 1934).

6. Secondary publications

Articles

Alexander S., 'Becoming a Woman in London in the 1920s and 1930s' in

D. Feldman and G. Stedman Jones (eds), *Metropolis. London: Histories and representations since 1800* (London, 1989), Chapter 10.

Bailey, V., 'Bibles and Dummy Rifles: The Boys' Brigade', *History Today*, Vol. 33 (October 1983), pp.5–10.

Benjamin, D. K. and Kochin, L. A., 'What went Right with Juvenile Unemployment Policy between the Wars: A Comment', *Economic History Review*, Second Series, Vol.XXXII, No.4 (November, 1979).

Benson, J., 'Work' in idem, *The Working Class in England 1875–1914* (Kent, 1985), Chapter 3.

Blanch, M., 'Imperialism, nationalism and organised youth' in J. Clarke, C. Critcher and R. Johnson (eds), *Working-Class Culture: Studies in history and theory* (London, 1979), Chapter 4.

Bond, R., 'Cinema in the Thirties: Documentary Film and the Labour Movement' J. Clark *et al.* (eds), *Culture and Crisis in Britain in the 30s* (London, 1979), pp.241–56.

Browning, H. E., and Sorrell, A. A., 'Cinemas and Cinema-Going in Great Britain', *Journal of the Royal Statistical Society*, Vol.117 (1954), pp.133–65.

Cohen, P., 'Historical Perspectives on the Youth Question Especially in Britain' in D. Dowe (ed.), *Jugendprotest und Generationenkonflikt in Europa im 20. Jahrhundert: Deutschland, England, Frankreich und Italien im Vergleich* (Dusseldorf, 1986), pp.241–59.

Cunningham, H., 'Leisure' in J. Benson (ed.), *The Working Class in England 1875–1914* (Kent, 1985), Chapter 5.

Davidoff, L. and Westover, B., '"From Queen Victoria to the Jazz Age": Women's World in England, 1880–1939' in idem, (eds), *Our Work, Our Lives, Our Words: Women's History and Women's Work* (Hampshire, 1986), Chapter 1.

Davies, A., 'Saturday Night Markets in Manchester and Salford 1840–1939', *Manchester Region History Review*, Vol.1, No.2 (1987), pp.3–12.

Drotner, K., 'Schoolgirls, Madcaps and Air Aces: English Girls and their Magazine Reading between the Wars', *Feminist Studies*, Vol.9, No.1 (Spring, 1983), pp.33–52.

Eichengreen, B., 'Juvenile Unemployment in Twentieth-Century Britain: The Emergence of a Problem', *Social Research*, 54 (1987), pp.273–301.

Feldman, D., '"There Was an Englishman, An Irishman and a Jew....": Immigrants and Minorities in Britain', review article in *Historical Journal*, Vol. 26, No.1 (March, 1983), pp.185–99.

Fowler, D. M., 'Teenage Consumers?: Young Wage–Earners and Leisure in Manchester, 1919–1939' in A. Davies and S. Fielding (eds), *Workers' Worlds: Cultures and Communities in Manchester and Salford, 1880–1939* (Manchester, 1992), pp.133–55.

Review of P. Stead, *Film and the Working Class: The Feature Film in*

British and American Society (London, 1989), *Social History*, Vol.16, No.3 (October, 1991), pp.407–8.

Review of H. F. Moorhouse, *Driving Ambitions: a social analysis of the American hot rod enthusiasm* (Manchester, 1991), *Journal of Transport History*, Vol.14, No.2 (September, 1993), pp.213–14.

Frith, S., 'Time To Grow Up', *New Society*, 4 April 1986, pp.12–14.

Garside, W. R., 'Juvenile Unemployment Statistics between the Wars: A Commentary and Guide to Sources', *Bulletin of the Society for the Study of Labour History*, 33 (Autumn, 1976), pp.38–46.

'Juvenile Unemployment and Public Policy between the wars', *Economic History Review*, Second Series, Vol.XXX, No.2 (May, 1977), pp.322–39.

'Juvenile Unemployment between the Wars: A rejoinder', *Economic History Review*, Second Series, Vol.XXXII, No.4 (November, 1979), pp.529–32.

'Youth Unemployment in 20th Century Britain: Protest, Conflict and the Labour Market' in D. Dowe (ed.), *Jugendprotest und Generationenkonflikt in Europa im 20. Jahrhundert: Deutschland, England, Frankreich und Italien im Vergleich* (Dusseldorf, 1986), pp.75–81.

Harrison, B., 'For Church, Queen and Family: The Girls' Friendly Society, 1874–1920', *Past and Present*, Vol.61, No.61 (November, 1973), pp.107–38.

Hay, J. R., 'Employers' Attitudes to Social Policy and the Concept of Social Control, 1900–1920' in P. Thane (ed.), *The Origins of British Social Policy* (London, 1978), pp.107–125.

Hebdige, D., 'Towards a Cartography of Taste 1935–1962' in B. Waites, T. Bennett and G. Martin (eds.), *Popular Culture: Past and Present* (1982, repr. Kent, 1986).

Hendrick, H., Review of J. R. Gillis's *Youth and History, Tradition and Change in European Age Relations 1770–Present* (New York, 1974) and J. Springhall's *Youth, Empire and Society: British Youth Movements, 1883–1940* (London, 1977) in *Social History*, Vol.3, No.2 (May, 1978), pp.249–52.

Higgs, E., 'Leisure and the State: The History of Popular Culture as Reflected in the Public Records', *History Workshop*, 15 (Spring 1983), pp.141–50.

Hoher, D., 'The Composition of Music Hall Audiences, 1850–1900' in P. Bailey (ed.), *Music Hall: The business of pleasure* (Milton Keynes, 1986), Chapter 4.

Horne, J., 'Youth Unemployment Programmes: a Historical Account of the Development of "Dole Colleges"' in D. Gleeson (ed.), *Youth Training and the search for Work* (London, 1983), Chapter 16.

'Continuity and Change in the State Regulation and Schooling of Unemployed Youth' in S. Walker and L. Barton (eds), *Youth,*

Unemployment and Schooling (Milton Keynes, 1986), pp.9–28.

Joyce, P., 'Work' in F. M. L. Thompson (ed.), *The Cambridge Social History of Britain, 1750–1950*, Vol. 2 (Cambridge, 1990), Chapter 3.

Knox, W., 'Apprenticeship and De-Skilling In Britain, 1850–1914', *International Review of Social History*, Vol.XXXI (1986), Pt.2, pp.166–84.

Laski, N., 'The Manchester and Salford Jewish Community 1912–1962', *Manchester Review*, Vol.10 (Spring 1964), pp.97–108.

Layton-Henry, Z., 'Labour's Lost Youth', *Journal of Contemporary History*, Vol.11 (July , 1976), pp.275–308.

Lee, A., 'Aspects of the Working Class Response to the Jews in Britain, 1880–1914' in K. Lunn (ed.), *Hosts, Immigrants and Minorities: Historical Responses to Newcomers in British Society, 1870–1914* (Kent, 1980), Chapter 5.

Linkman, A. and Williams, B., 'Recovering the People's Past: the archive rescue programme of Manchester Studies', *History Workshop*, 8 (Autumn 1979), pp.111–24.

McKibbin, R., 'Work and Hobbies in Britain, 1880–1950' in J. Winter (ed.), *The Working Class in Modern British History: Essays in Honour of Henry Pelling* (Cambridge, 1983), Chapter 7.

McKinlay, A., 'From Industrial Serf to Wage-Labourer: The 1937 Apprentice Revolt In Britain', *International Review of Social History*, Vol.XXXI (1986) Pt.1, pp.1–18.

More, C., 'Skill and the survival of apprenticeship' in S. Wood (ed.), *The Degradation of Work?: Skill, deskilling and the labour process* (London, 1982), Chapter 6.

O'Brien, M. and Holland, J., '"Picture Shows": The Early British Film Industry in Walthamstow', *History Today*, Vol.37 (Feb., 1987), pp.9–15.

Pearson, G., 'Perpetual Novelty: A History of Generational Conflicts in Britain' in D. Dowe (ed.), *Jugendprotest und Generationenkonflikt in Europa im 20. Jahrhundert: Deutschland, England, Frankreich und Italien im Vergleich* (Dusseldorf, 1986), pp.165–77.

Pope, R., '"Dole Schools": The North-East Lancashire Experience, 1930–39', *Journal of Educational Administration and History*, Vol.IX, No.2 (1977), pp.26–33.
'Education and the Young Unemployed: A Pre-War Experiment', *Journal of Further and Higher Education*, 2 (1978), pp.15–20.

Prynn, D., 'The Woodcraft Folk and the Labour Movement, 1925–1979', *Journal of Contemporary History*, Vol.18, No.1 (Jan., 1983), pp.79–95.

Pye, M., 'R.I.P. The Teenager, 1942–1978', *Sunday Times*, 30 July 1978.

Rees, G., and Rees, T. L., 'Juvenile Unemployment and the State Between The Wars' in T.L. Rees and P. Atkinson (eds), *Youth Unemployment and State Intervention* (London, 1982), Chapter 2.

Richards, J., 'The cinema and cinema-going in Birmingham in the 1930s' in J. K. Walton and J. Walvin (eds), *Leisure in Britain 1780–1939* (Manchester, 1983), Chapter 3.

Richardson, W. A., 'The Hugh Oldham Lads' Club, 1888–1958', *Manchester Review* (Autumn, 1954), pp.334–51.

Roberts, E., 'Learning and Living: Socialization Outside School', *Oral History*, Vol.3, No.2 (Autumn 1975), pp.14–28.

'The Family' in J. Benson (ed.), *The Working Class in England 1875–1914* (Kent, 1985), Chapter 1.

Seccombe, W., 'Patriarchy stabilized: the construction of the male breadwinner wage norm in nineteenth century Britain', *Social History*, Vol.XI (Jan., 1986), pp.53–76.

Springhall, J., 'Lord Meath, Youth and Empire', *Journal of Contemporary History*, Vol.5, No.4 (1970), pp.97–111.

'The Boy Scouts, Class and Militarism in Relation to British Youth Movements 1908–1930', *International Review of Social History*, Vol.XVI (1971), pp.125–58.

'"Young England, Rise up and Listen!": The Political Dimensions of Youth Protest and Generation Conflict in Britain, 1919–1939' in D. Dowe (ed.), *Jugendprotest und Generationenkonflikt in Europa im 20. Jahrhundert: Deutschland, England, Frankreich und Italien im Vergleich* (Dusseldorf, 1986), pp.151–63.

'Baden-Powell and the Scout Movement before 1920: Citizen Training or Soldiers of the Future?', *English Historical Review*, Vol.CII, No.405 (October 1987), pp.934–42.

Stedman Jones, G., 'Class Expression Versus Social Control? A Critique of Recent Trends in the Social History of "Leisure"', in idem, *Languages of Class: Studies in English working class history, 1832–1982* (Cambridge, 1983), Chapter 2.

'Working-class culture and working-class politics in London, 1870–1900: Notes on the remaking of a working-class' in idem, *Languages of class: Studies in English working class history, 1832–1982* (Cambridge, 1983), Chapter 4.

Taylor, P., 'Daughters and mothers – maids and mistresses: domestic service between the wars' in J. Clarke *et al.* (eds), *Working-Class Culture: Studies in history and theory* (London, 1979), Chapter 5.

Thompson, D., 'Courtship and Marriage in Preston between the Wars', *Oral History*, Vol.3, No.2 (1975), pp.39–44.

Thompson, P., 'The War With Adults', *Oral History*, Vol.3, No.2 (Autumn 1975), pp.29–38.

Thoms, D. W., 'The Emergence and Failure of the Day Continuation School Experiment', *History of Education*, Vol.4, No.1 (Spring 1975), pp.36–50.

Vigne, T., 'Parents and Children, 1890–1918: Distance and Dependence',

Oral History, Vol.3, No.2 (Autumn 1975), pp.6–13.

Voeltz, R. A., ""...A Good Jew and a Good Englishman": The Jewish Lads' Brigade, 1894–1922', *Journal of Contemporary History*, Vol.23, No.1 (January 1988), pp.119–27.

Warren, A., 'Citizens of the Empire: Baden-Powell, Scouts and Guides, and an imperial ideal' in J. M. MacKenzie (ed.), *Imperialism and Popular Culture* (Manchester, 1986), Chapter 10.

'Sir Robert Baden-Powell, the Scout movement and citizen training in Great Britain, 1900–1920', *English Historical Review*, Vol.CI, No.399 (April 1986), pp.376–98.

'Popular Manliness: Baden-Powell, scouting, and the development of manly character' in J. A. Mangan and J. Walvin (eds.), *Manliness and Morality: Middle-class Masculinity in Britain and America 1800–1940* (Manchester, 1987), Chapter 10.

'Baden-Powell: a final comment', *English Historical Review*, Vol.CII, No.405 (October, 1987) pp.948–50.

Waters, C., 'Manchester Morality and London Capital: The Battle over the Palace of Varieties' in P. Bailey (ed.), *Music Hall: The Business of Pleasure* (Milton Keynes, 1986), chapter 7.

Wild, P., 'Recreation in Rochdale, 1900–40' in J. Clarke *et al.* (eds), Working-Class Culture: Studies in history and theory (London, 1979), Chapter 6.

Wilkinson, P., 'English Youth Movements, 1908–1930', *Journal of Contemporary History*, Vol.4, No.2 (1969), pp.1–23.

Williams, B., 'The Jewish Immigrant in Manchester: The Contribution of Oral History', *Oral History*, Vol.7, No.1 (Spring 1979), pp.43–53.

Willis, P., 'Shop-floor culture, masculinity and the wage form' in J.Clarke *et al.* (eds), *Working-Class Culture: Studies in history and theory* (London, 1979), Chapter 8.

Books and Pamphlets

Abrams, M., *The Teenage Consumer* (London, 1959).

Bailey, V., *Delinquency and Citizenship: Reclaiming the Young Offender, 1914–1948* (Oxford, 1987).

Bell, T., *Pioneering Days* (London, 1941).

Benson, J. (ed.), *The Working Class In England, 1875–1914* (Kent, 1985).

Bogdanor, V. and Skidelsky, R. (eds), *The Age of Affluence, 1951–1964* (London, 1970).

Branson, N., *History of the Communist Party of Great Britain, 1927–1941* (London, 1985).

Branson, N. and Heinemann, M., *Britain in the Nineteen Thirties* (London, 1971).

Burnett, J. (ed.), *Useful Toil: Autobiographies of Working People from the 1820s to the 1920s* (London, 1974).

Buxton, N. K., and MacKay, D. I., *British Employment Statistics: A Guide to Sources and Methods* (Oxford, 1977).

Carr–Saunders, A. M., Caradog Jones, D. and Moser, C. A., *A Survey of Social Conditions in England and Wales* (Oxford, 1958).

Casson, M., *Youth Unemployment* (London, 1979).
Economics of Unemployment: An Historical Perspective (Oxford, 1983).

Chamberlain, M., *Growing Up In Lambeth* (London, 1989).

Clarke, J., Critcher, C. and Johnson, R. (eds), *Working-Class Culture: Studies in History and Theory* (London, 1979).

Cohen, S., *Folk Devils and Moral Panics: The Creation of the Mods and Rockers* (London, 1972).

Common, J., *Kiddar's Luck* (London, 1951).

Conran Foundation, *14–24: British Youth Culture* (London, 1986).

Constantine, S., *Social Conditions In Britain, 1918–1939* (London, 1983).

Cronin, J. E., *Labour and Society in Britain*, 1918–1979 (London, 1984).

Cross, G. (ed.), *Worktowners At Blackpool: Mass Observation and Popular Leisure in the 1930s* (London, 1990).

Croucher, R., *Engineers at War, 1939–1945* (London, 1982).

Crowther, M. A., *British Social Policy, 1914–1939* (London, 1988).

Curran, J. and Porter, V. (eds), *British Cinema History* (London, 1983).

Davis, J., *Youth and the Condition of Britain: Images of Adolescent Conflict* (London, 1990).

Dawes, F., *A Cry From The Streets: The Boys' Club Movement in Britain from the 1850s to the Present Day* (Hove, 1975).

Doherty, T., *Teenagers and Teenpics: The Juvenilization of American Movies in the 1950s* (London, 1988).

Dowe, D. (ed.), *Jugendprotest und Generationenkonflikt in Europa im 20. Jarhundert: Deutschland, England, Frankreich und Italien im Vergleich* (Dusseldorf, 1986).

Drotner, K., *English Children and their Magazines, 1751–1945* (New Haven, 1988).

Dunning, E., Murphy, P. and Williams, J., *The Roots of Football Hooliganism: An Historical and Sociological Study* (London, 1988).

Ehrlich, C., *The Music Profession in Britain since the Eighteenth Century: A Social History* (Oxford, 1985).

Everett, P., *You'll Never Be 16 Again: An Illustrated History of the British Teenager* (London, 1986).

Field, A., *Picture Palace: A Social History of the Cinema* (London, 1974).

Flint, R., *A Brief History of the Openshaw Lads' Club* (Manchester, 1948).

Foley, A., *A Bolton Childhood* (Manchester, 1973).

Frith, S., *Sound Effects: Youth, Leisure and the Politics of Rock* (London, 1983).
The Sociology of Youth (Ormskirk, 1984).
Music for Pleasure: Essays in the Sociology of Pop (Cambridge, 1988).

Frow, E. and Frow, R., *Manchester's Big House in Trafford Park: Class Conflict and Collaboration at Metro–Vicks* (Manchester, 1983).

Fyvel, T. R., *The Insecure Offenders: Rebellious Youth in the Welfare State* (Middlesex, 1961).

Garside, W. R., *British Unemployment, 1919–1939: A Study in Public Policy* (Cambridge, 1990).

Gifford, D., *The British Film Catalogue 1895–1970: A Guide to Entertainment Films* (Devon, 1973).

Gilbert, J., *A Cycle of Outrage: America's Reaction to the Juvenile Delinquent in the 1950s* (Oxford, 1986).

Gillis, J. R., *Youth and History, Tradition and Change in European Age Relations 1770–Present* (New York, 1974).
For Better, For Worse: British Marriages 1600 to the Present (Oxford, 1985).

Gittins, D., *Fair Sex: Family Size and Structure, 1900–39* (London, 1982).

Gloversmith, F. (ed.), *Class, Culture and Social Change: A New View of the 1930s* (Brighton, 1980).

Gordon, E., *Women and the Labour Movement in Scotland, 1850–1914* (Oxford, 1991).

Glucksmann, M., *Women Assemble: Women Workers and the New Industries in Interwar Britain* (London, 1990).

Graves, R. and Hodge, A., *The Long Week-end: A Social History of Great Britain 1918–1939* (1940, London, repro. 1990).

Gray, N., *The Worst of Times: An Oral History of the Great Depression in Britain* (London, 1985).

Greenwood, W., *There Was A Time* (Middlesex, 1969).

Hall, S. and Jefferson, T. (eds), *Resistance Through Rituals: Youth Sub-Cultures in Post-War Britain* (London, 1976).

Halliwell, L., *Seats In All Parts: Half a Lifetime at the Movies* (London, 1985).

Halsey, A. H. (ed.), *Trends in British Society Since 1900: A Guide to the Changing Social Structure of Britain* (London, 1972).

Hannington, W., *Never On Our Knees* (London, 1967).

Hendrick, H., *Images of Youth: Age, Class and the Male Youth Problem, 1880–1920* (Oxford, 1990).

Hobsbawm, E. J., *Industry and Empire: An Economic History of Britain since 1750* (London, 1968).

Hoggart, R., *The Uses of Literacy: Aspects of Working-class life with Special reference to Publications and Entertainments* (Middlesex, 1957).

Holmes, C. (ed.), *Immigrants and Minorities in British Society* (London, 1978).

Hopkins, H., *The New Look: A Social History of the Forties and Fifties in Britain* (London, 1963).

Howkins, A. and Lowerson, J., *Trends in Leisure, 1919–1939* (London, 1979).

Humphries, S., *Hooligans or Rebels? An Oral History of Working-Class Childhood and Youth, 1889–1939* (Oxford, 1981).

Humphries, S., *A Secret World of Sex. Forbidden Fruit: The British Experience, 1900–1950* (London, 1988).

Jeffery, T., *Mass-Observation: A Short History* (Birmingham, 1978).

Jephcott, P., *Girls Growing Up* (London, 1942).

Rising Twenty: Notes on Some Ordinary Girls (London, 1948).

Johnson, P., *Saving and Spending: The Working-Class Economy in Britain, 1870–1939* (Oxford, 1985).

Jones, S. G., *Workers At Play: A Social and Economic History of Leisure, 1918–1939* (London, 1986).

Jowitt, J. A. and McIvor, A. J. (eds), *Employers and Labour in the English Textile Industries, 1850–1939* (London, 1988).

Joyce, P. (ed.), *The Historical Meanings of Work* (Cambridge, 1987).

Kidd, A. J. and Roberts, K. W. (eds), *City, Class and Culture: Studies of cultural production and social policy in Victorian Manchester* (Manchester, 1985).

Kuhn, A., *Cinema, Censorship and Sexuality, 1909–1925* (London, 1988).

Le Mahieu, D. L., *A Culture for Democracy: Mass Communication and the Cultivated Mind in Britain Between the Wars* (Oxford, 1988).

Low, R., *The History of the British Film, 1906–14* (London, 1949).

The History of the British Film, 1914–1918 (London, 1950).

The History of the British Film, 1918–1929 (London, 1971).

Documentary and Educational Films of the 1930s (London, 1979).

The History of the British Film, 1929–1939: Film Making in 1930s Britain (London, 1985).

Lupton, T., *On The Shop Floor* (London, 1963).

MacInnes, C., *Absolute Beginners* (London, 1959).

England, Half English (London, 1961).

MacKenzie, J. M., *Propaganda and Empire: The Manipulation of British Public Opinion, 1880–1960* (Manchester, 1984).

Madge, C., *War–Time Pattern of Saving and Spending* (Cambridge, 1943).

Manchester and Salford Council of Social Service, *Golden Jubilee Over 60s Essays 1919–69* (Manchester, n.d. 1969?).

Manchester Evening News Special, *The Good Old Days*, 19 June 1976.

Manchester Grammar School, *Scouting at the Manchester Grammar School, 1912–1955* (Manchester, 1955).

Martin, B., *A Sociology of Contemporary Cultural Change* (Oxford, 1981).

Marwick, A., *British Society Since 1945* (1982, repr. Middlesex, 1987).

Mass Observation, *War Factory* (London, 1943).

Mayer, J. P., *Sociology of Film* (London, 1946).

British Cinemas and their Audiences (London, 1948).

Mays, J. B., *Growing up in the City: A Study of Juvenile Delinquency in an Urban Neighbourhood* (Liverpool, 1964).

McG.Eagar, W., *Making Men: The History of Boys' Clubs and Related Movements in Great Britain* (London, 1953).

Meacham, S., *A Life Apart: The English Working Class, 1890–1914* (London, 1977).

Moorhouse, H. F., *Driving Ambitions: A Social Analysis of the American Hot Rod Enthusiasm* (Manchester, 1991).

More, C., *Skill and the English Working Class, 1870–1914* (London, 1980).

Mulford, J., (ed.), *Worktown People: Photographs from Northern England 1937–38* (Bristol, 1982).

Mungham, G. and Pearson, G. (eds), *Working-Class Youth Culture* (London, 1976).

Partington, J., *The Two-Up and Two-Downer: The Story of the Crowded Life of a Lancashire Lad* (Manchester, 1972).

Pearson, G., *Hooligan: A History of Respectable Fears* (London, 1983).

Pollitt, H., *Serving My Time* (London, 1940).

Rees, T. L. and Atkinson, P. (eds), *Youth Unemployment and State Intervention* (London, 1982).

Renold, C. G., *Joint Consultation Over Thirty Years: A Case Study* (London, 1950).

Rhind, D. (ed.), *A Census User's Handbook* (London, 1983).

Richards, J., *The Age of the Dream Palace: Cinema and Society in Britain 1930–1939* (London, 1984).

Roberts, E., *Working Class Barrow and Lancaster 1890 to 1930* (Lancaster, 1976).
A Woman's Place: An Oral History of Working-Class Women, 1890–1940 (1984, repr. Oxford, 1985).

Roberts, R., *The Classic Slum: Salford Life in the First Quarter of the Century* (1971, repr. Middlesex, 1983).
A Ragged Schooling: Growing up in the Classic Slum (1976, repr. London, 1984).

Robertson, J. C., *The British Board of Film Censors: Film Censorship in Britain, 1896–1950* (Kent, 1985).

Rosenthal, M., *The Character Factory: Baden-Powell and the Origins of the Boy Scout Movement* (London, 1986).

Rowntree, B. S. and Lavers, G. R., *English Life and Leisure: A Social Study* (London, 1951).

Royle, E., *Modern Britain: A Social History, 1750–1985* (London, 1987).

Seabrook, J., *Working-class Childhood: An Oral History* (London, 1982).

Springhall, J., *Youth, Empire and Society: British Youth Movements, 1883–1940* (London, 1977).

Coming of Age: Adolescence in Britain, 1860–1960 (Dublin, 1986).

Stead, P., *Film and the Working Class: The Feature Film in British and American Society* (London, 1989).

Stedman Jones, G., *Outcast London: A Study in the Relationship between Classes in Victorian Society* (Oxford, 1971).
Languages of Class: Studies in English Working Class History, 1832–1981 (Cambridge, 1983).

Stevenson, J., *Social Conditions in Britain Between the Wars* (London, 1977).
British Society, 1914–45 (Middlesex, 1984).

Stone, R. and Rowe, D. A., *The Measurement of Consumers' Expenditure and Behaviour in the United Kingdom, 1920–1938*, Vol. II (Cambridge, 1966).

Thomas, M. W., *Young People in Industry, 1750–1945* (London, 1945).

Thompson, E. P., *The Making of the English Working Class* (1963, repr. Middlesex, 1979).

Tranter, N. L., *Population and Society, 1750–1940: Contrasts in Population Growth* (Essex, 1985).

White, C. L., *Women's Magazines, 1693–1968* (London, 1970).

White, J., *The Worst Street in North London: Campbell Bunk, Islington, Between the Wars* (London, 1986).

Willis, P. E., *Learning to Labour: How Working Class Kids get Working Class Jobs* (1977, repr. Hampshire, 1981).

Yeo, E. and Yeo, S. (eds), *Popular Culture and Class Conflict, 1590–1914: Explorations in the History of Labour and Leisure* (Brighton, 1981).

York Oral History Project, *York Memories of Stage and Screen: Personal Accounts of York's Theatres and Cinemas, 1900–1960* (York, 1988).

Zweig, F., *The British Worker* (Middlesex, 1952).

7. Unpublished work

Theses

Allcorn, D. H., 'The Social Development of Young Men in an English Industrial Suburb', unpublished PhD thesis, University of Manchester, 1955.

Barber, C., 'The Raising of the School-Leaving Age 1870–1947', unpublished PhD thesis, University of Manchester, 1976.

Canner, H. E., 'The Juvenile Employment Service in Manchester, 1910–1939', unpublished MEd thesis, University of Manchester, 1958.

Davis, J. '"The Favourite Age": A Study of the Emergence and Rise to Prominence of the Concepts of Adolescence and Youth in Modern Society with special reference to the Cult of Youth in Post-War Britain', unpublished PhD thesis, University of Essex, 1983.

Ferris, J., 'The Labour Party League of Youth 1924–1940', unpublished MA thesis, University of Warwick, 1977.

Fielder, A. E. H., 'Adolescents and the Cinema, Report of an Enquiry', Diploma in Social Studies, Department of Economics, University of Manchester, 1932.

Fowler, D. M., 'The Lifestyle of the Young Wage-Earner in Interwar Manchester, 1919–1939', unpublished PhD thesis, University of Manchester, 1988.

Harley, J. L., 'Report of an enquiry into the occupations, further education and leisure interests of a number of girl wage-earners from elementary and central schools in the Manchester district, with special reference to the influence of school training on their use of leisure', unpublished MEd thesis, University of Manchester, 1937.

Hayburn, R. H. C., 'The Responses to unemployment in the 1930s, with special reference to South-East Lancashire', unpublished PhD thesis, University of Hull, 1970.

Jackson, W. G., 'An Historical Study of the Provision of Facilities for Play and Recreation in Manchester', unpublished MEd thesis, University of Manchester, 1940.

Jones, S. G., 'The British Labour Movement and Working Class Leisure, 1918–1939', unpublished PhD thesis, University of Manchester, 1983.

Livshin, R. D., 'Aspects of the Acculturation of the Children of Immigrant Jews in Manchester 1890–1930', unpublished MEd thesis, University of Manchester, 1982.

McHugh, S. J., 'The Development of Secondary Education in Salford and Surrounding Districts (Eccles, Swinton and Pendlebury) 1902–1918', unpublished MA (Method I) Dissertation, University of Manchester, 1976.

Opie, L., 'Voluntary Effort to Help the Unemployed in the 1930s', unpublished MA thesis, University of Manchester, 1975.

Pope, R., 'The Unemployment Problem in North-East Lancashire, 1920–1938', unpublished MLitt thesis, University of Lancaster, 1974.

Power, J., 'Aspects of Working-Class Leisure During the Depression Years: Bolton In the 1930s', unpublished MA thesis, University of Warwick, 1980.

Rosamund, F. J., 'The Social and Economic Effects of Unemployment in Manchester, 1919–1926', unpublished MA (Econ) thesis, University of Manchester, 1970.

Schafer, S. C., '"Enter The Dream House": The British Film Industry And The Working Classes In Depression England, 1929–1939', unpublished PhD thesis, University of Illinois at Urbana-Champaign, 1984.

Solomon, H., 'The Aims, Methods and Achievements of the Manchester Jewish Lads' Brigade against the Background of British Youth Movements 1883–1914', Diploma in Local History, Manchester Polytechnic, 1984.

Tenen, C., 'Adolescent Attitudes to Authority at Work', unpublished MA thesis, University of Manchester, 1945.

Papers and Essays

Davies, A., 'Leisure and Poverty in Salford 1900–1939', paper prepared for an Anglo–German Conference at the University of Lancaster, 17–19 March 1988.

Findlay, F. T., 'Days That Used To Be' (Manchester, 1976), typescript, MCL, Local History Library.

Johnson, P., 'Working-class consumption and working-class collectivism in inter-war Britain', paper prepared for an Anglo-German Conference at the University of Lancaster, 17–19 March 1988.

Pead, E. W., 'Eighty-Nine Years On: London Federation of Boys' Clubs', typescript, n.d.

'Peaky Blinders and Scuttlers', transcript of a Radio 4 programme presented by Steve Humphries, 1987.

Richards, J., 'Cinemagoing in Worktown', paper prepared for an Anglo-German Conference at the University of Lancaster, 17–19 March 1988.

Roberts, E., 'Youth, Family and Work, 1890–1940', paper prepared for an Anglo-German Conference at the University of Lancaster, 17–19 March 1988.

Springhall, J., '"A School for Thieves"?: Commercial Entertainment and Juvenile Crime In Early and Mid–Victorian England', paper prepared for an Anglo-German Conference at the University of Lancaster, 17–19 March 1988.

Sutton, L., *Mainly About Ardwick*, Vol.I (Manchester, 1975), typescript, MCL, Local History Department.

Mainly About Ardwick,Vol.II (Manchester, 1977), typescript, MCL, Local History Library.

Welshman, J., 'Images of Youth: The Problem of Juvenile Smoking 1900 to 1939', typescript, n.d. 1984?

8. Other Sources

Manchester Studies Oral History Archive, Manchester Metropolitan University.

The following tapes proved the most useful on the issues discussed in this study: 70, 115, 189, 250, 486, 634, 660, 766, 780, 846, 856, 869, 996, 1001, J3, J7, J8, J20, J21, 324, 328, 340, 342, 343, 344, 378, 388, J124, J189, J214, J242, S1.

Index

209